TREND TRACKING

IS RIGHT ON TRACK!

*   *   *

"There is no better forecaster than Gerald Celente. The man knows what he is talking about."
—**Bob Berkowitz**
Host of Financial News Network (FNN)
"Focus"

*   *   *

"*Trend Tracking* is more soundly anchored in reality and more challenging than the *Megatrends* pabulum. What's more, Celente offers a checklist of nearly 200 'profit opportunities' from 'adult care' to 'zoning,' with a brief forecast for each."
—*Chicago Tribune*

*   *   *

"A book every executive should have as he prepares for the 1990s."
—**Robert L. Dilenschneider,**
President and Chief Executive Officer
Hill and Knowlton

*   *   *

"Has a way of turning events into opportunities ... offers tips on how to see connections and directions ... detailed ways to use change and trends beneficially to improve personal, corporate and world situations."
—*Seattle Times*

*   *   *

"I don't know how anyone can read *Trend Tracking* and then continue to view and live life in the same old way. This book is a must for both the corporate citizen and the American citizen."
—Barbara Singer
Vice President, Marketing
Footwear Industries of America
*   *   *

"Very readable and fact-packed."
—*Editor & Publisher*
*   *   *

"Very readable and personable. Goes beyond *Megatrends* by showing readers how to do it themselves."
—Leonard M. Fuld
Author of *Competitor Intelligence: How to Get It, How to Use It*
*   *   *

"In a complicated and hazardous world, this book makes planning ahead an easier challenge."
—Alfred L. Malabre, Jr.
Author of *Within Our Means*
*   *   *

"What separates Celente's book from other trend books is that he not only identifies trends but teaches his readers how to do it themselves and how to make money from it."
—*Poughkeepsie Journal*
*   *   *

"*Trend Tracking* goes beyond the rosy scenarios in *Megatrends 2000*."
—Gannett Newspapers
*   *   *

Today's most-quoted trend forecaster, GERALD CELENTE is director of the Socio-Economic Research Institute. Preeminent in its field, the Institute's trend forecasts are frequently featured by CNN, the *New York Times*, *USA Today*, *Wall Street Journal*, *Los Angeles Times*, FNN, and the BBC.

TOM MILTON, a senior fellow at the Institute and assistant professor of economics and finance at Mercy College, has been a consultant to multinational corporations, Third World governments, and small businesses.

TREND TRACKING

•

The System to
Profit from
Today's Trends

•

GERALD CELENTE
WITH TOM MILTON

WARNER BOOKS

A Time Warner Company

For the beautiful gift of love and love of life:
my parents, Louis and Marie,
and my precious partner, Mary Ann.

Originally published in hardcover by John Wiley & Sons, Inc.

Warner Books Edition
Copyright © 1990, 1991 by Gerald Celente with Tom Milton
All rights reserved.
This Warner Books edition is published by arrangement with
John Wiley & Sons, Inc.
Warner Books, Inc., 666 Fifth Avenue, New York, NY 10103

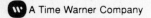 A Time Warner Company

Printed in the United States of America
First trade printing: September 1991
10 9 8 7 6 5 4 3 2 1

Library of Congress Cataloging in Publication Data
Celente, Gerald, 1940–
    Trend tracking : the system to profit from today's trends / Gerald
Celente with Tom Milton. — Warner Books ed.
      p.   cm.
    Reprint. Originally published: New York : Wiley, c1990.
    Includes bibliographical references and index.
    ISBN 0-446-39287-1
     1. Forecasting. 2. Quality of life. 3. Social prediction.
I. Title.
[H61.4.C45 1991]
003'.2—dc20
                                          91-4116
                                          CIP

Cover design by Andrew Carpenter

Contents

Acknowledgments

Our gratitude to our teachers: the ones who taught us both academics and how to live better lives, the ones who passed on their knowledge of life to us, and the ones who helped strengthen our weaknesses and improve our potential.

To the members of the Socio-Economic Research Institute of America who work to develop products and services for the betterment of humanity: Gary Abatelli, Mark Braunstein, Anthony Celentano, Curtis B. Wayne, Dr. Bruce Cohen, Fred Davidson, Burt Feinson, Don Hall, Gerard Harrington, Dr. Anne Landfield, Mary Ann Martinson, John Melia, Raul "Nacho" Oca, Steve Rosenberger, Dr. Mitchell Skolnick, Cynthia Stone, John Anthony West, and our pilots Captain Ed Allyn and Captain Jesse Reimer.

Our sincere appreciation to Carolyn Contois, our librarian, whose dedication has created one of the finest information systems we know of. To Lowell Miller, Inka Savrda, John Sperr, and Dr. Benjamin Weisman for their insights. To Gary Abatelli, who has given us the master key to many doors of knowledge. To Bill Hillsman, a founder and dear friend, for years of support, and Dr. Anthony F. Macchia for advice, guidance, and feedback in shaping the Globalnomic system. To Mark Contois, the head of our brain trust of gifted students, and G. Milton Cohen and Ray Shelton, our research assistants from Vassar College. Also, to Marc Eisenson and Nancy Castleman, who gave us the benefit of their experience.

Finally, our thanks to Marie Milton, our consulting editor, for her valuable advice along the way.

Preface to the Warner Edition

This book is about change. It shows you how to anticipate change, how to avoid being a victim of change, and finally how to profit from change. It shows you how to turn what looks like a disaster into an opportunity.

When I look at what has happened in the world just since this book was first published, I feel we can't be too aware of how quickly things change. In only little more than a year we saw a change in Germany from the fall of the Berlin Wall to a reunited country to a recognition of serious problems. In the same brief period we saw a change in our view of Mikhail Gorbachev from cautious hope to admiration to disappointment. And we saw a change in our Middle East policy from a pragmatic alliance with Saddam Hussein to a holy war against him.

If you had read this book before, you wouldn't have been surprised by these changes. If you read it now, you won't be surprised by the changes that are going to occur in the near future. You'll be able to anticipate them and profit from them. You'll be able to turn them into opportunities.

In this book we not only give you forecasts, we show you the trends shaping the future, so that you can pick them up and track them yourself. For example, we accurately forecasted the 1990–91 recession. But we also showed the trends that were leading to it. And now we show you how the same trends will shape our economy in the 1990s. Equipped with such tools, you can look ahead and see for yourself what's going to happen.

If you're a manager, an owner of a small business, a professional, an employee of a corporation, a skilled worker, a job seeker, a homemaker, a college student—whoever you are, you might want to plan for the future. But in this world of rapid change, how can you plan? How can you position yourself to profit from change? By trend tracking.

All things are connected,
like the blood which unites us all.

—Chief Seattle, 1855

I

HOW TO PROFIT FROM TRACKING TRENDS

$=1=$

Looking Ahead

Imagine yourself in a lifeboat, in a heavy surf, trying to make it to the shore. If you don't see the waves coming, they can swamp you. But if you do, and you position yourself for them, you can ride them.

It's the same with trends. If you don't see them coming, they can overwhelm you. But if you do, and you position yourself for them, you can profit from them.

To see them coming, you have to identify them, you have to track them. And I'm going to show you how to do it. That's what we do at the Institute: we not only track trends, we also show people how to do it.

The point is, you don't need an institute to track trends. You just need your own eyes and your common sense.

Tracking Trends

What is a trend? A trend is a definite, predictable direction or sequence of events, like the warming of the earth's climate. That's a trend.

We started tracking trends in the early 1980s. When people asked what we did, I would say we tracked trends for profit. I would explain that we identified trends by following social, economic, and political events, and that we showed our clients how to profit by translating trends into products and strategies. When people asked how we did it, they expected to hear that we used a highly complex system, with rows of computers and hundreds of analysts. And when they heard how simple it was, they were always surprised. They would ask me if that was really all there was to it, and I would tell them to try it. Some of them did, and they profited from it.

Tracking trends shows us how we got here, where we are, and where we're going. Take the warming trend, which I mentioned above. Most scientists agree that the earth's climate is getting warmer. Why is this happening? Because the emissions from our industry, transportation, and agriculture are producing what's known as the greenhouse effect. If you look at data on our use of fossil fuels, you can see how we got here. If you look at climatic data, you can see where we are. And if you look ahead, you can see where we're going, unless we do something to reverse the trend. But if you're tracking it, you'll be aware of such a change, and you'll see the new direction.

People often ask me if we have inside information. I tell them we don't, we just have the information that's available to everyone. But we know how to get it, and we know how to use it to identify and track trends.

Proacting versus Reacting

Change is a fact of life, yet many people don't want to think about it because they feel threatened by it. So when change comes, it takes them by surprise. By then they can only react to it, and unless they're lucky they suffer losses. If they're investors, they lose their money. If they're employees, they lose their jobs. If they're corporate executives, they lose their markets.

To react is to be taken by surprise and then to look for a solution, or a way out. To proact is to anticipate the future and to act accordingly. You can see these two different approaches in the stock market. Those who didn't anticipate the Crash of 1987 were taken by surprise, and like a crowd in a theater when someone yells fire they scrambled for the exits. They reacted. And of course they suffered enormous losses. But those who did anticipate the Crash got out of stocks and into cash or foreign currencies. They proacted. And they profited, or at least avoided losses.

Mostly, our government and corporate leaders don't look ahead any further than the next election or the next quarter. But if you don't look ahead, you can't proact, you can't develop effective policies. You can only react, you can only operate by crisis management. And your resources are dissipated in putting out fires, rather than utilized in achieving goals.

Look at our government. They're fighting a war against drug dealers, but they could have anticipated this problem. They could have seen that with the breakdown of the family and the decline of the school system, the underclass was growing, and that whether its escape mechanism was crack, or speed, or angel dust, the drug problem would grow with it. But they ignored these trends in the family and education, and now that they're reacting to the problem, they're not attacking its causes, they're only trying to relieve its symptoms.

Look at our corporations. They're playing financial games, and many of them are ignoring one of the most important trends in the world—globalization. It's a trend that emerged in the 1980s, and it's going to accelerate in the 1990s. The companies that only react to this change are going to be losers, while the ones that proact are going to be winners.

So why don't we all anticipate change? Because as we drive into the future, most of us have our eyes glued to the rearview mirror—a habit that causes accidents.

The Rearview Mirror

In school you learn about the past, but you don't learn how to relate it to the present, or how to project it into the future. You don't see how we got here, where we are, and where we're going. You only see the past, like a story that has nothing to do with you.

You take a course called current events, but it's just a lot of information, and you don't know what to do with it. You don't learn how current events are derived from history or how they form future trends.

It's the same in college. I remember asking a professor how the economic policy of the Johnson administration would affect our future. He looked at me as if I was trying to get him off the subject, and he dismissed me, saying: "You'll see." It was all right to look back, and at the present, but not ahead. The future was off limits.

And it's the same in a corporation. Managers are concerned about the present, about the next quarterly earnings, not about what's going to happen five years from now. So they have no use for people who look that far ahead.

That's why most people don't anticipate change. They've been conditioned at school and at work not to look ahead. But if you don't look ahead, you can't proact.

The Fall of the Shah

After I got out of college I ran the election campaign for a man who became mayor of my hometown, and then I served as assistant to the secretary of the New York state senate. In those positions I learned about politics, things they didn't teach you in school. I also learned that in analyzing a situation you should always consider the political aspect. This may seem obvious, but I've found that people are reluctant to bring politics into a discussion of another subject, maybe because they were asked not to talk about politics or religion at the dinner table. When you consider the political aspect, you have to let go of ideology. You have to step back and analyze the situation objectively. So I've become a political atheist. In other words, I don't believe in politics. I believe in government and in management, but not in politics. Just remember, if something is done for a political reason, someone gets rewarded at your expense. Of course, this applies not only to government but also to business.

A few years later, while working as a government affairs director for a trade association, I found that to keep abreast of the changes that would affect our industry, I had to read a lot. I read magazines and trade journals and newspapers, especially newspapers. As I gathered facts, I found that my opinions, and later my judgments, differed from those of the majority, as indicated by polls. I realized how opinions are formed by the media, which repeat a story over and over until the majority believe it, and how polls reflect what people have been told by the media.

For me, the turning point was the crisis in Iran. I had read about the Shah and his repressive regime. I had learned, not in school but from the newspapers, how we were involved in overthrowing a nationalistic leader there and replacing him with the Shah. He was our boy, and to leave no doubt about where we stood, our president and his wife spent New Year's Eve with him. On that occasion Carter said: "Because of the greatness of the Shah, Iran is an island of stability in the Middle East."

Political analysts predicted what would happen if the Shah fell. But they didn't believe that the Shah would fall. Lee Iacocca didn't believe it. In his autobiography he wrote: "In 1978, nobody could have imagined that by the next spring there would be havoc in Iran and the price of gas would suddenly double." Well, anybody who had been watching the situation objectively could have foreseen it. You don't have to be a foreign affairs expert to see that if millions of people are rioting in the streets, there's going to be change.

By reading the newspaper I learned that the Shah's police had no experience at riot control and no riot-control equipment. They had highly sophisticated military equipment, but nothing to control the riots. This fact was critical, and it wasn't repeated by the media, so if I hadn't been reading the paper front to back every day, I would have missed it. A lot of analysts must have missed it, because they were surprised by the Shah's failure to control the riots. After putting this fact together with all my other facts, I concluded that the Shah would fall, and that the new government would turn against us.

When the Shah did fall I wasn't surprised, except by my ability to make forecasts. I hadn't ever done it before, I hadn't ever followed a situation and looked ahead to see where it was going. And I wondered if I could do it again. I followed the hostage situation, and I watched Carter, knowing that he was in political trouble. He was being challenged by Ted Kennedy in the primaries, and I figured that if he lost in Pennsylvania, he would have to do something about the hostages. So I made a bet. I invested in gold, assuming that Carter would lose the primary, that he would invade Iran, and that the price of gold would then go up as people around the world panicked.

Carter lost in Pennsylvania, but nothing happened, and I had doubts. Three days later he lost again in Michigan, and right after that he ordered the ill-fated rescue mission. The price of gold shot up, and I was in the business of tracking trends.

One thing I learned from this experience is that the majority of people, led by politicians and the media, don't see the cause of a problem, they only see the symptoms. In the Iran crisis, they didn't see the grievances of the Iranian people over the fact that we had imposed the Shah on them, they only saw the hostages. And their natural concern for the hostages was manipulated by our leaders for political ends.

Another thing I learned is that the top executives of our corporations don't think globally. As most of us remember, the fall of the

Shah was followed by an oil shock, with higher prices, shortages, and gas lines. When it hit, the American auto companies were reluctantly complying with the government mileage requirements, but ignoring the trend toward small, fuel-efficient cars. The Japanese, who had a product to meet this demand, captured a good share of the market. The American companies were surprised by the change, and by then they could only react to it. But they should have foreseen it. If I could foresee it, they could have.

We hear a lot of talk about competitiveness. We hear a lot of reasons why we've lagged behind other countries. But one reason is, we don't look ahead. And unless we do, we'll always be surprised by change.

The Crash of '87

At the end of 1986 Reagan predicted a "second boom" in the economy. And people evidently believed him. Money poured into the stock market, driving it to record heights. But at the Institute we had doubts, and on January 20 we issued a press release stating that the market would crash.

We didn't have a crystal ball, we just looked at the facts. And what did we see? An international monetary crisis fueled by trade imbalances and debt. The highest number of bank failures, foreclosures, and bankruptcies since the Depression. A worsening of world conflicts. A deepening farm and industrial crisis. An oversupply of commercial real estate and a glut of high income properties. Stock market volatility.

We realized that the scenario presented by Reagan was mainly an illusion, and that the bull market would last only as long as people believed him. We saw that he had already lost credibility as a result of a series of incidents culminating in the Iran-Contra arms scandal. And we concluded that he wouldn't be able to maintain the illusion for much longer. At the time, we said: "For too long the many developments leading up to this crisis have been swept under the rug or dismissed by politicians, bureaucrats, and the private sector. 1987 will be the year it hits the fan."

We advised investors to get out of the stock market and into cash and foreign currencies. Those who followed our advice profited, or at least avoided losses. Those who didn't were surprised, and when they called their brokers the lines were busy.

Our forecast of the crash impressed people. How did we do it? We looked at the facts, we used our eyes and our common sense.

The Baby Boomers

As we approach the end of this century, it's natural for us to be more than usually curious, and perhaps anxious, about the future. When we talk about the past, we give names to centuries that characterize them. We call the fifth century B.C. the Golden Age of Greece, the sixteenth century the Age of Discovery, the eighteenth century the Age of Reason, as if the turn of a century were the boundary line between two ages. So we look to the 1990s, the last decade of this century, as if it will be the swan song of our present age or the prelude to a new age.

Actually, the fundamental change began in the 1980s, with the aging of the World War II generation and the maturing of the baby boomers. You could see this in the 1988 Republican candidates. Bush was a pilot who flew battle missions in World War II, and he appealed to his generation as a war hero. But if Quayle hadn't come on like a hawk, it wouldn't have mattered to his generation that he had avoided going to Vietnam by serving in the National Guard.

Why are the baby boomers different? Because so many of them went to college. This was partly a result of economic prosperity, and partly a result of Vietnam. Children of immigrants, children of people who hadn't finished high school went to college. Young men who otherwise might have been drafted went to college. Young women who didn't want to end up like their mothers went to college. So they became educated en masse.

The parents of baby boomers grew up during the Depression, and the thing they wanted most for their children was an education. They kept saying: "Finish high school, go to college, get as much education as you can." In this respect, the children followed their parents' advice. But at college they learned to question their parents' values, and they raised the issues of the 1960s: civil rights, Vietnam, women's liberation, the environment. Their parents were shocked. They wanted their children to have an education so that they could get good jobs, not overturn their world.

The baby boomers did get jobs, and got married, and had children, and some of their younger brothers and sisters became yuppies. But most of them didn't abandon the values of the Sixties. They still want equal rights for people. They still oppose war. They're still concerned about the environment. They still care more about life-style than about money. And now that those at the leading edge of the baby boom are in their 40s, they're in a position to implement their values.

That's why things are going to change. The people who are coming into power have a different mentality than the previous generation. Of course, we're at a transitional stage, and many of our leaders still have a World War II mentality. They're still looking back to the good old days of the 1940s and 1950s, instead of ahead to the future. But within this decade the Sixties mentality will have taken over, and it will characterize the next century, the Global Age.

= 2 =

Identifying Trends

Throughout our history, people have tried to predict the future, using different forms of magic, religion, and science. We even have experts who call themselves futurists. It's interesting to go back and read some of their predictions about the 1980s. One group predicted that by the middle of the decade we would land men on Mars. Well, that's typical—they get carried away by the exotic possibilities of high technology, while they ignore mundane problems.

At the Institute we're not futurists, we're trackers of trends. Futurists look beyond the present and make predictions. We look at the present, at the current events that form future trends, and we make forecasts. We're concerned with how the events of today will affect our immediate lives tomorrow. So we follow present trends and project them into the future.

Where Trends Come From

Some researchers maintain that trends come from the bottom up, and that they originate in California, Seattle, and other key trend centers, then move eastward. We've found that they come from the bottom up, the top down, and the middle out, and that they originate in Teaneck, New Jersey, or Ames, Iowa, or Waco, Texas, or anywhere else. To spot trends, we don't just look at demographic segments, we also look at social, economic, and political events.

World leaders are important trendsetters. To a great extent, Ronald Reagan determined the course of the 1980s. He was one of the most trusted and best liked presidents in modern history. And because he was so popular, he was able to steer the country in the direction that he wanted to go. He changed the national priorities from social programs to defense. He advocated a policy of downsizing the public sector and deregulating the private sector, moving the economy toward a laissez-faire system. He was a strong anti-Communist, and he led the country toward intervention in Grenada, Nicaragua, Angola, and Afghanistan. These were trends, and they affected every level of our society.

Mikhail Gorbachev is a trendsetter in the Soviet Union. With *perestroika* (restructuring) and *glasnost* (openness), he's steering his country in a different direction. It's not just image, it's a real change, and it's coming from an intellectual level. We can see trends forming: the pullback of troops, more freedom of the press, the policy of building the economy rather than the military. And we can track them as they develop.

Trends also come from the middle class. One trend in middle America is known as NIMBY (not in my backyard), as people across the nation organize to protect their neighborhoods from pollution and overdevelopment. The battle of Love Canal demonstrated the power of the middle class when they're united in such a cause. Similar battles followed. It became clear that Love Canal had been a major event, the beginning of a trend that's still developing.

From the lower classes we often see music trends emerge. Jazz, rhythm and blues, rock, punk, heavy metal—these came from the bottom of society and percolated up through every level. A recent trend is the salsa beat, which came from the rapidly growing Hispanic population and is now finding a mass audience, mixing with rock. We also see fashion trends emerge from the inner city. If you want to forecast the next rage in sneakers, go to Harlem, or Watts, or Overtown, and see what the kids are wearing there. Before long, it will spread to suburbia and middle America.

So trends come from everywhere, from every class, from every group. And if you watch for them to emerge only in Marin County, or only in the upper classes, you'll miss a lot of them. In this respect, we differ from other trend researchers. They use a narrow focus, we take a broad view.

Seeing Trends

Anna Novak, a friend of mine, studies primate behavior in tropical forests. Last year she was working in a Panamanian forest, observing monkeys. She had seen a lot of monkeys there, but never a snake. And she began to wonder if there were any snakes in that forest.

One day a colleague who studies snake behavior went into the forest with her. They hadn't gone ten steps when her colleague spotted a snake. When they had gone a few steps farther, he spotted another. By the time they reached her study area, they had seen more than fifty snakes. Anna was puzzled, and she asked her colleague why she hadn't ever seen them before. And he said because she was looking for monkeys.

Field biologists have a word for it. They say you have a "search image" for whatever you're looking for. If you have a search image for monkeys, you'll see monkeys. If you have one for snakes, you'll see snakes. And if you have one for trends, you'll see trends. You just have to know what you're looking for so that when you see it, you recognize it. A trend, as I said, is a definite, predictable direction or sequence of events. It follows logically, even inescapably, from causes that usually span a number of fields or disciplines.

That definition won't enable you to identify a trend, but it gets you started. If a trend is a "direction" or "sequence of events," then you know that one event doesn't make a trend. You need at least two points to plot a direction, at least two events to form a sequence. So at first you won't know if what you're seeing is a trend.

Suppose you read in the newspaper that 85 percent of the high school graduates who applied for jobs with a local company failed a test of basic skills. That's an event, but it's not a trend. A year later, you read that 90 percent of them failed the same test. That's beginning to look like a trend.

Once you have a direction or sequence of events, you then have to test it, just as a field biologist has to test a specimen to make a positive identification. The basic test is whether the apparent trend has social, economic, and political significance. You can decide this by asking two questions. What caused it? What likely effects will it have? If the answers are trivial, it's not a trend.

It's important to realize that you often find the causes and the effects of a trend outside of its field. A cause of the decline of our public school system is the breakdown of the nuclear family. An effect is our loss of competitiveness in the global market. So if you want to identify trends in education, you have to look beyond that field.

That's how we identify trends. We look at events, and we watch for a direction or sequence. Then we look for its causes and effects. And if it has social, economic, and political significance, it's a trend.

What if an apparent trend only has political significance? Then it's not a trend by our test. To be a trend, it has to meet all three conditions.

Trends versus Fads

We distinguish trends from fads, which are unpredictable, short-lived, and without social, economic, and political significance. For example, Cabbage Patch dolls were a fad. And Reagan-inspired patriotism was a fad.

Detecting fads can also be profitable. If you get in front of it at the right time and ride its crest, you can make a lot of money on a fad. So even though they don't have the staying power and influence of trends, fads are interesting. But if you invest in one, just be sure to recognize a fad for what it is. Don't begin to believe it's a trend.

Coleco, the toy company, made that mistake. They were known for their ability to capitalize on fads. They were masters at it. But they evidently began to believe their own hype. They tried to build a whole business on a passing fad, Cabbage Patch dolls, and when the fad ended so did the company.

Smart investors recognize fads for what they are, they get in and out. So if you're smart, you can profit from them.

The Yuppie Craze

A big fad that politicians as well as businessmen mistook for a trend was the yuppie craze. That's one reason why Gary Hart fizzled out in the presidential primary of 1984. He mistook the yuppie craze for a trend.

On September 27, 1983, we issued a press release in which we identified Hart as a leading dark horse candidate. Our report directly contradicted the conventional wisdom of the day. The media were running articles about John Glenn's right stuff and Walter Mondale's credentials. But as we saw it, they epitomized what the real silent majority hates about politicians.

The real silent majority are independent voters and independent thinkers, who don't practice a party religion. In our research we found that baby boomers were fed up with politics as usual. They were looking for a candidate who offered both an intellectual and a practical approach for dealing with the country's problems, present and future. Hart appeared to be that candidate.

Trends research was relatively new at that time, but Hart recognized its importance. He built a candidacy around "his vision of the future." Mondale and Glenn just talked about their past achievements and what was wrong with the present administration. They were the front runners, but only because the media declared them as such and people didn't know who else was out there.

In analyzing the situation, we recognized early that Hart would emerge as an odds-on favorite. We immediately notified the campaigns of both parties that Hart would do well in Iowa and that he would gain strength. We projected that he would win in New Hampshire.

When it happened, it took the pundits by surprise. They didn't know why Hart had won. We knew why. As we had said in our press release, the real silent majority wanted a candidate who was concerned about the future. But the media, in just two weeks, came up with another explanation. It had been yuppies. And that's how the yuppie craze started.

We pointed out that only about four million out of the 76 million baby boomers had incomes high enough to qualify as yuppies, as defined by researchers. So Hart's success had nothing to do with yuppies. But the media didn't want to hear the facts. They preferred their own explanation.

It may be hard to believe now, but until then no one had ever heard the term yuppie, except a handful of researchers. But overnight everybody was talking about yuppies. Before you knew it, everybody was a yuppie expert. Marketers, advertisers, and manufacturers refocused their strategies on the lucrative but virtually nonexistent yuppie market.

With our research that showed why people were gravitating toward Hart, we went to Washington to meet with his staff. When we walked into his campaign headquarters, it was like entering a Kennedy museum. The walls were adorned with John and Bobby pictures. In our discussion with his staff it became clear that they were selling an image. And the image was being fashioned to appeal to yuppies.

I told them that the majority of people don't know anything about Hart. They like his looks, they like the way he loosens his tie and carries his suit jacket on his shoulder. But that's not what the election is about. The sizzle stuff will wear off quickly. Until New Hampshire, he was just an image, but now that he's solidly in the forefront, he's going to be dissected by the press and challenged by his opponents. People are going to want to know what he really stands for, and they're not going to be satisfied with nice sounding phrases.

The campaign was riding high, the egos of the staff were over-inflated. They had reached the point where they believed their own hype. So they didn't listen, and they continued to sell an image, without worrying about substance.

A few weeks later, Mondale demolished Hart by demanding, "Where's the beef? Where's the beef?" And he was right: there was no substance to the Hart campaign.

Nor was there a yuppie trend. It was just a fad, started by the media to explain something they didn't understand. This is a classic example of what we call historical engineering, that is, cutting off the toes of history to fit the glass slipper of the media.

The Globalnomic System

There are other professionals who analyze data and make forecasts, including economists, market researchers, and pollsters. They do valid work, which we use in our analyses. But by themselves they often arrive at the wrong conclusions, because they look at the world through the narrow eyes of their profession.

Economists have this limitation. They make forecasts using economic data, ignoring social, political, and other data. That's why their forecasts are often wrong—the real world is more complex than their quantitative models, however elegant. When we have an economic problem, they have solutions. But they're like doctors who only prescribe a drug for the symptom instead of taking a holistic approach and looking at the patient's body, mind, and spirit.

Market researchers also have this limitation. They study a particular market, and they can tell you all about it. But they're not looking at other fields. When something happens that will affect that market, they don't see it. For example, they didn't see the trend that led to the movement against drunk driving in the early 1980s, which has affected sales of alcoholic beverages. Nor did they see the trend that led to the recent surge in demand for natural foods.

Pollsters have the same limitation. Opinion polling is a snapshot in time, and the focus is set by the pollsters. The typical polling interview is artificial. People are asked specific questions about issues that they probably haven't thought about much. And often they respond as they think they're supposed to.

Politicians rely on polls. Before his defeat in the 1984 presidential primary, John Glenn's pollster said that "pols will follow the polls." He presumably meant that Glenn would address the issues that mattered to the mainstream, and that he would rely on polls to tell him what those issues were. But the polls weren't telling him what really mattered to the mainstream because of their flawed and limited design. People were just parroting back what the media had told them, and the media were just repeating what the politicians had told them. So a candidate who relied on polls was only getting an echo of his own rhetoric.

The same thing happened in the 1986 election. Early that summer the White House decided to present the drug problem as a major issue. The media were invited to help publicize the issue, and they responded with enthusiasm. From June until election day the public was drugged with the drug problem. Politicians jumped on the bandwagon. A few went undercover to show how easy it was to buy drugs— and make headlines. The polls showed that drugs were a major issue for the voters. But this was only a response to the media hype. Relying on the polls, the politicians failed to address the economic and other issues that most people worry about.

In 1988 a national candidate asked us to review his campaign and determine if he was on the right course. We analyzed his speeches and position papers, and we interviewed him for three hours on videotape, asking him a battery of questions. We then gave him 30 issues to rank according to his own values. When we analyzed the results, we found that he was politicking even with us. He ranked the issues in the same order as his constituents had ranked them in one of his polls. He wasn't projecting his own values, he was only following the polls. And when we studied the videotapes, we found "leakage" in his nonverbal behavior, which indicated that he was lying.

The fundamental problem with economic forecasting, market research, and polling is that they ignore information from other fields. The economist who sees the world through the eyes of his profession ignores everything outside of his field. The market researcher ignores everything outside of his field. And so does the pollster.

Our system of forecasting goes beyond the limits of a single discipline. It looks beyond economics and incorporates social, political, and other factors. We recognize that economic data result from an interaction of trends from fields that at first glance seem unrelated to economics. But trends developing in these fields will influence economics. These trends are global, so we call our method of integrating data from many fields the Globalnomic system.

The word is derived from the Latin *globus*, meaning ball, or the whole world, and the Greek *nemein*, meaning to manage. It's a multidimensional system of tracking trends, making forecasts, and proacting. It's not passive, we don't just watch things happen. We take positions, or we try to reverse what's happening. In fact, the biggest secret about trends is that they can be reversed. So Globalnomics is more than an analytical tool, it's a management system.

The key to our system is making connections between seemingly unrelated fields. In our system, thinking globally means making such connections. When the futurists of the 1960s predicted that by now we would be working only 22½ hours a week, they were projecting advances in technology. But they ignored trends in the family, in education, and in the economy that would affect the number of hours people have to work just to stay even. They took a one-dimensional view, they looked only at technology.

That's the flaw that the Globalnomic system is designed to overcome—the failure to see the effects of trends in other fields on the field you're concerned with. With our system, you look at trends in many fields, you make connections, you anticipate effects, and you proact.

= 3 =

Developing a System

Friedrich von Schiller said: "In today already walks tomorrow." At the Institute, we say current events form future trends. That's the basis of our system. We identify and track trends by following current events. We've found that if you understand the present, you can anticipate the future. If you know where you are, and how you got there, you can see where you're going.

But there are two main obstacles. First, you're given so much fantasy and so much hype by the media. Second, you're given so much information, most of which is irrelevant. As a result, your view of current events is blocked, your vision of the real world is blurred. So if you want to detect trends, you have to distinguish reality from illusion, and you have to screen out all that irrelevant information.

Getting Information

As we dress in the morning, or as we drive to work, we listen to the news, and we get some bites of information, which last about 20 seconds. As we relax in the evening, we watch the news, and we get more bites of information, which the networks have prepared for our entertainment.

There's a term used in information processing called GIGO, which means garbage in, garbage out. In other words, the quality of the input determines the quality of the output. From scraps of garbage, we form opinions on major issues.

Think about it. We get more information from a waiter in a restaurant about what to order than we get from news programs about current events. We wouldn't make an investment, accept a job, or choose a mate after getting only 20 seconds of information. So why should we form an opinion on a major issue after only 20 seconds? But that's what most people do.

We get information from four worlds: the media world, the political world, Disney world, and the real world.

The media world includes the news divisions of the three major networks, as well as CNN, Fox Broadcasting, radio, newspapers, and magazines, such as *Time* and *Newsweek*. These are the primary sources of information for most people.

The political world has its own network, C-SPAN, and free mailing privileges. These are the outlets for politicians who try to impress us on cable television and send us junk mail, which of course we pay for.

Disney world is entertainment, the prime-time TV shows, movies, music, magazines, and amusements that are targeted at mass market audiences. But while they entertain us, they also form public opinion. They give us images, they create illusions that many people accept at face value.

The real world is the facts, events, and ideas that affect our lives. The other three worlds are little more than fantasy factories. Yet they dominate the flow of information. They stand between us and the real world, making it hard for us to see the important social, economic, and political events that are forming trends.

Headline News and Junk News

Most people get their news from television, radio, or tabloid newspapers. But what kind of news do they give us? Headline news and junk news.

Headline news is sensational. Trends don't make headlines unless something dramatic happens. For example, Chernobyl was headline news, but the trend that led to Chernobyl had been developing for years.

Also, headlines are often misleading. You can find extreme examples of this by glancing at the tabloids while you're in line at the supermarket. The headlines tell you that a four-year-old girl came back from the dead and had nine children before she was five, but inside the paper you learn that she was in a coma and there's no mention of any children. But even the best papers are often unable to capture the essence of a story in a few words. At times headlines are simply uninformative, as in the following example: "New Fed Report on the Economy Shows Signs of Both Weakness and Strength," which tells you nothing.

Junk news is titillating, exploitative, often depressing, and never important. It gives us a diet of sex, crime, and disaster. It also gives us fare like the baby sagas: Baby in the Well, Baby Doe, Baby M. We get more junk news than any other kind of news, yet it gives us no nourishment. Like junk food, it can fill us up and leave no room for anything else. In the fall of 1987 a poll reported that 69 percent of those surveyed said they were following the story about the Baby in the Well, while less than 15 percent said they were following the presidential campaign.

The media, by their nature, must jump ahead to the next hot story, so they're hooked on headline news and junk news. TV stops covering events that are no longer sensational, newspapers relegate them to the back pages. When an April 1983 report on education documented the failure of our school system and urgently called for reform, it made headlines, and it was a hot story for a while. Then it disappeared from the front page, giving the impression that the problem had gone away. But the problem hadn't gone away.

You have to screen out the headline news and junk news and focus on the real news, the current events that are forming future trends. Real news rarely appears on television, and it rarely makes headlines. It's usually in the middle of the better newspapers, or in specialized publications. There you can find warnings of a crisis months or years before it makes headlines. Years ago you could have found warnings of the savings and loan crisis in the two-inch stories about the failures of minor banks around the country. In the summer of 1989, you could have found a warning of another possible crisis in an item at the bottom of the editorial page of the *Wall Street Journal*, in which a senior Housing and Urban Development official said that the mortgage portfolio of government-sponsored Fannie Mae was "the country's biggest insolvent savings and loan."

The Basic Requirements

Before I show you how we track trends, remember—we do it for a living, so we work at it more than you will. Unless you want to be a trends analyst, I recommend that you simply incorporate trend tracking habits into your daily routine.

There are three basic requirements.

1. *You must have an open mind.* You must be willing to suspend your beliefs so that you can be as objective as possible. If you're reading about an election, you have to forget that you're a Democrat or a Republican. You have to be skeptical about politicians. "Sometimes I wonder," said Mark Twain, "if the world is being run by smart people who are putting us on or imbeciles who really mean it." Try to maintain that kind of attitude. If you look at events through the distorted lens of an ideology, you won't be able to see trends.

2. *You must be willing to accept change.* If you are, you can take advantage of it. But if you reject it, you'll be swept away by it. Now, that doesn't mean you have to accept every change. For example, you don't have to accept the decline of our school system. But you have to accept the fact that it's happening before you can do anything about it. You can't deny it, and you can't ignore it.

3. *You must practice tracking trends.* It's like playing a sport or a musical instrument. If you want to be good at it, you have to practice. But you don't have to spend the kind of time that professional athletes or musicians do. You only have to spend about an hour a day, which you should be able to fit into your routine. In fact, you probably already spend an hour a day reading the paper or magazines or watching TV. So you only have to make better use of that time.

Selecting Fields

The first step in developing your own system is to select the fields in which you want to track trends. I suggest you start with the broad fields that we analyze in Chapters 5 through 13. You can pick up the trends that we've identified and track them yourself. And you can identify trends yourself.

At the Institute we're tracking trends in 187 different categories, most of them within these broad fields. The number changes, since trends have life cycles: they're born, they grow, they reach maturity,

Save $79 off the cover price

☐ 12 issues of <u>Inc.</u> for $12
(You save $24 off the cover price)

☐ Check here for even bigger savings –
3 years of <u>Inc.</u> for only $29.
(You save $79 off the cover price)

Name _____

Company _____

Address _____

City _____ State ____ Zip ____

☐ Payment Enclosed ☐ Bill me

Please allow 4-6 weeks for delivery of the first issue.
Canadian Residents: Add $12.00 per year for postage and GST.

4BMM

BUSINESS REPLY MAIL

First Class Mail   Permit No. 19   Boulder Colorado

Postage will be paid by addressee

**Subscription Service
Department**
P.O. Box 51534
Boulder, Colorado 80321-1534

they hit old age, and they finally die. So categories are added and deleted.

One of our fastest growing categories is the homeless. We put this in the field of the family, but it has causes and effects in other fields, such as politics, health, and the economy. Our fastest growing categories in the environment field are the greenhouse effect, the ozone layer, and toxic waste. Our fastest growing category in the world field is Europe 1992, a subject that emerged only in the spring of 1988.

We also have categories for apparent trends that fizzled out. For example, the patriotism stimulated by the hostage crisis in Iran and skillfully exploited by politicians looked like a trend, but it didn't meet our test. It didn't have economic significance, since it didn't make people buy American goods. So we considered it a fad.

The fields will give you a broad framework for classifying information, and the categories will develop as you identify trends yourself. Your natural tendency will be to add categories that are of special interest to you. This is fine, but don't ignore trends that look as if they won't affect you. If they're really trends, they will affect you, and if you learn to think globally, you'll see how. Remember the key to our system—making connections between fields.

Let me give you an example, using some of our categories. Under A, we have advertising, agriculture, AIDS, airlines, AT&T, and autos. How are they related?

Take advertising, agriculture, and AIDS, which at first glance don't seem to be related. But advertising strategies change because of AIDS, and researchers look at the chemicals used in agriculture for possible causes of the breakdown of the immune system.

Airlines and autos and AT&T are related because work and travel patterns are changing. From these trends, new communications vehicles will emerge. Auto and airline travel will become more difficult as the roads and skies become more congested. The growing concern for the environment will block the expansion of highways and airports. The growing concern for safety will also play a role. So more and more of the travel load will be shifted to communications.

That's how we use the Globalnomic system: we expand the range of our perception of cause and effect, we make connections between fields, we think globally.

Setting Up Files

You read about a possible job opportunity, a possible investment, a new product, or a new process, and later you wish you could remember where you read it. Well, if you can't put your hand on the information, you can't use it. But if you can reach into a file and take it out, you can track trends. So as you develop categories, set up files.

You don't need a computerized data base. You just need a file cabinet or a desk drawer with hanging folders. Set up a folder for each of your initial categories and have room for expansion behind them, so that as you add categories your system can accommodate them.

Suppose you read an article about an election, and it states a candidate's position on an issue that could affect your business. Clip that article and file it under politics, unless you already have a specific category for the issue. Watch for further information on the issue, from that candidate and the other candidates. Follow it.

You might be wondering why you shouldn't just use a clipping service rather than go through all the trouble of reading and clipping articles yourself. There are several reasons.

First, it's important to get the information in the context of the day's news. If you know exactly where the story came from, and what was around it, you'll have a feeling for how it fit in, and how important the editors considered it.

Also, if you use a clipping service, you have to tell them what to look for. But often when you read a newspaper using our method, you'll find things you haven't thought of, things you haven't told the clipping service to look for. So if you rely on them to do it, you'll miss things.

Finally, you should get the news fresh. By the time you get it from a clipping service, you might not be able to take full advantage of it.

You can't rely on someone else to track trends for you. It's like relying on someone else to diet or exercise for you. When I was little, I often wished my parents were rich enough so that I could hire someone to go to school for me. But as much as I hated it, now I'm glad I went myself. And that's why you have to track trends yourself.

You don't have to clip the articles yourself. If you have a secretary or a receptionist, they can do it. And they'll start tracking trends. They'll read and learn about things that they otherwise might not have known about. They'll become more knowledgeable, more valuable to the company.

If your files become unwieldly, you may need to purge information from your system. But be selective. You should keep records of how a trend developed, so that later if you want to know about it, you only have to review your file.

What to Read

At the Institute, we get our information from sources that are available to everyone. Unlike those people on Wall Street who have made headlines, we don't use inside information, we use public information.

Mainly, we read the newspapers. Every day we read the *New York Times* from front to back. We skip the classified ads, and we're very selective in reading editorials. We also skip stories on murders, disasters, and other junk news, since they're not important for tracking trends. They have no social, economic, or political significance.

Our method differs from that of trends researchers who rely on content analysis. They measure the importance of a story by the number of times it gets printed and the number of words in the story. They're bean counters, who take a purely quantitative approach. But no matter how many times a story on the Baby in the Well gets printed, it will never be important. As much as we sympathize with the child and her parents, it has no social, economic, or political significance. So we don't waste our time reading it.

We always read the Saturday paper. Saturday is actually the best day to read a paper. For one thing, they put less headline news and junk news into the Saturday paper, since they're selling it less on newsstand appeal. Also, the government releases a lot of important economic data on Friday afternoon after the markets have closed. And they hold back other important information that might upset people, releasing it for Saturday when not many people read the paper.

"With the readership of Saturday newspapers the lowest of any day of the week," the Associated Press wrote, "and the viewership of weekend television newscasts below that of any weekday, Friday is the first choice for state and federal officials who'd just as soon have no one notice some announcements."

Since we read the paper every day, we don't have to read the Sunday paper so thoroughly. We read the first section, and we read feature stories in the business, real estate, arts, and living sections. Also, we go through the book reviews looking for sources of information. But we're very selective, even more than during the week. We don't want to spend the whole day reading the paper.

Of course, you don't have to read the *New York Times*. Depending on where you live, you could read the *Los Angeles Times*, the *Washington Post*, the *Chicago Tribune*, the *Boston Globe*, the *Atlanta Constitution*, or another such paper. Wherever you live, we highly recommend that you start the day with *USA TODAY*, which covers a wide variety of subjects. I don't know of any other paper, at least in English, that covers so much in so little space. For our system, which makes connections between fields, the content and format of *USA TODAY* is almost ideal. We start the day with it, since it gives us a quick overview of the important events in different fields. Later, we read the *Times* for more details.

We read the *Wall Street Journal*, which is the best daily source of business and economic news. We don't read all of it. We read the front page, except for the news summaries, and we go through it, looking for stories that meet our test. We read the features on international subjects. And we read the commodities page, since the prices of food, fuel, and other commodities are good indicators of inflation.

We also read our local papers to keep up on issues of local concern. When we travel, we always buy the local papers not only to get a view of local issues but also to get another view of national and international events.

In addition to newspapers, we read a number of magazines and journals that have different points of view, ranging from the *Utne Reader* to the *National Review*. We look for sources of information that are out of the mainstream, since we want to have a broad perspective. You'll find these alternative sources in the directory at the back of this book.

What about *Time*, *Newsweek*, and *U.S. News & World Report*? They can be useful if you've missed the papers for a few days, or if you want to get some additional background on a crisis. But if you've been reading the papers every day, you really don't need these magazines. And by cutting them out of your routine, you can save time.

On the other hand, trade journals are very useful. You should read the trade journal of your industry, but you should also read *Advertising Age* or *Ad Week*. By reading one of them, you can learn the strategies of major companies, what they're going to do and why. If you're in a small- or medium-size business, you can see what the big guys are doing. Say you're in the pizza business and you learn that the strategy of Pizza Hut is to focus more on home delivery. How will this affect you? How should you respond?

Newsletters are also useful. As a start, we recommend the *Newsletter on Newsletters*, which tells you what newsletters are available. Then you can get the ones you want.

Finally, if you have a computer and you know what you're looking for, you can tap into data sources. But these are not a substitute for reading newspapers, magazines, and journals. For all our advances in information technology, there's still no substitute for reading hard copy.

You might be wondering how you'll ever find the time to do all this. Well, it will be easier than you think. For one thing, you'll recover the time you're spending now on less useful sources of information. And with our method, you'll read much more efficiently.

How to Read a Newspaper

One of the strains of living in today's world is what we call information overload. The sheer quantity of information available makes it a chore to sift through all that dirt, looking for nuggets of gold. But with the Globalnomic system, you're reading for a purpose, not just reading. You have a framework for deciding what to read, what not to read. So you don't waste your valuable time getting useless information.

When you read the paper, always have a marking pen, and underline or highlight what's important. There are two reasons for doing this. First, it helps you to retain the information. Second, when you go back to the story you don't have to read the whole thing to find what you're looking for. You can just pick it out of the text.

You'll be surprised how much of a story is filler and how little is fact. But always read to the end of a story, because the most important fact of all could be buried there. If an opposition view is presented, it will be there.

After reading the story, write in the blank space above the headline the category under which it should be filed. Then go on to the next story, using our test. Does it have social, economic, and political significance? If not, skip it.

To show you how we read a newspaper, I'll go through an issue of the *New York Times*. Look at the headlines: "U.S. Pledges $2 Billion in Rescue of Biggest Insolvent Savings Unit." The bailout of the thrift industry is going to have a major effect on the federal budget, since it's going to cost at least $500 billion. This story has social, economic, and political significance. "After five days of intense negotiations that often began early in the morning and went late into the evening . . ." Do we really have to know how much beer and pizza they sent out for? ". . . the agency said it had reached an agreement to sell the $30 billion American Savings & Loan Association of Stockton, California, the nation's largest insolvent thrift association . . ." Underline that. ". . . to a group headed by Robert M. Bass of Fort Worth. The chairman of the bank board, M. Danny Wall, said in a telephone interview that it would provide assistance equal to $2 billion to the Bass group." Underline that. "The agreement today is the fourth such transaction involving $1 billion or more that the bank has participated in during the last three weeks." For years we've been following this situation in the back pages and in the Saturday papers. Now it's on the front page, and a lot of people are surprised because they weren't tracking the trend, they weren't anticipating the crisis. After reading the story, we mark it "Thrifts" for filing.

Look at the rest of the front page. "Misery Rises with Rivers in Bangladesh." This is significant, but it's nothing new. We know that Bangladesh is having problems, so this story won't add to our knowledge. The headline is enough to remind us what's happening there.

"Kindness is a Closed Subject as Campaign Officially Opens." We'll read this story quickly, and then we'll mark it for our file on why people hate politicians.

"Compromise to Halt Fines Eludes Yonkers Mayor and City Council." This is about a court-ordered plan to redistribute low-income housing, which is heavily concentrated in one area of the city. It has been resisted for many years, so once you know the story, the headline is enough.

But look at this one. "Price of Illiteracy Translated to Poverty and Humiliation." It's about the effects of illiteracy on our society, a very important trend. We now have 72 million people who are functionally or borderline illiterate, and the number is rising. It's going to result in unemployment, crime, drug abuse, and other problems. So we read this story, and we mark it for filing under "Education."

We've read the front page and found only three stories that are worth filing.

On the second page we find a story about Israel. We'll read this because what happens there affects us. Until the basic issue is resolved, the Middle East is going to be an ignition point of international conflict. This is an example of a story that's no longer on the front page.

But the problem is still there, and taking it off the front page won't make it go away.

"A Citadel of Privilege, Where Now the Masses Marry." This is about the Soviet Union. We'll read this because of what's happening there. Gorbachev is saying their system doesn't work, it needs to be changed. And what he's doing will affect us. Almost anything about the Soviet Union is worth reading.

"Japan in the World: Applying Assertiveness Training to a Foreign Policy." We'll read this. We'll read anything about Japan because they're now a world power. In many ways, our whole future is bound up with theirs.

"Iraq Asserts its Authority in Kurdish Stronghold." We've been following this for eight years, so we only have to check the lead paragraph to see if there's been any change.

"NATO Spy Fiasco Bonanza for Warsaw Pact." We'll skip this. It's just another spy story.

"Greece and U.S. Delay Talks on Military Base." This is an important trend. We're going to lose more and more military bases as the world demilitarizes. How will this affect us? In our budget, for one thing. We'll spend less money on defense, and that will help reduce the deficit.

"In San Diego Developers Profit as Homeless Get Low-Cost Housing." Homeless and housing are two of our categories. We'll read this whole story, underlining the key facts. "By relaxing its building codes and offering low-interest loans to the builders, the city has made it profitable again for private developers to build and operate single room occupancy hotels." So how does this affect you? Are you a contractor? A developer? An investor? Do you put your money into real estate ventures? This might be a good opportunity. In San Diego, developers have found that they can make money on something other than condos and townhouses. And it might work in other cities.

"Effects of Drought Linger on in Mississippi." We'll read this. It's part of the long-term warming trend, and it's going to affect everyone.

There's an editorial about the budget deficit. A major issue. So we'll read that one.

Well, we just read the first section of the *New York Times*. How long did it take? Not as long as it takes to watch the evening news on television. And we got much more information.

The key is to read the paper for a purpose. Use the framework of your categories. Look at the stories and see if they pass the test of significance. If they do, then read them and later file them. If they don't, then skip them.

You'll find that if you track trends, you'll get a lot more out of the paper. And you'll enjoy reading it.

What About TV?

We watch TV for mainstream information. Remember, about 66 percent of the people rely on TV as their primary news source, and if you know what they're being told about current events, you can predict their reactions.

Television is also useful during a crisis, since it can give you the latest developments more quickly than a newspaper. But we don't recommend it for daily information. Even people within the industry don't recommend it. Gene Mater, a senior vice president of CBS Broadcasting, said: "I don't think evening news should serve as the primary source of news. People should be more open to other news sources, such as newspapers and magazines."

In our files we have this story from the *Times*: "Rescue teams and Army helicopters searched yesterday for 300 elk hunters cut off by heavy snow in Washington State while a winter storm barrelled into the southwest dumping 11 inches of snow in Arizona. One hunter died of apparent carbon monoxide poisoning as he huddled in his pickup truck." The story was relegated to the back pages of the paper, as it should have been, but it was the lead story on all three morning network news shows. If you rely on TV for information, this is what you get.

In 1986 every weeknight 38 million Americans watched one of the network evening news programs. They got 22 minutes of news and eight minutes of commercials. Each minute represents about 160 spoken words, which means that the total number of words in a TV newscast would fill a bit more than half of a typical newspaper page. That's how much you get from TV, and most of it is junk news. In the time it takes you to listen to a TV news broadcast, you could read at least half of the newspaper and get a lot more information.

So if you want to be informed, read newspapers, magazines, and journals. Don't rely on TV.

= 4 =

Profiting

Now that you have an idea of how we identify and track trends at the Institute, let's see how we profit from them. Our method has four phases: trend tracking, forecasting, planning, and implementing strategies.

In trend tracking, we identify and track a trend, using the technique we've just described. In forecasting, we project the trend into the future. In planning, we develop strategies to take advantage of the projected change. In the last phase, we implement them.

The process may sound familiar because the last three phases are used by corporations in long-range planning. But their forecasting is based on economic data and market research, while ours is based on data from a number of fields. They build their plan on one or two footings, we build ours on a broad foundation.

Rather than talk about the phases one at a time, I'll show you how the process worked in some actual cases.

The Iran Crisis

I told you how I started tracking trends during the Iran crisis of 1979, and I'll use that as a simple model.

Trend tracking. I was following the political trend in Iran. I was also following the trend of our declining ability to make the world conform to our image, which had become evident in Vietnam. And I was following economic trends, especially inflation.

Forecasting. Projecting the political trend in Iran into the future, I expected that the Shah would fall. Because he was our boy, I could see that this would raise further doubts about the viability of the pax Americana. People in Europe and the Middle East, whose security depended on us, would be further disillusioned. They would feel exposed, and they would take measures to protect themselves. What could they do? They could convert their assets into dollars, as they had done in earlier crises. But with the high inflation, the dollar was rapidly losing its value, and another oil shock would make things worse. So there would be a flight to gold.

Planning. I developed a simple strategy to profit from these trends. I would buy gold, as much as I could, and I would hold it until its price was driven up by people reacting to the fall of the Shah and the consequences.

Implementing strategies. I called a broker, opened an account, and started buying gold. And having proacted, I watched the events unfold as I had expected.

That's the process: trend tracking, forecasting, planning, and implementing strategies.

Mario Who?

Let's take a case from domestic politics. In 1982, when Ed Koch decided to run for governor of New York, it looked like a sure thing. He only had to beat Mario Cuomo in the primary. In an earlier race for mayor, he had trounced Cuomo, so as far as the media and political experts were concerned, Koch was already governor, and they were busy speculating who would be the next mayor.

Trend tracking. At the time there was supposed to be a trend toward conservatism, based on Reagan's defeat of Carter. But we were skeptical. We looked at what was happening in the real world. We were having a severe recession. Many people were out of work, and many more were worried about losing their jobs. In this situation, we saw a rising number of single parents, women who had come into the work force out of necessity, women who couldn't afford day care for their children. The people out of work and the single parents were the victims of two powerful trends: the restructuring of the economy and the breakup of the nuclear family.

Forecasting. Based on these trends, we forecasted that the major issues of the New York election would be the needs of displaced workers and the split family. We believed that in view of what was then happening, people would be more inclined to vote for a candidate who offered to help them than for one who preached the doctrine of self-help.

Planning. We saw what kind of a strategy would win the election. The candidate would talk about the real issues and offer programs to help people—not the programs of the 1930s or the 1960s, but programs for the 1980s—education, job training, and day care for working mothers.

Implementing strategies. As we listened to the candidates, we realized that Cuomo was more attuned to the real issues. Cuomo was talking about the needs of the family, while Koch was trying to ride the conservative wave. In June 1982 we met with Andrew Cuomo, the campaign manager, and we showed him why people would respond to his father's campaign. Though Cuomo was then trailing Koch by 32 percent in the polls, we forecasted that if he stuck to his strategy, he would win. We also recommended that Cuomo avoid getting pinned with the liberal label. He did, and he won.

Buy American

Here's a case from research we did for a consumer products company. Among other things, they wanted us to evaluate the use of patriotism as a theme in advertising.

Trend tracking. We traced the resurgence of patriotism to the outrage provoked by the Iranian hostage crisis in 1979. We saw it as a factor in the 1980 presidential campaign, in which Ronald Reagan responded to America's need to regain its self-respect. We followed this apparent trend as it rose in the early 1980s, climbed with the 1984 Summer Olympics, and peaked with the Statue of Liberty celebration in 1986.

Advertisers were pushing the theme of Buy American, especially in industries that had been hardest hit by imports, such as apparel and automobiles. But our researchers found little evidence that people were buying American products for patriotic reasons. In fact, only 6 percent of people surveyed in January 1985 believed that the country of origin was very important when selecting a product. And our growing trade deficit proved the failure of the Buy American theme.

Forecasting. Based on our analysis, we concluded that patriotism was only a fad, and we forecasted that it would abate. Like the drug issue, it was being exploited by political candidates, but once the elections were over, it would recede into the background. We also pointed out that even at its peak, patriotism hadn't been an effective selling theme.

Planning. We advised our client not to use patriotism as an advertising theme, since we questioned its efficacy. We recommended that they use other themes for marketing their products.

Implementing strategies. We developed an ad campaign for our client. It had a global theme, reflecting the trend away from patriotism.

Sports and Hobbies

In another case, we examined trends that would affect the recreation industries, especially manufacturers of sports equipment, sports apparel, and hobby products.

Trend tracking. We traced the growth in sports and hobbies to the baby boom generation. We noted that Americans had been consistent in the proportion of disposable income they spent on recreation. Between 1970 and 1985, the proportion varied only one-tenth of 1 percent, according to the Census Bureau. The growth followed demographic trends and the general rise in national income. We also noted the growing concern about health and nutrition.

Forecasting. We projected that as the baby boomers aged, they would lose interest in sports and become more interested in hobbies. We projected a decline in tennis and other exertive sports, along with a decline in jogging, and an increase in golf, along with an increase in walking as a form of exercise. We projected that gardening would be one of the fastest growing hobbies. This trend tied into the health and nutrition trend. As people became more concerned about the food they ate, they would want to grow more of it themselves. We also projected growth in arts, crafts, photography, and other hobbies that didn't require physical exertion.

Planning. For companies that made sporting goods, we recommended a shift in emphasis from products such as tennis rackets and running shoes to products such as golf clubs and walking shoes. For companies that used sports tie-in promotions, we recommended more selective approaches to reach the less numerous market of young people. And for companies that sold hobby products, we recommended a broad appeal to the growing market of baby boomers.

Implementation. In this case, our work stopped here. But in other cases, we translate trends into products for our clients.

Business News

This is the story of how we failed to convince CBS to start a business news radio network.

Trend tracking. We were tracking a trend that had begun to worry the major networks (ABC, CBS, and NBC), their declining share of the audience. We saw the public turning to FM radio and cable TV for information and entertainment. In particular, we saw a growing appetite for business news.

Forecasting. Projecting the trend, we forecasted that the major networks would continue to lose share of the audience to programs aimed at special niches, such as business executives and professionals who wanted real news, not junk news.

Planning. We developed a unique programming concept for an All Business Information Radio Network and presented it to CBS in the spring of 1987. Almost immediately, we found resistance to the project—maybe it was the "not invented here syndrome," or maybe it was just the typical large corporate attitude toward new ideas. In any case, after months of discussion, Laurence Tisch told us he wasn't interested.

Implementation. A year later, NBC announced that it was going to start a business news cable channel. And business news radio programs began to appear around the country.

For CBS, the story ends on October 20, 1987, the day after the stock market crash, with Tisch sitting in his office on the 35th floor of the Black Rock. "In the background," wrote the *New York Times*, "the single television set was tuned to the Financial News Network, which was airing a Wall Street report." The head of CBS was tuned to another network, evidently unable to get business news from his own network.

The Snack Foods Industry

Recently, we did some research for the snack foods industry, and using our method we developed strategies for them to profit from trends that will affect them.

Trend tracking. One of these trends is the changing composition of the family, along with the changing roles of its members. Data show that the nuclear family that produced the baby boom generation is no longer the dominant social unit. One-third of the 91 million American households are headed by single adults, and one-fifth of them consist of one adult living alone. In today's society, with 65 percent of the mothers working outside the home, many children are virtually on their own. As many as seven million children under 14 are left unsupervised while their parents work, and this number is increasing.

Another trend that will affect the snack foods industry is the increase in home entertainment. For a variety of reasons, including the cost of outside entertainment, technological advances in audio and video equipment, fear of crime and social disease, and less spendable income, Americans are staying at home more. A 1987 poll of adults from age 18 to over 60 showed that 57 percent prefer to spend their leisure time at home instead of going out. The figure was higher for those over 60, but was surprisingly high for the age 18–29 bracket (43 percent).

Another relevant trend is the changing distribution of income. Our research shows that the middle class is shrinking, while the lower and upper classes are growing. The middle class is moving up, while the lower class has been losing upward mobility because of a lack of education. So income distribution is beginning to acquire a barbell shape.

Another relevant trend is the growing concern for health and fitness. Sales of health publications and video fitness programs have been growing by more than 25 percent annually. Health food products and vitamins now appear on the shelves of most supermarkets and pharmacies. This trend emerged with the baby boomers, and it has been spreading, though it hasn't reached some minorities and the under-educated. Nor does it have much impact on teenagers and preteen-agers.

Another relevant trend is immigration. Data show that immigrant groups are the fastest growing sectors of the population, especially Hispanics. The actual rate of increase is far beyond what the Census Bureau estimates. In 1986 the border patrol caught 1.8 million illegal aliens. Think how many they didn't catch. The impact of this trend has already been felt by the snack food market, in which corn chips have been gaining on potato chips.

Forecasting. Based on the trend of changing family composition and roles, we projected a change in the patterns of grocery shopping. In particular, we projected an increase in teen shopping. At the time of our study, 80 percent of all teens made at least one daily meal for themselves. Four years earlier, only 64 percent did. With both parents working, or with the single parent working, children are being given a lot of money to do grocery shopping. In 1989, they were given $31.7 billion to shop for food. We projected that this would increase as the proportion of working mothers increases. We also projected less leisure time and more home entertainment. In particular, we projected an increase in home parties. And we pointed out that this would be an opportunity for the snack food industry.

Based on the income distribution trend, we projected that the most important growth in demand would be at the low end of the market, with less significant growth at the high end. We projected a decline in faddish gourmet food items. In the middle class, we projected a demand for back to basics.

From the health and fitness trend, we projected that shoppers would prefer products with natural ingredients and without additives, especially at the high end of the market. We projected that this trend would grow stronger as the baby boomers face the problem of how to care for their aging parents. They're getting a preview of what will eventually happen to them. With the splintering of the family, with fewer children, or no children, they can foresee that in their old age they may have no one to take care of them. So they'll be taking better care of themselves.

Based on the immigration trend, we projected higher rates of growth in segments of the market that reflect ethnic preferences, especially in the Hispanic sector. With economic stagnation and social upheaval expected in most of Latin America, the volume of Hispanic immigrants will increase, and their population will grow at about five times the rate of other sectors.

Planning. To profit from these changes, we recommended the following strategies:

1. Develop and market products that appeal to teenage shoppers. The objective was not only to take advantage of their growing importance as shoppers today, but also to start building brand loyalty among them.

2. Focus on the low end of the market and look for niches at the high end, where gross margins tend to be higher. Go back to basics in the middle.

3. Develop products, or new versions of existing products, with natural ingredients and few or no additives.

4. Target products in the corn chip and other segments that originate from high-growth immigrant sectors.

Implementation. Since we did this work recently, we haven't had time to see the effect of the strategies that were implemented. But we were right about the markets, which are evolving as we forecasted.

These cases should give you an idea of how the process works: trend tracking, forecasting, planning, and implementing strategies. Of course, the key is trend tracking, since the other three phases depend on that.

In the next section, we're going to identify some major trends in a number of fields: the media, politics, the family, education, health, the environment, the military, the economy, and the world. We're going to see the causes and effects of these trends, using the Globalnomic system of making connections between fields.

As you read this section, remember that virtually all the information came from newspapers, mainly the *New York Times*, *USA TODAY*, and the *Wall Street Journal*, as shown in the notes at the end of the book. We got the information by reading for a purpose, and you can do the same.

II

THE MAJOR
TRENDS
SHAPING OUR
FUTURE

= 5 =

The Media

We follow trends in the media because they're our primary source of information on current events. To a great extent, our knowledge of the world depends on what information the media give us and how they present it.

At the Institute we've identified three trends in the media that have social, economic, and political significance. The first is a concentration of mainstream sources, including television, newspapers, magazines, and book publishers. The second is government control of information. And the third is the presentation of news as entertainment.

These three trends are interrelated. The concentration has resulted in less diversity and lower standards. It has brought a tabloid mentality that recognizes only headline news and junk news. With their mass audiences, the media conglomerates have a lot of political influence, but at the same time, as they depend on the government for information, they can be manipulated by politicians. In fact, the relationship between the media and politicians has become so close, it's hard to tell who is controlling the other.

Of course, if you're the government and you want to control information, it's easier to deal with a few large corporations than with thousands of independent journalists. And if you want to deny reality, it's easier to create and maintain illusions with an industry whose mission is to entertain than with one whose mission is to inform. I'm not saying that there has been a conspiracy between them, I'm just saying that they have evolved in the same direction. The media world and the political world have become more like Disney world.

Concentration

The concentration of any industry eliminates competition and diversity, resulting in a lack of innovation and a failure to respond to public needs. But it's especially troubling in the media because they're our source of information, and information is knowledge, and knowledge is power.

This trend was already under way in the early 1980s when it was accelerated by the takeover mania. It's exemplified by Rupert Murdoch, the tabloid king, who has built an international empire that now includes newspapers, magazines, a news service, a broadcasting network, TV stations, and book publishing. His purchase of *TV Guide*, with circulation of 17 million, gave him an even wider access to the mass audience, and you can be sure that this won't be his last acquisition.

Other media conglomerates have been buying newspapers, magazines, book publishers, film studios, TV and radio stations, and whole networks. As a result, more than 70 percent of our daily newspapers are owned by about a dozen chains. Most of the magazines are owned by a few large corporations. The merger of Time Inc. and Warner Communications will create one of the largest media empires in the world.

The concentration in ownership is being extended to cable TV as the major networks acquire interests in cable networks. ABC, for example, has interests in ESPN, the Arts & Entertainment Cable Network, and Lifetime Network. NBC has started a cable channel (CNBC), and it has agreed to form a joint venture that will merge the new channel with the news, sports, and entertainment services of Cablevision Systems, a major cable operator.

In the cable industry the system operators have interests in broadcasting networks, cable channels, and programming services. Tele-Communications Inc., the largest cable operator, has interests in American Movie Classics, Cable News Network, the Discovery Channel, Headline News, the Fashion Channel, Home Sports Entertainment, and other services. Time Inc., the next largest cable operator, owns

HBO and Cinemax, with interests in Movietime, the Travel Channel, and Viewers' Choice as well as interests in Cable News Network, the Fashion Channel, and other services in which the major operators all have interests, including Turner Broadcasting System.

So the concentration is not only within each medium but across the different media: broadcasting, newspapers, magazines, book publishing, and movie or TV production. "This reduces public access for independent productions," wrote Ben H. Bagdikian, author of *The Media Monopoly*. "It reduces critical reporting among what used to be competitive media. It reduces diversity of content because the cross-owning company prefers to use and re-use its original material in as many media as it owns. A book manuscript becomes a mass paperback, a TV series, a movie, and so on."

We forecast that unless the government stops the trend of concentration in the media by enforcing the antitrust laws or passing new ones, our access to information will be controlled by a half dozen giant conglomerates. We agree with Nicholas Nicholas Jr., president of Time Inc., who predicted: "There will emerge, on a worldwide basis, six, seven, eight vertically integrated media and entertainment megacompanies."

Government Control

Control of information by the federal government is another ominous development. As Thomas Jefferson said, "Our liberty depends on freedom of the press and that cannot be limited without being lost."

As we look through our file on the media, we can track this trend. "A month ago today," wrote the *New York Times* in late 1983, "the Reagan Administration released a contract that has no precedent in our nation's history to be signed by all government officials with access to high-level classified information. It will require them for the rest of their lives to submit for government review articles or books they write."

A few years later the Reporters Committee for Freedom of the Press issued an alert on the restriction of public access to government information. The report listed 135 specific actions that had occurred since 1981, including threatened prosecution of the press for publishing classified information, proposed amendments to weaken the Freedom of Information Act, and the use of lie detectors.

In 1987 the American Library Association gave a six-year chronology of acts that cut off the free flow of information compiled or controlled by the federal government. The report noted that 78 items had been added to the government's secrecy list. It strongly criticized efforts to restrict and privatize government information, such as public documents and statistics.

That same year the People for the American Way, a public interest group, released a study on the trend toward secrecy in government. It pointed out the unprecedented controls on information, not only on defense and foreign policy issues, where legitimate secrets do need to be protected, but on a host of topics vital to our daily lives from toxic wastes to occupational hazards, from new technology to the health of our children.

A report issued in December 1988 by the International Press Institute said: "One of the saddest truths facing the media around the world today is the growing trend toward government interference in democratic countries." Among other examples, it cited "efforts to limit public access to information held by the American government."

At times, when the government does release information on vital issues, it has been known to distort the facts. For example, in the spring of 1989 it changed the testimony delivered to Congress by Dr. James E. Hansen, director of the Goddard Institute for Space Studies, making his conclusions about the global warming trend appear less serious and less certain than he had intended. This was done by the White House's Office of Management and Budget, which favored a wait-and-see approach to the problem of global warming. "It distresses me that they put words in my mouth," Dr. Hansen said. "There is no rationale by which OMB should be censoring scientific opinion."

Attitude toward Public

The basic problem of the media, especially television, is their attitude toward the public. They think we have no brains, no education, and very short attention spans.

Dave Marsh, a contributing editor of Rolling Stone, said: "I know that most people in the United States aren't stupid, but the people who program radio stations think they are. And the people's anger is rising. They want to change things, but they don't know how."

"Most television executives, on both the local and network level, underestimate the intelligence of the viewer," said Bill Kurtis, a former

CBS co-anchor on the morning news. "The thinking on our program, for instance, is that the interview should last only three minutes because of limited attention span. I don't buy that at all, and it's very frustrating because you really can't get into anything in three minutes."

"The reality is," said Dave Marash, a former TV anchorman, "we live within large systems, public and private, and most local television news coverage of these systems is like the blind man's description of the elephant—a bit of trunk, a bit of leg, a bit of tail. Most local news operations will not expend the time required to understand how these parts add up, nor will they devote the necessary air time required to explain these systemic failures to the viewing audience. They prefer stories with immediate impact and lingering emotional residue."

In an address at Middlebury College in Vermont, Ted Koppel of ABC News said: "We celebrate notoriety as though it were an achievement. What is largely missing in American life today is a sense of context. There is no culture in the world that is so obsessed as ours with immediacy. Most of our journalism is such that the trivial displaces the momentous because we measure the importance of events by how recently they happened." Koppel is saying that our culture is shallow, while admitting that the media are just as bad. But like other TV news performers, he mistakenly assumes that the public shares his values.

If you watch the stars of TV news, the anchormen and anchorwomen, you can see their attitudes toward the public. They have a lot of information, but they only give you little bites of it, as if you couldn't handle any more. And they assume that you want to be entertained, not informed.

News as Entertainment

The trend toward news as entertainment was identified by Edward R. Murrow in 1958. At the time he urged his managers and colleagues to "get up off our fat surpluses and recognize that television . . . is being used to distract, delude, amuse, and insulate us." But they didn't listen to him.

This is a trend that started at the top, with the decision by TV executives that people didn't want hard news, they only wanted entertainment. In December 1984 CBS hired Phyllis George, a former Miss America, and made her the co-anchor of the "Morning News." When TV critics attacked the network for this decision, Ed Joyce, president of CBS News, told them: "If we have learned anything, it's that hard news broadcasting doesn't work in the morning." Well, they hadn't learned anything. The public tuned out, and CBS is still last in the morning ratings.

Network veterans also criticized the decision. Richard Salant, who was president of CBS News for 16 years in the 1960s and 1970s, said: "For CBS News to reach outside the ranks of broadcast journalism demeans our business. If they want to do that, put the show in the entertainment division, the record division, or the toy division, but get it out of news. Once we start playing those games, we lose all credibility."

Commenting on the general trend to hire performers rather than reporters, Walter Cronkite said: "Main stations are not looking for qualified people. Probably the majority are looking more for glamour than substance." And that's what they give you, those unreal people with their blow-dried hair that never moves, never falls out of place.

"Since the mid-1970s," Tom Brokaw said, "two distinct breeds of television reporters have evolved. People serious about their craft and people interested principally in being performers on local television news, where the emphasis is on performance rather than re-porting." From what I've seen, the first breed is almost extinct, while the second has proliferated. The people who give you the news could have stepped out of a commercial, or off the set of "General Hospital." They're actors rather than journalists, and they're not even good actors.

Before he left CBS for public television, Bill Moyers said: "The line between entertainment and news steadily blurred. Our center of gravity shifted from the standards and practices of the news business to show business."

The programmers of these shows love disasters, especially hurri-canes. The guy from hurricane control tells you how Hurricane Bobby got upgraded from a tropical storm. Then they show you footage of palm trees swaying, building up the drama until the climactic moment when the hurricane is scheduled to hit the coast.

They also love stories about mass killers. They exploited the rash of child slayings in Atlanta for more than it was worth, and then they brought it back as a docudrama, just to squeeze a little more out of it.

Even worse, if the story isn't dramatic enough, the programmers have been known to fake the news, or do what they call a "simulation." For example, last summer while Felix Bloch was the subject of an espionage investigation, ABC News showed faked footage of an American diplomat handing a briefcase to a Soviet agent. Viewers were only later told that the footage was a simulation. In the meantime, they might have concluded from the footage that Bloch was guilty. Commenting on the use of simulations, Reuven Frank, former president of NBC News, said: "They now subscribe to the gospel of do anything for an audience. It's marvelous for drama. For news, it's lies."

Extending the idea further, NBC and CBS are planning to do what they call "re-creations," or dramatizations of news events that are completely simulated. These will be seen on NBC's new "Yesterday, Today and Tomorrow," and on CBS's "West 57th." Sid Feders, executive producer of NBC News, said that re-creations are "a natural next step" in TV news. Well, he's right, they're a natural next step in the trend of "infotainment."

There's a saying in economics that bad money drives out good money. We say that junk news drives out real news. The junk news comes first, and then if there's time, you might get a nibble of real news. The other night, the lead story on the 11:00 news was about a woman who had killed two of her children. They spent almost five minutes on this story. Then they had a story about a drug murder, and this was followed by a story about AIDS. Finally, just before the weather, they mentioned briefly that Gorbachev had made some changes in the Soviet form of government. This event was important, the equivalent of our restructuring the House, Senate, and administration, but it got only ten seconds. The junk news got 19 minutes and 50 seconds.

Homogenization

Have you ever switched from channel to channel during the news? You find that the networks are all covering the same stories, in the same order, in the same way. You can almost go from one to the other without missing anything.

I pick up *Time* magazine, and I see that it has the same person on the cover as *Newsweek*. At times they not only have the same person on the cover, they also use the same words. For example, in March 1987 they both had Reagan. *Newsweek* said: "Reagan's Failure: Can He Recover?" *Time* said: "Can He Recover?" The exact same words.

When you look at prime-time programming, you can see how the networks copy each other. If one has a hit, the others copy it. And they copy themselves. If a program works, they give you more of the same. It's like the movies: Rocky I, Rocky II, Rocky III ... Rocky XXIX. They would rather imitate their competitors, or repeat themselves, than try something different. They would rather stop with a success than move forward from that point. They keep giving you more of the same, more of the same. And they wonder why people get tired of it.

Have you ever wondered why newspapers are so much alike? Because they get news from the same source, the Associated Press (AP), which serves 84 percent of the nation's dailies. AP is a network of news and photo bureaus that transmits an estimated four million words a day to an audience of one billion people. Its stories are used not only by newspapers but also by radio and television stations. The decline of its rival, United Press International (UPI), has left AP in a dominant position. If you look at your local newspaper, you'll probably see that more than half of its news was provided by AP.

Have you ever wondered why TV news programs are so much alike? Because they all copy the same model. "In TV-land," wrote *USA TODAY*, "there's no inclination to break the mold, because local television news thrives on imitation. And a station can spend up to $50,000 for a full make-over to look like every place else. Entire companies exist just to make sure that happens. These specialized TV service firms will travel to your station, armed with brochures, cassettes, sales pitches to convince general managers and news directors to keep up with the Joneses."

It's bad enough if the news programs all have the same format and the same content, but it's really insidious if they all have the same point of view. That means they're giving you opinions presented as facts, and they're giving you only one set of opinions.

Whenever the issue of media bias comes up, they're usually accused of being liberal. But they're more conservative than people think. In fact, it's more accurate to characterize their point of view as "establishment," rather than use the liberal or conservative labels, which the media love. Look who owns the media: Capital Cities, GE, the Lowes Corp., Rupert Murdoch, the Hearsts, Gannett, Knight-Ridder, Newhouse, Time Inc., and so on. They're large corporations, which aren't noted for being liberal.

"If anything, journalists bear slightly to the right of center," Dan Rather said, in an interview for *Playboy* magazine. And this is from a member of the club. So we're not getting a liberal bias, we're getting an establishment bias.

Labeling

Because they think we have no brains, the media use labels, such as leftist, terrorist, or environmentalist, to simplify the world for us. Of course, they're giving us their interpretation of the facts. And in doing this, they plant a bias.

By calling someone an environmentalist, they imply that the person belongs to a special interest group or a lunatic fringe. But clean air isn't a special interest, it's a common interest. In a recent poll 86 percent of the people expressed concern about the environment. So the label is misleading, as well as prejudicial, since a great majority of the people are now "environmentalists."

When there's a revolt against a government, the media usually characterize the rebels as leftists, regardless of their actual political orientation. They give us an image before we've even had a chance to form our own opinion, and after they've repeated the label over and over, we tend to accept it. If this doesn't upset you, remember that it was Hitler's tactic to repeat something over and over until people believed it.

For example, in our file on Japan we have a photo of a crowd of people wearing helmets and armed with bamboo poles and metal pipes. They're labeled as "left-wing radicals," but what are they protesting? The expansion of the Narita Airport into neighboring farmland. And who are they? Mainly farmers, who don't want to give up their land. Is this radical? But once they've been labeled, we might have already formed an opinion, and we might not ask such questions.

Because they're trying to entertain us, rather than inform us, the media cast the protagonists of a story as good guys or bad guys. Again, they want us to take a side on an issue before we've had a chance to understand it, and after we've been duped into taking a side, we're unlikely to change it.

Ted Koppel expressed the media attitude when he explained the success of "Nightline" in presenting controversial topics. "People," he said, "like to reduce the news to good guys and bad guys." How does he know what people like? The fact is, the media like to reduce the news to good guys and bad guys, because they think that's what people like.

The "Nightline" formula of controversy was adopted by Morton Downey, Jr. and Geraldo Rivera, and it has degenerated into trash TV. Its purpose is not to inform people but to stir up passions. If you want to study the use of labeling, tune in to one of those programs.

In September 1983, I complimented John Chancellor of NBC for an editorial he did on the use of labels by the media to report on the war in Lebanon. He said: "You raise one of the most vexing and persistent problems with the press. We tend to use shorthand to label everything, and sometimes it can be very misleading—as in the case of the factions in Lebanon. I wish there were something which could be done about it, but am not hopeful in the short run." And things have gotten worse since then, with the media using labels more than ever.

Historical Engineering

People in the media have a saying that there's nothing older than yesterday's news. This is another reflection of their attitude toward the public, who are supposed to have a limited attention span. So they go from one hot story to the next. What happened yesterday no longer matters, all that matters is what's happening now. This attitude makes it easier for the media to do what we call historical engineering, or rewriting history. Because of the lack of continuity in news coverage, people forget what really happened.

An example of historical engineering is what they did with Dan Quayle. At the time he joined the National Guard, almost everyone who was eligible for the draft was looking for a way to avoid going to Vietnam, and the media found nothing wrong with this. In fact, they made celebrities of the protesters. But 20 years later they acted as if Quayle had done something terrible, no doubt assuming that we wouldn't remember what they had said back then. It didn't seem to matter that one-third of the congressmen had also joined the National Guard.

Another example is what they did with Nixon. In April 1988 the Gannett News Service reported: "Richard Nixon is back. It's hard to turn on the TV or pick up a news magazine these days without seeing the former president. After nearly 14 years of living almost as a recluse in California and now in New Jersey, Nixon has resurfaced to assume the mantle of elder statesman." They drove him out of office in disgrace, and now they've brought him back as an elder statesman.

The Future of TV

Ten years ago, the three major networks (ABC, CBS, and NBC) had a 90 percent share of the audience. During the 1990–91 season they had a 63 percent share, according to Nielsen Media Research. Projecting this trend, we forecast that by 1995 the three major networks will have only a 50–55 percent share of the audience.

They're losing audience for all of the reasons given earlier, plus the increase in the number of commercials. Now that they're selling 15-second spots, the networks are bombarding us with 320,000 commercials per year, up 20 percent over 1985. This is driving viewers away, as it did in the 1988 Summer Olympics, when NBC gave us almost one minute of commercials for every four minutes of sports. As I sat with my remote control, evading the blasts fired by sponsors, I wondered what happened to the Olympics.

Cable TV is gaining audience. Cable now reaches 57 percent of American households. Almost half the households have access to more than 30 channels, so people have a lot of choices. And now that 72 percent of households have remote control, it's easy for people to switch channels, to "graze" through the programs until they find something that interests them.

VCRs are now found in 65 percent of American households, which gives people still another option. VCRs are not just a fad, they're a strong trend, and they're one of multiple uses of the TV box, which will eventually be linked to many different sources of information and entertainment.

With more and more competition, the major networks will appeal mostly to the young, the uneducated, and the elderly. In 1983 we put out a release in which we said that "the continued entertainment product shortfall will hasten networks toward the proliferation of news-talk formats. As these expand, network television will become characteristically similar to AM radio, while cable television will become the mirror image of FM radio." We predicted that network TV would become more titillating, more exploitative, with elements of *True Confessions*, *People Magazine*, and the *National Enquirer*.

It's already happening. "Television has gone tabloid," the *Wall Street Journal* wrote in May 1988. "The seamy underside of life is being bared in a new rash of true-crime series and contrived-confrontation talk shows." These shows focus on the sleazy, the sordid, and the downbeat. Two of the most popular shows are "A Current Affair" and "America's Most Wanted," both produced by Fox Broadcasting, which is controlled by tabloid king Rupert Murdoch. Of course, violence is nothing new to TV, but now instead of being mainly fictional, it's real life violence, like the kind you see in the tabloid papers. There has recently been a backlash against the tabloid shows, with more and more national advertisers refusing to buy time on them. But even if they become less offensive, they've set the trend for network TV, and it will continue.

Also, in the 1990s the networks will be challenged by new technologies, such as satellite dishes and fiber optics. An estimated 2.2 million homes get their TV via satellite dishes, and the number will grow as the size and cost of dishes are reduced. This technology will enable viewers to get programs directly from producers or syndicators, bypassing the networks as well as the cable operators. Fiber-optic cable will greatly increase the number of channels a viewer could get, while offering services such as video shopping and data retrieval. If telephone companies are allowed to transmit programming over fiber-optic lines, then the networks and the cable operators will have new competition. But the industry will be dominated by a few giants, offering the same Disney world entertainment in a variety of ways. So viewers will have to seek out the cable channels that offer real information.

= 6 =

Politics

Before I started tracking trends, I worked in the political world, and I got an inside view of it. I observed politicians, and I studied their behavior patterns, just as my friend Anna Novak studies monkeys, and after a while I could predict what they would do. In fact, there's no one more predictable.

If a problem arises, politicians will ignore it. They'll try to divert your attention from it by raising other issues, the ones they've devised to control the agenda of public discussion. If you remind them of the problem, they'll play the rosy scenario, and they'll delay taking action as long as possible. When the problem has finally become so big that they can no longer ignore it, they'll react to it, but they won't attack its cause, they'll only give you symptom relief.

From reading history, I've concluded that politicians have always been like this. So what's new? What's new is the power to form and manipulate public opinion that they've acquired through television. What nuclear weapons were to the art of war, television is to the art of politics.

Politicians discovered television in the 1960s, but they didn't harness it for routine purposes until the 1980s. Now they depend on it. They use it to run for office, they use it to divert our attention from problems, they use it to play the rosy scenario, and they use it to give us symptom relief. But in the process something has happened to the politicians. They've become creatures of the media, like the characters in prime-time TV shows. They've fallen under the control of their handlers, the image makers and pollsters and spin doctors. You begin to wonder who's running the country, the people who get elected, or the people who produce them.

What has happened is, the political world and the media world have been merging. As I said earlier, they've become more like Disney world, which deals in illusions. The whole purpose of Disney world is to entertain us, to divert us from reality. That's why Reagan was so effective at creating and maintaining an illusion of prosperity—he was operating in the world he knew as an actor. Other politicians have used TV in the same way, though not as well as the master.

At the same time, the use of TV advertising in political campaigns has raised the ante for those who want to run for office. I'm not talking about a slight increase, I'm talking about a quantum jump that has changed the game—since 1976, the amount spent for political ads on TV has more than quadrupled. To finance their campaigns, candidates rely on contributions from special interest groups, who naturally expect something in return. It's a system that breeds corruption. Not only that, it undermines the whole idea of representative government, since politicians who have been financed by special interests are no longer responsive to the general public. In fact, an incumbent member of Congress no longer has to worry about being challenged in the next election.

This is where we are. We have a system that isn't working, and people know it. Just as they're tuning out of the major networks, they're turning away from the two major political parties. They're realizing that the Republicans and Democrats don't have all the answers, and that bipartisan solutions aren't the ultimate way of dealing with our problems. They're looking for alternatives. And if those parties don't reform, they're going to have competition.

Political Solutions

The phrase "political solution" is a contradiction in terms. If an action is political, then it's not a solution, it's just an attempt to relieve the symptoms of a problem.

Politicians are the last ones to recognize a problem. They prefer to ignore it, but if you point it out to them, they deny it, as Reagan did with the unemployment problem. He cited the hundreds of ads in the Sunday paper, offering jobs. "That means," he said, "there are employers looking for people to go to work." But those jobs required skills that most of the unemployed didn't have.

Politicians say there's no evidence that a problem exists, as they did with acid rain, the greenhouse effect, the ozone layer. They kept citing a lack of scientific evidence, until they were overwhelmed by it.

Politicians divert attention from a problem, as they did with the need for day care. They talked about traditional family values, but not about the family problems of the 1980s.

That's what politicians do. They ignore problems, deny them, or divert attention from them. They play the rosy scenario, creating illusions of health and wealth, while in the real world people are homeless.

When they can no longer ignore a problem, they react to it, as they did with the trade deficit. But instead of attacking its cause—our excess consumption–they only relieved the symptom by devaluing the dollar. This action had side effects, as foreign investors took advantage of the favorable exchange rate and snapped up our assets at bargain prices.

Politicians don't think globally, they don't look for cause and effect beyond the field where the problem arises. If they want to make our country strong, they build up the military at the expense of other areas. They fail to see that a nation's strength depends on its economy, its family structure, its education, its health care system, and so on. They don't make connections between these areas.

So watch them, and listen to them. But don't wait for them to tell you about a problem, and don't accept their solution to it. If you do, you'll be swamped by a wave.

The Savings and Loan Crisis

To understand how politics can affect trends in other fields, look at the savings and loan crisis.

This crisis had been building for years. It made headlines briefly in 1985 when a large number of savings and loans in Ohio were closed to avoid a panic. Then it seemed to go away, since it was no longer making headlines.

The original function of savings and loans, also called thrifts, was to take deposits from savers and make loans to home buyers. The thrifts paid interest on the deposits, which they held in the form of passbook savings, and they charged interest on the loans, at rates 2 percent to 3 percent higher than they paid on the deposits. This difference gave them an interest spread, the key to profitability.

From the late 1940s to the mid-1960s, an era of stable interest rates, the industry prospered. It paid fair rates on deposits, and it made mortgage loans at fixed rates of 5 percent to 6 percent. It helped to finance the homes in which the baby boomers were born and raised.

Then interest rates began to go up, which put the thrifts in a bind. The rates they paid on current deposits were going up, while the rates they received on earlier loans were fixed. So their interest spread was narrowing.

The government reacted to the problem by imposing ceilings on the rates that banks and federally chartered thrifts could pay on deposits. This was a typical political solution. Instead of attacking the cause of the problem, inflation, they administered symptom relief. If rates on deposits are going up, a symptom of inflation, put a ceiling on them. Forget the cause, just stop the effect, and maybe the problem will go away.

Well, it didn't go away, and the side effects of the government's reaction were very harmful. By imposing that ceiling, the government prohibited the thrifts from paying a fair rate on deposits, and soon the rate of inflation was higher than the ceiling. While prices rose by 7 percent depositers earned only 5.5 percent. They were losing money, their savings were being eaten away.

Some people realized that, and they withdrew their money. But most people didn't. They left their money in savings accounts, trusting the system. They had been told that it was wise to save, even virtuous, and they kept saving.

Meanwhile, the thrifts weren't adjusting to the new conditions. Lulled by the rosy scenario and protected by the ceilings, they waited for rates to go down again.

But rates went up further, driven by inflation, and as the gap between market rates and the ceiling grew wider, more people withdrew their money from the thrifts. They were the ones who had enough money ($10,000) to invest in Treasury bills, which paid market rates. The ones who didn't have enough money were stuck with the ceiling rate. In other words, the government was subsidizing home owners at the expense of small savers, who had no options except to stop saving.

In the early 1970s money managers found a way for people to get out from under the ceiling. They formed mutual funds that took small "deposits" ($500), pooled them together, and invested them in Treasury bills and other money market instruments. They were called money market funds, and they paid market rates. They grew rapidly, and by 1978 they had $45 billion of savings, a lot of which had been withdrawn from the thrifts. At that point the thrifts faced a crisis. Their depositors were withdrawing money, but their funds were tied up in mortgage loans, payable over 20 to 30 years. If the trend continued, they would soon be unable to meet the demands of their depositors.

Again, the government reacted. In 1980 it passed a law that removed the ceiling. As the thrifts offered market rates, they stopped losing deposits. But over the next few years, the rates they paid on current deposits went up to 17 percent, while the rates they received on earlier loans were fixed at about 8 percent. So now they faced another crisis. With the wide negative interest spread, they were losing money, and the media were estimating the number of months individual thrifts had left before they became insolvent.

Remember that from 1966 to 1980 the thrifts operated under a ceiling on interest rates. Their basic function was still the same—to take deposits from savers and make loans to home buyers. For 14 years, while the world was changing, the government froze the industry in time, no doubt hoping that the good old days would come back and everything would be all right. Then finally they recognized that the industry would have to change, since the good old days weren't coming back. They reacted to one crisis, the loss of deposits, and produced another.

In 1982, at the height of this crisis, 250 thrifts failed. Again, the government reacted. They permitted the industry to diversify into other areas. They also approved more lenient accounting practices, which allowed the thrifts to hide their problems. The politicians didn't want to see the problems, they wanted to play the rosy scenario, and they pointed to the better looking balance sheets as evidence of improvement.

For a while the media stopped talking about the thrifts. Their problems seemed to have gone away. But within a few years the problems came back, compounded. With deregulation, many thrifts had rushed into areas in which they had no experience, such as real estate ventures. Now their mistakes were showing up. Also, in its troubled state, the industry had attracted people who shrewdly realized that the government guarantee of deposits was a license to steal. Now their misdeeds were coming to light.

The crisis made headlines in 1986, and Congress began to debate how to increase the resources of the Federal Savings & Loan Insurance Corporation (FSLIC), the agency that insures the industry's deposits. They were still debating at the end of the year when it was found that FSLIC's liabilities exceeded its assets by $6 billion. At that time the cost of bailing out the thrifts was estimated at $16 billion.

Once again, the crisis was defused, and it didn't make headlines again until after the 1988 election. As the facts were revealed, the chairman of the House Banking Committee, Henry Gonzalez, admitted that in 1988 he and other lawmakers were aware of the staggering losses that the thrifts faced but failed to act because it was an election year. "The decision last year," he said, "was that you don't rock the boat."

"Members of Congress," the *Wall Street Journal* wrote, "after years of sweeping the S&L problem under a rug, know they must finally confront it. If they don't raise bank insurance premiums, they must put more of the rescue cost on the backs of taxpayers and possibly have to make offsetting cuts in spending on popular domestic programs." They knew they must finally confront the problem because it was headline news, but they came up with yet another political solution.

Here's a problem that arose in 1966, and they still haven't done anything about it. They haven't attacked its causes, they've only tried to relieve its symptoms, and in the process they've made it worse. But listen to them. Instead of admitting their mistakes, they're blaming the people who ripped off the industry. They're going after these people, just as they're going after the people who supply drugs. Symptom relief, that's all they know.

We estimate that political solutions to the problems of this industry will cost us at least $500 billion. When you pay your taxes, remember that.

Media Campaigns

There was a time when "political campaign" and "media campaign" were different things. Now, with the merger of the political and the media worlds, they're the same thing. They have the same attitude, and they use the same techniques. They even involve the same people. "Old politicians don't die or fade away any more," said Eddie Mahe, a political consultant. "Now they just go on the networks."

Like the producers of prime-time television, the handlers of political candidates have a low regard for the public. They program candidates for the mainstream, or what they imagine as the mainstream—couch potatoes, with no brains, no education, and very short attention spans.

"I represent the mainstream," Bush said during the 1988 campaign, "the mainstream views and the mainstream values. If I win it will be a mainstream mandate. That's what this election is about." But when someone asked him what the mainstream was, he had trouble describing it. He talked about family values, about school prayer, and about the death penalty for killing a police officer. That was all. He didn't say anything about the issues, about the problems in our society.

Playing to an imaginary audience, political candidates evade the issues and talk about values. They surround themselves with family, they wrap themselves in the flag. They make claims about our way of life. But real people want to hear about jobs, housing, health care, and education. That's why after listening for a while, they tune out.

The candidates not only evade the issues, they create false issues to divert the public. Remember what a big deal they made about the pledge of allegiance? Was that a real issue? If it was, what happened to it? As soon as the election was over, the politicians and the media stopped talking about the pledge of allegiance and started talking about the real issues. They're talking a lot about them now, especially the savings and loan crisis. But do you remember one word that either candidate said about the problem during the campaign?

Like the media, the candidates stayed with proven formulas. We heard Dukakis comparing himself and Bentsen with Kennedy and Johnson, the winning combination of Massachusetts and Texas. We heard Quayle compare himself with Kennedy. It's the same mentality that gives us sequels like Rocky II and Rocky III. They try to sell us JFK II and JFK III. They even tried to sell us Nixon II. In 1988 I saw teeshirts that said: "He's tan, he's rested, he's ready—Nixon in '88."

I talked about how the major networks copy each other and give viewers the same programs. The two major political parties do that too. They copy each other, and at times you can't tell them apart. As pollster Pat Caddell said, we don't have two political parties, we have the Washington Beltway party. "It's like the NFL," he said. "It has two conferences, the Democrats and the Republicans. The second string is the press. The Washington press corps have become players."

If you want to see how politicians and the media play together, look at the presidential debates. The nonpartisan League of Women Voters used to sponsor them, but in 1988 they pulled out because they felt that the debates no longer served the public. The two major political parties formed a commission to sponsor them, and with the media they worked out a format that suited both of them. So instead of debates, we got media events.

Actually, the whole campaign was just a series of media events, carefully staged to project an image, while avoiding productive discussion of the issues. Instead of getting the details of his position on defense, we saw Dukakis riding in a tank, with a helmet covering most of his head. Instead of getting the details of his position on education, we saw Bush speaking at a high school, with a line of cheerleaders doing their routine. Instead of getting information, we got entertainment, Disney world.

With the merger of the political and the media worlds, the dialogue between the candidates has been reduced to one-liners. Instead of getting thoughtful discussion of the environment, we got a one-liner about the pollution of Boston Harbor. And of course we also got labeling. A main strategy of the Bush campaign was to pin the liberal label on Dukakis, while creating a negative perception of it.

This raises the subject of negative campaigning. I think most observers agree that the 1988 campaign was extremely negative, not only at the national level but also at the local level. Eddie Mahe gives us the rationale: "The incumbent is the product the voters are now using. If they're perfectly happy with that product, they're not going to switch. So before a challenger can get his message across, before he can even get people to pay attention to him, he has to explain why they should be dissatisfied with what they have. That means negative ads. . . . The bottom line is negative works."

Negative ads aren't new. In the 1964 campaign Johnson ran the now-famous ad in which a little girl with a daisy was about to be obliterated by a nuclear blast, implying that this would happen if Goldwater got elected. But the ad was broadcast only once. In the 1988 campaign the ads were repeated over and over, and they had an effect. "Polls have shown negative ads work," wrote *USA TODAY*, "even though voters say they dislike them."

The 1988 campaign had almost all the elements of network TV: the 20-second bites of information, the staged events, the proven formulas, the labeling, the commercials. The only thing missing was a laugh track.

Special Interests

As television has become the dominant medium for political campaigning, the cost of running for office has escalated at both the national and local levels. In 1988 the presidential candidates spent $500 million, the congressional candidates spent $457 million. To pay these expenses, they have to raise money, and just as the sponsors of TV programs influence their content, the sponsors of political candidates influence their behavior. So we end up with a government that represents special interests.

Who are these sponsors? They're political action committees (PACs), representing businesses, labor unions, and trade associations that contribute money to election campaigns. In 1990 they contributed about $180 million to congressional candidates. They gave it to the candidates who could help them the most. For example, in the past three elections, PACs of the savings and loan industry gave almost $4.5 million to House and Senate candidates. The major recipients included Fernand St Germain, former chairman of the House Banking Committee, and Don Riegle, chairman of the Senate Banking Committee, as well as other members of these committees. What did the industry get for its money? Benign neglect, perhaps? While hundreds of thrifts were going under amid charges of mismanagement and fraud, Congress looked the other way. "The big story of the S&L crisis," said Edwin Gray, former chairman of the Federal Home Loan Bank Board, "is how Congress didn't listen to regulators because we didn't make contributions."

By sponsoring candidates the special interests not only get representation, they keep it. Look at the House, which is supposed to be responsive to the public. Instead, it has almost no turnover. In the 1990 elections 96 percent of the incumbents won, and in 83 of the 435 contests the incumbent was either unopposed or had only token opposition.

A study by the Center for Responsive Politics showed that the 1988 congressional election winners outspent losers by as much as ten to one. On average, the House winners spent more than three times as much as the losers. Only six House incumbents lost, and most of them were defeated because of ethics scandals. On average, the Senate winners spent more than twice as much as the losers. Only four Senate incumbents lost. "What we are talking about," said Ellen Miller, executive director of the center, "is the buying and selling of elections."

It takes money to buy an election, and PACs clearly favor incumbents. In the 1988 House elections they gave $82.2 million to incumbents and only $9 million to challengers. Why do they prefer to back incumbents? "Political action committees want to put their money where it will do the most good," the *New York Times* explained, "and incumbents are a good risk."

Amitai Etzoni, director of George Washington University Center for Policy Research, said: "Most members of Congress accept frequent campaign contributions in exchange for doing the work of special interests. Political action committees openly pride themselves on not really going after votes, but electing friends and defeating enemies. The result is actually more detrimental to the democratic process than buying votes one at a time." It certainly is. If you buy votes one at a time, you're only corrupting the system. If you buy representatives, you're destroying it.

"Here, sir, the people govern," Alexander Hamilton wrote, describing the function of the House. "Here they act by their immediate representatives." Now the special interests govern, acting by their representatives.

The Revolving Door

Another reason why our system isn't working is that too many important government positions are filled with political appointees. Typically, they come from the private sector, work for an agency that procures from their industry or regulates it, and then go back to the private sector at a higher level than before. They seem to regard their appointments as stepping stones, rather than as goals.

One of the many revolving door stories in our file is about a man who worked for a firm of naval architects and then became assistant secretary of the navy. While in that position, he approved some large noncompetitive contracts for General Dynamics. Then he left the government for a position as senior vice president at General Dynamics. That's the pattern, the revolving door.

Again, this problem isn't new. Its underlying cause is that in our country government service doesn't have a lot of prestige, and it doesn't pay as much as the private sector. Also, government service has become highly politicized, which discourages people from making long-term commitments. So it doesn't attract the best and brightest, at least for careers. It attracts opportunists who use their positions to advance themselves, rather than to serve the public.

We saw an effect of the revolving door syndrome in the Department of Housing and Urban Development (HUD) scandal, which made headlines in the summer of 1989. What emerged was a pattern in which former government officials, including at least one cabinet member, used their political influence to obtain millions of dollars from federal low-income housing programs in return for large consulting fees from developers. The media characterized their behavior as "influence peddling," which may be legal but certainly raises questions of ethics. Is it right for former government officials to peddle their influence? Is this the purpose of working a few years for the government as a political appointee?

There's also the problem of incompetence. We hear about the conflicts of interest, but we don't hear about the bad decisions—until we have to pay for a bailout. Look at the HUD programs, which were supposed to provide low-income housing. How well did the people running those programs spend the money? How competent were those political appointees? Ask the homeless.

After the 1988 election we read about how Bush had to fill 5,000 administrative positions, and there wasn't even a change in party. That gives you an idea of the turnover in government positions at the management level. Instead of being filled by career people, most of these positions are filled by political appointees. Where do they come from? Well, if the position is in a regulatory agency, they often come from the industry being regulated, or from its lobbying group. For example, two former chairmen of the now defunct Federal Home Loan Bank Board, which regulated the thrift industry, came from the U.S. League of Savings Institutions, its powerful lobbying group.

The practice of filling management positions with political appointees perpetuates a vicious circle. It leads to a high rate of turnover, and at the same time it discourages the best and brightest from pursuing careers in government service, since they don't have a path to the top positions. So when Bush had to fill those 5,000 positions, he had trouble finding enough qualified people within the government.

"We are not attracting first-rate people in the same depths that we were," said Paul Volcker, former chairman of the Federal Reserve. He attributed this problem to the trend toward more political appointments at upper levels, which bred morale problems. "Would you want to be bossed around by a deputy assistant secretary who was an advance man?"

Corruption

There has always been corruption in public office, but recently we've seen more and more of it. We see it at every level now: in the cabinet, in Congress, in the federal agencies, in the Pentagon, in the state and local governments, in the judiciary.

Michael Deaver, an aide to the president, was convicted of perjury.

Edwin Meese was found by the Justice Department to have engaged in conduct that "should not be tolerated of any government employee, especially not the attorney general."

Jim Wright, the Speaker of the House, resigned after an investigation of his financial dealings, and Tony Coehlo, the House Majority Whip, resigned after media reports questioned the propriety of a 1986 junk bond investment. But don't feel bad for either of them: Wright gets a $200,000 annual allowance from taxpayers, and Coehlo has a $1 million job on Wall Street.

Mario Biaggi, congressman from New York, was sentenced to two and one-half years in prison for accepting illegal gratuities and for obstruction of justice.

Harold E. Ford, congressman from Tennessee, was indicted by a federal grand jury on charges of conspiring with two former bankers to commit mail, bank, and tax fraud. The former bankers were C. H. Butcher and Jacob F. Butcher, brothers who once controlled 27 banks in Tennessee and Kentucky. Both of the Butchers were convicted of fraud.

James Traficant, congressman from Ohio, was found liable for federal taxes of $108,000 in bribes accepted from reputed organized crime figures while sheriff of Mahoning County.

Pat Swindall, congressman from Georgia, was convicted on nine counts of lying to a grand jury investigating charges involving the laundering of drug money. The conviction is under appeal.

Dan Walker, former governor of Illinois, pleaded guilty to fraud and perjury charges resulting in part from improper loans arranged for him from his own savings and loan association before it went bankrupt. He's serving seven years at a minimum security federal prison in Duluth.

David Friedland, a New Jersey state senator, was convicted of fraud. To avoid prison, he fled the country. He was later found on a resort island south of India, where he owned a scuba shop and led diving trips for tourists.

R. Budd Dwyer, former treasurer of Pennsylvania, made news when he blew his brains out during a televised news conference the day before he was to be sentenced on 11 bribery charges.

Robert Garcia, congressman from New York, was convicted of extorting cash, loans, and jewelry from Wedtech Corporation, a defunct defense contractor. Before he was sentenced to three years in prison, he resigned from Congress.

Samuel Weinberg, a Brooklyn civil court judge, collapsed into his wife's arms moments after he pleaded guilty to federal racketeering charges.

I could go on, but you've probably had enough. The bottom line is, people have become cynical about government. In a 1989 poll, about half the people estimated that 40 percent or more of our congressmen are corrupt.

Breakdown of System

In recent years, politicians have been losing their audience. During the 1988 conventions, more than two-thirds of the prime-time viewers were watching something else.

Among the major democracies, we have the worst record of voter turnout. In the 1960 presidential election only 63.1 percent of the eligible voters cast ballots. In 1988 only 50 percent did. In off-year elections, voter turnout is even worse. In 1990 only 36 percent of the eligible voters went to the polls. This was the second lowest turnout since 1942, a wartime election.

The experts who analyze the low voter turnout blame poll times, polling places, and voter registration procedures, but they never blame the candidates, they never blame the pollsters and handlers who advise the candidates not to talk about the issues. And like the producers of network TV shows, they wonder why people are tuning out.

Disgusted with the system, people are abandoning the two major political parties. In the 1986 election 43 percent of the voters said they were independent, compared to 23 percent in the 1980 election. That's a trend.

About one-half of the baby boomers say they're independent. Even blacks, who maintained a strong loyalty to the Democratic party, have begun to drift away from it. A poll taken in October 1988 found that blacks were less committed to the Democratic party than they were four years earlier. The decline was especially evident among young blacks.

The problem is, our two major parties are living in the past, they have a World War II mentality. They're not addressing the present issues, let alone the future issues. And if they don't change, we're going to see new parties in the 1990s, formed around issues like health and the environment. It has happened before, as in the case of the Republican party, which was formed around the issue of slavery. Projecting present trends, we forecast that it will happen again.

It's happening in Eastern Europe. The system wasn't working, so now it's being changed. The changes aren't coming from political parties, they're coming from coalitions of people who are fed up with the system. As we watch these changes from a safe distance, we understand them, since we can see how the Communist system had broken down.

But whether or not we can see it, there's ample evidence that our own system has broken down. We have a high divorce rate and a high teenage pregnancy rate. We have a high rate of mental illness among our children. We have a 30 percent dropout rate in our schools. We have 27 million people who are functionally illiterate. We have 32 million people living below the poverty level. We have a high crime rate and a drug problem. We have polluted air, we have contaminated food and water. We have the highest infant mortality rate as well as one of the shortest life expectancies among industrialized nations. We have unaffordable and inadequate health care. We have homeless people.

Politicians ignore these problems. They hide behind the shield of office, they sneak out back doors so they won't have to confront the press, they rarely take questions from live audiences, they stage most of their public appearances to exclude people with contrary views. Using the media, they give us the fantasies of Disney world rather than the facts of the real world.

They not only ignore the problems, they also contribute to them, as we saw in the case of the savings and loans. Politics is a cause of problems, in business as well as in government. H. Ross Perot, the Texas billionaire who tried and failed to change things at General Motors, said: "My greatest regret is over the maneuvering and politics and power-grabbing going on inside the corporation, which distracts them from making the finest cars in the world." Well, my greatest regret is over the politics going on in the government, which prevents us from being the finest society in the world.

In my talks around the country I get a strong response to what I say about politics. People realize that our system isn't working, and they understand why. They're tired of the political hype. They're sick of the lies, the corruption, the waste. And they're going to demand changes.

As we look around the world, we see changes in countries whose leaders have sensed the public mood. We see changes in the Soviet Union, with *perestroika*, which means a restructuring of the system. It's coming from the leader, Gorbachev. Remember Brezhnev, who epitomized the old order, the old mentality, the World War II generation, with all the medals on his coat? Well, when we look at Gorbachev, we don't see medals, we see the beginning of a new mentality.

We also see the beginning of a new mentality here, though it hasn't been welcomed by the media. They write admiringly about Boris Yeltsin, the former Moscow party leader, who wants to accelerate the process of change in the Soviet Union. But when we have a candidate who wants to do the same thing here, they label him as a radical. They applaud what's happening in Eastern Europe, portraying the intellectuals, artists, and students who have led the demonstrations as heroes. But when we have demonstrations here, they characterize the leaders as extremists.

In the 1990s we'll have new national leaders. What will they be like? We can get an idea by looking at the state of Mississippi, where a new order has emerged from the baby boom generation. Led by Governor Ray Maybus, they've replaced the old order in a state that was known for resistance to change. In running for office, they addressed the issues, they appealed to the public's intelligence. They avoided the traditional negative campaign tactics of Mississippi politics. Maybus was elected with 82 percent of the vote, which shows that people will respond to a positive campaign.

We expect to see candidates from the baby boom generation emerge on a national level by 1992. In the last election, Bush picked a baby boomer as his running mate, and looking at the vice presidential candidates you could see the difference between the old and the new generations: Lloyd Bentsen led a bomber squadron in World War II, while Dan Quayle was obviously not a war hero. The age of war heroes is over.

Catalyst for Change

When you look at history, you realize that tax issues have often been the catalyst for reform movements and revolutions. For example, there's the Magna Carta, the French Revolution, the American War of Independence. Looking at the current trend, we predict that the tax issue, or spending issue, will be the catalyst for change in the 1990s.

The Disney world story is that taxes have been reduced, but the real story is that the tax burden on working people is heavier now than ever before. In fiscal 1988 the total tax bite was a record 32.2 percent of GNP, despite lower income tax rates. Each year the Tax Foundation, a Washington-based research group, calculates the number of days that the average American must work to pay federal, state, and local taxes. For 1989 the magic number was 125. This means that from January 1 to May 4 the average American is working for the government.

Not only that, but more and more of the tax burden is being carried by people without regard to their ability to pay. In other words, taxes have been getting more regressive. The Social Security tax, which falls most heavily on low- to middle-income workers, has been steadily increasing. Sales taxes, imposed by the states, have been increasing. Property taxes, which bear no relation to income or spending, have been increasing. They're draining income from current home owners and making it harder for people to become home owners. They've become so high that many of the elderly can no longer afford to stay in their homes, after struggling all their lives to pay off mortgages.

Public reaction to the Tax Reform Act of 1986 was less than enthusiastic. In a survey of households by the Conference Board, 53 percent said the new law was less fair than the old law, 14 percent said it was fairer, and 33 percent said they saw little change. So in spite of all the hype about tax reform, most people realized that it hadn't lightened their tax burden.

Beyond that, people are aware of the gross injustices in our tax system. They know that the "reform" favored people in the higher income brackets. In fact, some people earning between $10,000 and $40,000 actually had to pay higher taxes, while people earning more than $200,000 benefited from huge tax cuts.

While they see wealthy individuals successfully avoiding taxes, average people are being harassed by the IRS (which recently joined the lengthening list of government agencies tainted by scandal). Responding to complaints, four lawmakers in early 1987 introduced a taxpayers' bill of rights for protection against abusive, overreaching, and heavy-handed IRS practices. One of the sponsors, Senator Pryor from Arkansas, said: "The public is rapidly losing faith in our system."

I'm always amazed when they come out with these polls showing that 45 percent of the people wouldn't mind paying more taxes to reduce the budget deficit. Well, I don't know how they pose the question, but I don't know anyone who wouldn't mind paying more taxes. If you want to know how people really feel about taxes, look at what happened to Mondale in the 1984 election. He said he was going to raise taxes, and he got wiped off the map.

Correctly reading the mind of the public, Bush said there would be no new taxes. Being a politician, he broke his promise, and he ignited an explosive issue. Though people were distracted by the prospect of war in the Middle East, they organized in hundreds of cities to protest against higher taxes. And in the 1990 elections they sent a message to candidates who were associated with a policy of raising taxes.

The tax issue, or spending issue, is now the main topic of debate at the state and local levels of government. Thirty states are facing budget deficits this year, and more are expected to be in this position next year. Most of them are considering tax increases as well as spending cuts, and some people are already feeling the effects—for example, the teachers and health workers who are being laid off.

As taxes rise and services decline, the public is becoming more conscious of the fact that we have limited resources and that therefore we must set priorities. That's where the public is going to get involved, in setting priorities. That's where the changes are going to occur.

At this point it's clear that the tax issue, which is really about the allocation of resources, is going to be the major issue of the 1992 elections. So track what's happening now in our states, cities, counties, and towns.

= 7 =

The Family

Politicians like to talk about the family. It's a lot safer than talking about the economy, and people respond, as they responded to "The Waltons." Remember that? It showed a family in the 1930s, three generations living happily under one roof: the father, who worked within shouting distance of their house, and the mother, who took care of them, and the five or six children, who got along, and the grandparents, who helped the parents. That was an extended family, which by the time of the program no longer existed. In fact, by then the nuclear family, portrayed in "Happy Days" and "Family," was breaking down. But this is the kind of family politicians talk about, the mother and father who stay together, raise their children, and care for their parents. Like "The Waltons," they're appealing to nostalgia.

The nuclear family, with father as breadwinner, mother as home-maker, and children, is no longer the norm, except in Disney world. In the real world it represents only 10 percent of American households. It has been replaced by two-income families, single-parent families, and other arrangements. We can see the causes of the two-income family by looking at economic and social trends. One of these causes was the decline in real personal income, which made it difficult, if not impossible, for families to maintain their standard of living without a second income. Another cause was the rising aspirations of women for the psychological, intellectual, and monetary rewards of a business or professional career. We can see a cause of the latter trend in the number of women who went to college during the 1960s, and we can see the effects of the two-income family on our society. It has shifted more of the burden of raising children and caring for the elderly to institutions, the expenses of which are largely borne by the general public.

While politicians talk about family values, as if we were still living in the world of "Happy Days," the breakdown of the family has contributed to many of the social and economic problems we now confront: high school dropouts, poverty, crime, drugs, the homeless. If you think globally, you can see the connections. In fact, you can see the feedback between the family and education, which determines future income. Single mothers are twice as likely as married mothers not to have graduated from high school. Single-parent families are likely to be living below the poverty level. Children living with single parents are likely to drop out of school. So the cycle keeps feeding on itself.

We hear proposals to fight drugs, or to improve our schools, or to care for the homeless, but these are usually political solutions, symptom relief. They don't attack the causes, many of which are in the family. I'm not saying that the government should get involved with the family, I'm just saying that they should develop policies that help the new forms of family raise children and care for elderly. But first our leaders have to recognize that these are now the prevailing forms, that the days of "Ozzie and Harriet" are over.

Meanwhile, we see adjustments in the two-income family, as women in their 30s start having children. By now they've been working for 10 to 15 years, and depending on whether they've saved anything, they're likely to take a leave of absence, or work at home, or work part-time. They want to spend more time with their children. This shift in priorities looks like a back-to-the-family trend, but it won't be the old nuclear family. It will be a family in which men and women will no longer play the specialized roles of breadwinner and home-maker.

For the single-parent family, unless there are changes in government policy, things will get worse. The children will have less opportunity to break out of the poverty cycle, and they'll join the ranks of a growing underclass. The middle class, with fewer recruits from the lower class, will continue shrinking as its members move up. We'll develop a class structure that looks like a barbell, with many people at the high end and the low end, but few in the middle.

Working Mothers

The extended family was the victim of the prosperity and mobility that followed World War II. In the 1950s it evolved into the nuclear family. Typically, the parents in a nuclear family no longer lived where they had grown up. They separated themselves from grandparents, uncles, aunts, and cousins, so they lost the support structure of the extended family. Women, who had joined the work force in large numbers during the war, went home to raise children, run a household, serve the community, and care for the elderly, while men provided all the income. This system worked because in the 1950s and 1960s a middle-class family could live on one income, and though some women went back to work once their children had grown up, it usually wasn't out of sheer economic necessity.

In the 1970s the pattern changed as the economy faltered and real personal income declined. By the end of the decade, mothers could no longer afford to stay at home and raise children. Whether or not they were "liberated," the economic situation drove them back into the work force. And the trend continued into the 1980s, with more and more mothers working. According to the Census Bureau, in 1970 less than one-third of married mothers with children under age six worked outside the home. By 1980 more than one-half did, and by now about two-thirds do. Even more significant in terms of the need for child care, in 1976 about 30 percent of mothers with infants worked outside the home, and by 1988 almost 50 percent did.

Most families need two incomes just to keep up. Without the second income, they would sink out of the middle class. So from economic pressure, the nuclear family has evolved into the two-income family, and women who work outside the home try to raise children, run a house, and care for the elderly at the same time. Women did all these things in the past, but they had an extended family to support them. Now they have only a husband, if that.

The Single-Parent Family

In 1960 one out of every ten children under the age of 18 lived with a single parent. In 1980 one out of five did, and now it's one out of four. But this doesn't tell the whole story, since many of the children who are counted in two-parent families go through periods of living with a single parent. Almost 60 percent of all children spend at least one year in a single-parent family before turning 18.

Single-parent families have been increasing because of divorces and because of births to unmarried women. One out of two marriages ends in divorce, and births to unmarried women now account for 22 percent of all births. That's more than one out of five births. Compounding the problem, the unmarried mother is often a teenager. In fact, each year one-half million teenagers have babies, and more than 60 percent of them are unmarried. That's a change from the 1970s, when fewer than one-third of the teenage mothers were unmarried. Back then, if you were an unmarried teenager and you had a baby, it was a mistake. Now it's an accomplishment. For some girls, it's the only way they can see of gaining an identity.

Whatever the cause, the single-parent family has a rough time economically. There's only one income, and it's provided by a woman, who typically doesn't earn as much for the same work as a man does. It's lower if the woman is young, and it's getting even lower. For single mothers under age 25, real income has declined by almost 20 percent over the past 15 years. One out of three single mothers is living below the poverty level.

A study by Sheila Fitzgerald Krein and Andrea H. Beller of the University of Illinois at Urbana found that the more time children, especially boys, spend in a single-parent family, the less schooling they're likely to complete. "Time spent with a single parent during the formative preschool years seems to have a particularly negative impact on the boy's future education," the researchers said. Since education determines future income, time spent with a single parent may have economic consequences. And six out of every ten children are likely to spend at least a year with a single parent. Here's a connection between the family, education, and the economy, which you can see by using the Globalnomic system.

Child Care

In the two-income family and the single-parent family, there's a need for child care that didn't exist in the nuclear family when the mother stayed at home. While the new family forms have become more common, replacing the old nuclear form, neither the market nor the government has met that need.

It's estimated that the average family can afford to spend about 10 percent of gross income on child care. The actual cost of most services is higher than that, as much as 25 percent. Whatever the cost, it's an extra burden, since 20 years ago the average family spent virtually nothing on child care. And now the costs of housing, health care, and taxes absorb a much higher percentage of income. So the need for child care has emerged at a time when the average family is being squeezed.

For the two-income family, the problem is availability. For the single-parent family, the problem is affordability. But it's the same problem—the need for child care is greater than the present system's ability to provide it. And the need is growing every year.

The government has reacted in the usual way, refusing to admit that there is a problem. In April 1988 a task force of the Labor Department concluded that there wasn't a problem in child care availability. Well, maybe there wasn't a problem for them. There are ten day-care centers in Washington for children whose parents work for Congress or federal agencies. They're available to high-ranking employees and members of Congress, who make $90,000 or more a year.

But for those who don't receive such benefits, there is a problem. In fact, it's so bad that some parents leave their children in public libraries. A 1985 survey in Los Angeles found between 1500 and 2000 unattended children in libraries each day. By early 1988, because of concerns over legal liability, libraries discouraged and even banned children who were not accompanied by adults.

One reason for the shortage of good day-care facilities is the low pay for workers, who typically earn between $10,000 and $12,000 a year. They get paid less than just about anyone you can think of, which indicates something about the values of our society. Yet if they got paid more, fewer families could afford day care. So raising salaries alone won't solve the problem.

What's needed, especially by single-parent families, is financial support for day care. But at the Institute we don't expect it to come from the federal government, which is unable to meet existing commitments out of revenues. And we don't expect it to come from state and local governments, which are overextended as a result of the federal government's policy of shifting responsibilities to them.

That leaves the private sector. Today about 3,300 companies with more than 100 employees offer child care benefits, including on-site day care, financial assistance, flexible work schedules, and family leave options. This is a significant increase over the 600 employers that offered such benefits in 1982. It's estimated that one-half of all the medium and large companies are considering day-care benefits.

Facing labor shortages, many companies offer child care benefits to attract and retain women employees. Large companies are more likely to establish day-care centers, while small businesses are more likely to allow flexible hours, extended leaves, job sharing, and part-time arrangements to enable employees to care for their children. Service businesses are more likely than manufacturers to offer child care benefits, since 50 percent of employees in the service sector are women, compared with less than 30 percent in manufacturing.

Federal law mandates maternity leave with a guaranteed job upon return for the period of disability due to pregnancy and childbirth, which is usually four to eight weeks, with the same sick pay as other disabled employees. But most women want leaves from three to six months, which corresponds to the period of bonding between a mother and her baby. With 60 percent of new jobs being filled by women of childbearing age, employers will have to respond to their needs.

Latchkey Children

According to one account, the term "latchkey children" was introduced in 1944 to describe children whose fathers were off at war and whose mothers were off at work. They were named for the house keys the children often wore around their necks. The term now refers to school-age children whose mothers work outside the home. The national Parent Teacher Association estimated that as many as seven million children from age 5 to 13 are in this situation.

After school they're free to do whatever they want, and mostly they watch television. In the years from kindergarten through high school, they watch an average of 21,000 hours of TV. That's 9,000 hours more than they spend in school—if they don't miss a single class. Both parents and teachers agree that the lack of supervision is detrimental, as shown by a 1988 survey sponsored by the Metropolitan Life Insurance Company. Teachers ranked "children being left on their own after school" as the leading cause of problems in school.

At the same time, many of these children have household responsibilities, such as food shopping and making dinner. About 13 percent of children between the ages of six and 15 regularly make their own dinner. If you know what kind of food they like, you know what they eat.

Because they do much of the shopping, teenagers account for a large percentage of spending on groceries and household items. Discretionary spending by teenagers in 1989 was estimated at $56 billion, which is more than the combined GNPs of Portugal, New Zealand, Panama, Chile, and Iceland. They're spending not only family money but also their own, since three-fourths of the teenagers enrolled in school also have jobs.

In the process they've learned to appreciate the value of money. But they've also become obsessed with it. In a 1987 poll, 82 percent of teenagers said that their primary concern was money.

Teenage Problems

You can see the effects of the breakdown of the family in teenage problems: insecurity, conduct disorders, substance abuse, depression, and suicide.

While teenagers have always had problems, most adults feel that teen problems have been getting worse. A survey conducted by the National Association of Private Psychiatric Hospitals found that 72 percent of adults feel that today's teenagers face far more serious problems than they faced. "There's less structure for teens today, what with working mothers, single parents, availability of drugs, and the impersonal nature of modern life," said John Meeks, medical director of the Psychiatric Institute of Montgomery County in Rockville, Maryland.

Some researchers have found that infants who spend a lot of time in care away from their parents are likely to have problems later on. A study released in 1987 by Jay Belsky, professor of human development at Penn State, found that infants who spend 20 hours or more a week in care away from their parents during the first year are likely to become problematic children, who display "heightened aggressiveness, noncompliance, and withdrawal in the preschool and early school years."

Other researchers have found that children who are routinely left unsupervised for long periods are prime candidates for clinical depression. They tend to have feelings of abandonment, frustration, anger, and despair. "Whether that's because they're alone a lot or because the family's in disarray is uncertain. Maybe the two come together," said Lynette Long, a researcher at American University.

The number of children between the ages of 10 and 19 who have been treated in psychiatric hospitals jumped 43 percent from 1980 to 1987. Here you can see not only a trend in teenage problems but also a trend in the way families deal with them. "Family turmoil—divorce, remarriage, frequent migration—and two-career households," wrote the *Wall Street Journal*, "have left many parents either too busy or too distracted to deal with adolescents. Psychiatric treatment has lost some mystery, and insurance for inpatient care has become more widespread as churches, schools, and other institutions that helped guide earlier generations through adolescence have lost influence."

How many teenagers are in this situation? A 1987 government study estimated that 15 percent of the children under 18 needed treatment for mental health problems. In other words, about ten million children. They were described as "children who are too aggressive or too withdrawn, who have problems learning in school, or who get in trouble with the law." The study concluded that these disorders were not simply the passing problems of childhood but were mental health problems.

A symptom of these problems and the failure of society to deal with them is teenage suicide. A survey conducted by the Department of Health and Human Services in 1988 found that suicide is the leading cause of death for people 15 to 24 years old. Almost 20 percent of the girls and 10 percent of the boys said they had attempted suicide, while 42 percent of the girls and 25 percent of the boys said they had seriously thought about it. Another survey of 11,000 eighth and tenth graders found that 18 percent of the girls and 11 percent of the boys had attempted suicide. Still another survey of the 2,024 teenagers in "Who's Who Among American High School Students" found that 30 percent of them had considered suicide.

Back to the Family

In a 1988 survey 73 percent of working parents said that one of them would stay home if money weren't a factor.

"I think this says that there are a lot of parents working out of economic necessity or perceived economic necessity," said Cheryl

Hayes, a child care expert at the National Academy of Sciences. "And parents—especially of very young children—have doubts about whether their children should be cared for outside the home."

These doubts have led to a countertrend. Among married mothers, we see what looks like a trend of back to the family. We don't mean back to the nuclear family, but to a family in which the roles of men and women have become more flexible. Men, no longer the sole breadwinners, are more inclined to help with child care. Working mothers, who have tried to have it all, have found that when you juggle a career and a baby, they both suffer. So we see women leaving their jobs for extended periods to care for their children. We see them working part-time or working at home.

In various ways parents are becoming more involved in child care and education, not only because they have to, but because they want to. Many of them are baby boomers reasserting the values that they developed earlier in their lives. The man who protested against the war and the woman who marched to save the whales are realizing that if you want a better world, you have to start with the family.

Grandmother

You live in a house that has three bedrooms. It's more than you need, since you're alone, but you have no alternative. You've looked at some apartments, but you can't afford the ones that have been designed for the elderly, and you would be afraid to live in the others, which aren't in the safest neighborhoods. But you can barely afford the house, with property taxes and maintenance costs going up every year.

You have a daughter who lives in Nashville. She calls you every other week, and once a year she visits you. She used to bring her children, your grandchildren, but now they're grown up. One lives in Atlanta and the other in Dallas. You'll probably never see them again. But when your daughter calls you, she tells you about them, so you feel you almost know them. It only takes some imagination.

You also have a son who lives in Omaha. He calls you twice a year, on your birthday and on Christmas. He hasn't come to visit since your husband died, which was eight years and seven months ago. But he has his own problems. His third wife just left him, and his latest job didn't work out.

It's hard to get up in the morning. When you put your feet down on the floor, you wonder if your legs will hold up. You totter into the bathroom and lower yourself onto the toilet. When you have to get up again, you wish they made toilets higher. You wish they made a lot of things different.

It's hard to get dressed, but you always do, though you hardly ever go anywhere. You refuse to be like those old ladies who sit around all day in their robes. You put on a dress with a zipper on its side. You have trouble with buttons, since you have arthritis. You also have trouble pulling anything over your head, so you wear cardigan sweaters.

You go downstairs, holding the rail. Your daughter keeps suggesting that you turn the family room into a bedroom and sleep there, so you wouldn't have to use the stairs. But the room doesn't have any closets, and there's only a small powder room downstairs, so it really wouldn't work. Besides, your doctor says going up and down stairs is good exercise, as long as you're careful. And you are careful.

In the kitchen you open the refrigerator. You only use the top two shelves, since you can't bend down and reach the others. The crispers are less than a foot off the ground, completely inaccessible.

You take out the apple juice and see you're almost out of it. You'll have to get groceries. You can't drive anymore because of your eyes, and you can't walk to the supermarket, which is six or seven miles away. There used to be a grocery store within walking distance, but it went out of business. The only store left in the neighborhood is a pizza place, and you can't eat pizza, it upsets your stomach.

Luckily, one of your neighbors, a nurse whose husband left her with two small children, takes you shopping with her. She goes once a week, depending on what days she's off. Without her, you'd have a problem getting food.

You take your pills with the apple juice—five in all. You don't remember what each is for, you only know them by the colors.

Then you walk to the front door and get the paper, which the boy leaves in the mailbox so you can reach it.

You read the paper while you eat breakfast, a cup of herb tea and an English muffin. You sit at the table opposite the place where your husband always sat.

You remember the morning he fell asleep there. For the past few months, he had been falling asleep at odd moments. He had always snapped out of it. But this time he didn't. When you couldn't wake him up, you called the paramedics.

On the way to the hospital he finally woke up. But he didn't know who he was. They kept him in the hospital for a few days, doing tests. They concluded that his brain had somehow been damaged, and when they released him, they told you he would need nursing care.

For a while you tried to provide it yourself, but you just didn't have the strength or the energy. You tried a home care service, which wasn't any good. You tried another, with better results. But it was expensive. It cost you a $100 a day, and it wasn't covered by your insurance, even though you had a special policy for extended care. It covered only medical care, and he was getting custodial care. So you had to pay for it.

Your savings lasted for three months. Then you borrowed against his life insurance, as much as you could, and this lasted for five months. Then you borrowed against your house.

Before you ran out of this money, he got an infection in his bladder. They put him into the hospital again, and then into a nursing home, where he could get medical care. So for a while the insurance covered it.

Then you were going to bring him home. But your children advised you not to. They convinced you to leave him in the nursing home and put him on Medicaid.

You wish you hadn't, though you would have had to sooner or later, when your money ran out. It still hurts to remember his face when you left him there after a visit. It was as if you were abandoning him.

You went to see him every day, and you made sure that they treated him well. But as nice as they were, they robbed him of his dignity. They called him by his first name, girls who could have been his grandchildren. They humored him as if he were crazy. And they tied him to his wheelchair.

Now, as you stare across the table, you're terrified of ending up like that. And you swear that if they ever put you in a nursing home, you'll starve yourself.

Care for the Elderly

Baby boomers have seen their parents end up like this, and looking ahead they can see themselves in the same position. They know they're not going to be like the grandparents in "The Waltons," who lived with their children and grandchildren. They're going to be on their own, with no one to take care of them. They can preview what will happen to them, and this *previewing* is the main force driving their concern for health, nutrition, and fitness. They don't want to end up as inmates in nursing homes. And they believe that if they take care of themselves now, they won't have such a hard time later. So their concern isn't just a fad, it has deep, powerful motives behind it.

Here's a connection between the family and health. The cause is the breakdown of the family, the effect is the concern for health that has changed the behavior of many people. If you think globally, you can see how the breakdown of the family led to the surge in natural foods. You can also see how it will lead to a higher rate of savings, which will have a profound effect on the economy. You only have to make the connections.

As we look ahead, the problem of child care is nothing compared to the problem of care for the elderly. By the end of the 1990s, about 50 million people in this country will be age 65 or older, and 30 percent to 50 percent of them will eventually need long-term care. In another era, their families would have provided it, but if people don't have time to care for their children, how are they going to find time to care for their parents?

Somehow they do find the time, since 95 percent of the elderly live at home, with family members providing virtually all of their care. Most of the burden falls on daughters, who outnumber sons by three to one among children caring for their parents. Many of these women work full-time, and many are single. It's hard for them to carry the burden, and it will get harder. The number of people over age 85, who are most in need of care, is the fastest growing segment of the population. But families have been having fewer children. In fact, the average couple now has more parents than children. "The result," said a report issued by the Older Women's League, "will be a significant decline in the number of family care givers at the same time the need increases dramatically."

When families are unable or unwilling to care for the elderly, the solution is to have others take care of them. About 1.5 million elderly people are in nursing homes, many of them for custodial care. But it costs about $25,000 a year to stay in a nursing home, so most people can't afford it. Data show that 70 percent of single people run out of money within three months of being admitted to a nursing home, and 50 percent of couples run out of money within six months of one spouse being admitted. They sign away their Social Security benefits, then go on Medicaid. But as costs go up and the number of elderly people increases, where will the Medicaid money come from?

Most of the elderly would rather stay at home. According to the Census Bureau, most of them stay in their houses until they reach their mid-70s, and even then they only leave because they can no longer manage by themselves. If they could manage, most of them would rather stay where they've been living. So there's a growing demand for home care.

But there are problems of availability and affordability, just as with child care. Home care workers are paid as little as child care workers, so people aren't attracted into the field. Yet if they got paid more, fewer people could afford home care, and few can afford it now.

When a 70-year-old man won the lottery in Florida, they asked him what he was going to do with all the money. "Now," he said, "I don't have to go into a nursing home."

As people realize that help from the government will be limited, they're going to want insurance plans to cover the cost of long-term care. At present there are only about 500,000 such policies, most of them held by the elderly. But we can see an enormous market for them among the baby boomers, who don't want to end up like their parents. In a study we did for the Health Insurance Association of America, we predicted that the long-term care policy would be the hottest insurance product of the 1990s.

We're going to see corporations provide support for elderly care as well as child care to attract and retain good employees. They could have day-care centers for children and adults together, with the old helping to care for the young and the young stimulating the old.

We're going to see more ECHO (Elder Cottage Housing Opportunity) units. These are small cottages placed temporarily near a family's main house, with a special zoning permit. They're an option for people who don't need a nursing home but do need some care, which they couldn't get living miles away. They can live in their own homes and have some independence, as well as the care they need. The form of housing, a pre-fabricated unit, is inexpensive. A one-bedroom unit with living room, kitchen, bathroom, and porch—specially equipped for the elderly—would cost from $25,000 to $30,000. The idea originated in Australia, spread to Canada, and is now being tried in New York, Pennsylvania, and a few other states.

We're going to see more group residences. These provide the amenities of a hotel as well as the benefits of a community. They don't have health services on the premises, though nurses and doctors visit them. The emphasis is on communal dining, arts, crafts, and other activities. They're an option for people who are in good health but don't want to live alone. But of course they're expensive.

For those who can't afford group residences, boarding houses will reemerge. This type of housing receded with the affluence of the 1950s and 1960s, but it will come back as the middle class shrinks.

The Homeless

Every time I go into the city, I'm struck by the number of people lying in doorways or begging in the streets. You didn't see them years ago, but now they're everywhere, from New York to Seattle. You find them not only in the cities, but also in the suburbs. And they greet you, asking: "Spare some change?"

When people lived in extended families, there was a home for everyone: the unemployed son, the unmarried daughter, the retarded aunt, the alcoholic grandfather. If you had a problem, you could depend on your family. As the poet Robert Frost said, home was the place where, when you had to go there, they had to take you in. But now, with the family broken up, there no longer is such a place for a lot of people.

Who are the homeless? They're the elderly, the unemployed, the mentally ill, the physically disabled—people who in another era would have been living with their families. A large number of them are children, with a single parent or on their own. And many of them are Vietnam veterans. So we're not just talking about bag ladies.

How many homeless people are there? The estimates are now as high as four million, and that's growing by as much as 40 percent a year. In the summer of 1989 the American Affordable Housing Institute warned that the number of homeless could triple in a minor recession.

The causes of the problem are not only in the family but also in politics, education, health, and the economy. One cause in particular is the federal government policy that led to a shortage of low-income housing. From 1981 to 1986 HUD funding for such housing fell from $30.2 billion to $10 billion—the largest budget cut for a cabinet-level department in the Reagan administration. During that same period, HUD-subsidized housing starts plunged from 144,348 units to only 17,080. It doesn't take a genius to see that if we're building fewer low-income units while the number of poor people is increasing, more and more of them will end up living on the streets.

Local governments have reacted to the problem by getting the homeless off the streets and into temporary housing, whatever the cost. In many cases, people have been lodged in hotels and motels at a great expense to taxpayers. Again, instead of attacking the causes of a problem, the government administers symptom relief. If you get the people off the streets, the symptom goes away. But the problem doesn't, it keeps getting worse.

Recently, local governments have begun to do what they should have done years ago—plan and develop subsidized housing. But they're still not thinking globally, they're still not making connections. They still don't see that the homeless are a symptom of chronic problems in many areas of our society. And unless they attack the causes, the homeless will be the fastest growing segment of our population.

= 8 =

Education

Our school system was designed to meet the needs of a growing industrial society. It taught people how to read, write, and do some arithmetic. More important, it taught them how to follow instructions and be good employees. It didn't teach them how to think. It didn't teach them how to ask questions, how to analyze problems, or how to find solutions. It didn't have to, since management did all the thinking.

As long as working for a business was like being in the army, this system worked. But the needs of our society have changed, and our school system no longer meets them. It doesn't even meet the needs of our army, let alone our economy. While we're living in a high-tech society that requires knowledge, adaptability, and creativity, our school system is still doing what it did 50 years ago, though not as well. At least back then, it taught people how to read, write, and do some arithmetic.

If you think globally, you can see causes and effects of the decline of our school system. You can see a cause in the breakdown of the family, which has shifted more responsibilities to the schools, and in the rising aspirations of women, who have stopped providing a virtually captive reservoir of talent for the teaching profession. You can see effects in the economy. But politicians ignore the problem, or they just use it to make headlines. And the bureaucrats who run the school system haven't been receptive to change.

When there have been changes, they've been fads, like the "new math" and "relevance" fads. With new math, a kid in third grade was supposed to be able to do calculus. Then we find out that after he graduates from high school, he can't even calculate a percentage. With relevant courses, they were supposed to learn about the real world. Then we find out that they can't even locate their country on a map.

Why has this happened? Because the system is run by administrators who view the world through the eyes of their profession. They didn't look outside of their field and see what was happening in the family or in the economy. They didn't see how trends in other fields were going to affect education. They didn't proact, they only reacted. Instead of changing the system, they only expanded the bureaucracy and tinkered with the curriculum.

There's a growing awareness of the problem. President Bush, in response to the public clamor, has said he would give a higher priority to education. The First Lady has made a cause of eradicating illiteracy. But they won't change the system. What will change the system is pressure from businesses, which are the market for its products. The system was designed to meet their needs, and with their support and involvement, it will be redesigned in the 1990s.

In Loco Parentis

With the breakdown of the family, the schools have been burdened with functions that used to be family responsibilities. They've also been getting less support from parents in their primary function of education.

Working mothers, who have less time to spend with their children, rely on the schools not only to teach them but also to counsel them. If you want to see the effect of this, just look at the budget of your local school. It probably has more guidance counselors than science teachers. And parents wonder why the schools aren't teaching their children more.

At the same time, parents have become less involved in the education of their children. In this age of specialists, they expect the schools to do the job. But the schools never did the job by themselves, and they never will. They need support from parents. When they get it, they can be successful, within the limits of the system. When they don't get it, they can only try—and hope for miracles.

In a survey by the Carnegie Foundation for the Advancement of Teaching, 90 percent of the teachers said that lack of support from parents was a major problem at their schools. Ernest L. Boyer, president of the foundation, commented: "Teachers repeatedly made the point that in the push for better schools they cannot do the job alone, and yet there is a growing trend to expect schools to do what families, communities, and churches have been unable to accomplish."

That's thinking globally, making connections between fields. Here we can see how the schools have been affected by the breakdown of the family. The schools need support from parents, but they're not getting it. Yet they're expected to assume more of the burden of raising children. So if you want to understand what's happening to the school system, you have to look outside the field of education.

The Teaching Crisis

Compounding the problem, the quality of teachers has declined. Low pay is one reason. At entry level the average salary of a public elementary or secondary school teacher is significantly lower than that of the next lowest paid professional, and after that the gap only widens. Low status is another reason, which hasn't been helped by the shift in the burden of raising children. In many situations teaching has been degraded to baby-sitting.

While pay and status lagged, women who in the 1960s would have gone into teaching were attracted to law and finance and business, which became more open to them in the 1970s. At the same time, values changed from social concern to material success. In the 1960s everyone wanted to be a speech therapist. In the 1980s everyone wanted to be an investment banker.

"The severe crisis in teaching relates directly to the fact that the best and the brightest are not choosing teaching anymore," said Dr. Emily Feistreitzer, author of a 1983 Carnegie Foundation report.

"For the most part," said Albert Shanker, president of the American Federation of Teachers, "you are getting illiterate, incompetent people who cannot get into any other field."

The quantity of people interested in teaching has also declined. In the late 1960s almost 25 percent of college students wanted to be teachers. In 1982 less than 5 percent did. The result is a shortage of teachers, especially in math and science. To fill positions, schools use people who aren't qualified. A survey by the National Education Association in April 1987 found that one out of every six teachers wasn't qualified in the subjects he or she taught.

The training of teachers is "notoriously ineffective," according to a 1988 report by the New York school board, which found that the least experienced teachers were often sent to the city's most troubled schools.

"The crisis has to do with salaries, with the preparatory process, with credentialling (which is a mess), and most important, it has to do with morale," said Ernest L. Boyer, commenting on a 1988 survey of teachers by the Carnegie Foundation. Teachers, he said, "are concerned about loss of status, bureaucratic pressures, negative public image, and the lack of recognition and rewards."

Among the causes of the problem, three out of five teachers said there was too much political control over the school system. There it is again—politics.

Misplaced Priorities

During the 1980s the federal government put a low priority on education. In fact, it wanted to eliminate the Department of Education. From the beginning, the Reagan administration proposed to cut spending on education. Congress resisted, and they compromised. That was the pattern for the next eight years: proposed cuts, resistance by Congress, and compromise. So while spending on education increased from $14 billion in 1980 to $23 billion in 1990, it barely kept up with the rate of inflation, and its share of the total budget declined.

Meanwhile, the government increased defense spending to an annual level of $300 billion, 15 times the amount allotted for education. Their objective was to make us stronger, and they believed that the way to do this was to build up the military. But they weren't thinking globally, they didn't see that by favoring the military over education, they made us weaker, not stronger. They didn't understand that our strength depends on the economy, which depends on education.

Terrell Bell, secretary of education in the early 1980s, tried to get the administration to make these connections. "I tried to convince the president and his people of the bonds that tie together education, the economy, and military strength," he wrote after resigning. "But notwithstanding the fact that I had been a teacher for much of my adult life, I never succeeded in getting this lesson across to them."

In 1988 we spent about $330 billion on education, most of which was financed by state and local governments. At the same time, we spent about $350 billion on defense, including military research and military uses of the space program. We spent more than $250 million on a single B-1 bomber, which would have paid for one year of college for more than 25,000 students. Think of what we could have done if we had reallocated only a quarter of our defense budget to education.

Some people say that money won't solve the problems of our school system. But these same people will spend money on weapons that are just as deficient as our schools. So why not spend it on education? Why not spend it on something that at least could give us a return? It's all a question of priorities, and unless we change them, we're going to continue getting weaker.

Dropouts

About 30 percent of our children drop out of school. In urban areas 50 to 60 percent of them drop out. Now, even with a high school diploma it's not easy for a young person to get a decent job. But without a diploma it's almost impossible. A report by the Department of Labor in July 1988 found that students who drop out of high school were far more likely to be unemployed later, often for longer periods of time than those who graduate. "Many dropouts do not participate in the job market at all," said James Markey, of the Federal Bureau of Labor Statistics. "Of those who do, one in four is unemployed."

Here's a connection between education and the economy. A lack of education affects not only individuals, it affects our whole society. It creates a shortage of qualified people, which constrains economic growth. At the same time, it drains public funds to support or rehabilitate such individuals. So it has a doubly negative effect—the loss of benefits and the payment of costs.

A study of dropouts in New York found similarities in their backgrounds. "They come from communities where poverty is the norm," said Victor Herbert, director of the high school dropout prevention program, "where the presence of drug and alcohol abuse is commonplace, and where the likelihood of living with a single parent and several brothers and sisters gives them more reason not to go to school than to go."

Again, a connection between the family and education. We can see the relationship between the single-parent family and the dropout rate, which in turn affects the individual's economic future. If we remember that a single parent is likely to have dropped out of high school, we can see how the cycle of poverty is repeated.

With 50 percent to 60 percent of urban children dropping out of school, the underclass is rapidly growing. Terrell Bell warned us about it: "This ominous plague, the dropout plague."

Illiteracy

According to the Department of Education, more than 27 million Americans over the age of 17 are illiterate, and another 45 million are barely competent in basic skills. So more than 72 million Americans may lack the reading and writing skills they need to find work. And the number is growing annually by more than two million.

Who are they? They're immigrants, they're dropouts, they're even people with high school diplomas. They're the ones who have fallen through the holes in our system of universal free education. Like the homeless, a group with which they overlap, they're a symptom of chronic problems. And like the homeless, they're costing us. Estimates of the cost of illiteracy are in the hundreds of billions of dollars a year. The Institute for the Study of Adult Illiteracy at Penn State said the cost is at least $225 billion a year, in terms of lost productivity, welfare, crime, and prison expenses.

The Business Council for Effective Literacy, a corporate-sponsored group, has documented instances in which employees misordered millions of dollars in parts, overpaid bills, and endangered the work place. In one case, a feed lot operator who misread a label killed a pen full of cattle by giving them poison instead of grain. If that could happen in a feed lot, I wonder what could happen in a fast-food restaurant.

Illiteracy in the work force is going to be a major problem in the 1990s. In a 1990 study by the Conference Board almost 20 percent of the companies surveyed reported that they have problems finding people who can read. Unless this trend is reversed soon, it will have a devastating effect on our society.

The Underclass

Assessing his effort to improve the school system, Terrell Bell said that the reforms of the 1980s didn't do "a darn thing" for students at the bottom of the economic scale, most of whom are concentrated in urban schools.

A report from the Carnegie Foundation for the Advancement of Teaching concluded in 1988 that the reforms had "bypassed" urban schools. It said that the systems were plagued by stifling bureaucracies, unmotivated students, and crumbling facilities. "No other crisis—a flood, a health epidemic, a garbage strike, or even snow removal—would be as calmly accepted without full scale emergency intervention," the report said, calling for a crusade on behalf of urban education.

Here again, if you think globally, you can see how the failure of urban education begins with the family. Making this connection, the Committee for Economic Development, a group of corporate and educational leaders, addressed the needs of disadvantaged preschool children. Its 1987 report, entitled "Children in Need: Investment Strategies for the Educationally Disadvantaged," urged more spending on prenatal care for pregnant teenagers, instruction for parenthood, better child care programs, and quality preschool programs. The committee warned: "We are creating a permanent underclass of young people who cannot hold jobs because they lack fundamental literacy skills and work habits."

It goes beyond that. People who can't find or hold jobs are likely to get into drugs and crime. That's why declaring war on drugs is not a solution, that's why putting more cops on the beat is not a solution. Those are only political attempts to relieve the symptoms. If you really want to solve a problem, you have to attack its causes. And one of the causes of drug abuse and violent crime, which are often related, is the failure of our school system to teach children the skills that will enable them to find and hold jobs.

When I think about the millions of immigrants who came here years ago not speaking a word of English, and how their children went to school and learned what they needed to function in our society, I'm impressed by the way the system worked then. But now the children of immigrants aren't learning what they need. According to a report by the National Coalition of Advocates for Students, they aren't even learning how to read, write, and speak English. Instead of improving their position in society, these children may end up joining the underclass of native-born Americans.

The Needs of Our Society

Recently, there has been a lot of talk about the fact that many of our college students aren't being exposed to the ideas and works that form the basis of our civilization. This is something to worry about, but it's nothing compared to the fact that many of our high school students aren't learning how to function in everyday life.

A report from the National Assessment of Educational Progress said that almost one-half of the 17-year-old students tested in 1985 and 1986 were incapable of handling eighth grade math. Only 20 percent of the students could write an organized job application letter, and only 4 percent could read a bus schedule.

The Department of Education found that only 43 percent of people ages 21 to 24 could decipher a street map, and only 37 percent could get the main point of a newspaper article.

A 1988 Gallup poll revealed that most Americans were unaware of world geography. Almost 75 percent of them couldn't find the Persian Gulf on a map, and 45 percent couldn't find Central America. Some of them couldn't even find their own country. "You've heard of the lost generation," said Gilbert M. Grosvenor, president of the National Geographic Society, which commissioned the poll. "Well, we've found them. And they haven't the faintest idea where they are."

The Committee for Economic Development reported that one-half of our high school graduates couldn't read well enough to handle moderately complicated tasks. Xerox Chairman David Kearns, a member of the committee, said that businesses must hire workers who "can't read, write, or count," and then spend billions of dollars to train them. "One-fourth of the graduates," he said, "are barely able to read their diplomas."

A study conducted by the Center for Public Resources and Finance, entitled "Basic Skills in the United States Work Force," concluded that American industry is being severely hampered because young people entering the work force lack basic skills in reading, writing, mathematics, and science.

Some companies, recognizing that they can't find enough skilled workers, are doing what they call "dumbing down." For example, fast-food outlets have pictures of the item rather than a digit or a word on the cash register, so that you just hit the picture. If it's a hamburger, you hit the picture of a hamburger. If it's french fries, you hit the french fries. It's like the subways in Mexico, where the stops are identified by pictures of animals because so many people can't read.

The National Alliance of Businesses estimated that three out of four jobs now require education beyond high school. Manufacturing jobs require a higher level of technical skills, while service jobs require higher levels of reading, writing, speaking, and computing. If our schools don't produce graduates who have such skills, we'll have labor shortages. We already have them in some areas. For example, the Motor Vehicle Manufacturer's Association reported that in 1988 there was a shortage of 30,000 mechanics. Ten years ago a high school dropout could learn to be a good mechanic, but now you need a two-year college degree in electronics just to get by, since cars have so many computers and high-tech devices.

The widening gap between the products of our school system and the needs of our society has become a constraint on economic growth. So if you do an economic forecast, you have to take this into account.

Competitiveness

"The educational foundations of our society are presently being eroded by a rising tide of mediocrity that threatens our very future as a nation and as a people."

This is the theme of a 1983 report by the National Commission on Excellence in Education. The report, titled "A Nation at Risk," pointed out that American students suffer by comparison with those in other industrialized countries, at a time when we face strong competition in the global market. "If an unfriendly foreign power had attempted to impose on America the mediocre educational performance that exists today," the report said, "we might have viewed it as an act of war."

A 1983 study by the National Task Force on Education for Economic Growth concluded that Japan and other industrialized countries have superior educational systems. It found that 95 percent of the Japanese graduate from high school, compared to about 70 percent in this country, and that because they have a longer school year, as well as a longer school week, the typical Japanese high school graduate has the equivalent of roughly four full years more than an American high school graduate. If you add to that the greater stability of the Japanese family and the greater involvement of parents in education, you can see why they're outperforming us in many areas of the economy.

"If we are serious about economic growth in America, about improving productivity, about recapturing competitiveness in the basic industries and maintaining it in the newer industries, about guaranteeing to our children a decent standard of living and a rewarding quality of life, then we must get serious about improving education," the task force declared. "And we must start now."

That report was in 1983. A study released by the National Science Foundation in March of 1988 showed that American high school students ranked near the bottom among students in industrialized nations. "These findings emphasize again the troubled state of science education in the United States," said Erich Bloch, director of the NSF. "America's future as a world technological and economic leader and the quality of life we enjoy depend on confronting the real problems in science education with vigor, determination, and a sense of urgency."

Another study, part of a 20-year educational assessment program sponsored by Congress, found that American students had a "distressingly low" understanding of science. The report said that most 17-year-olds were poorly prepared to handle jobs requiring technical skills, and that only 7 percent could handle college level science courses. It warned that we are producing a generation of students who lack the intellectual skills necessary to assess the validity of evidence or the logic of arguments. "It's a national disgrace," said Bassam Shakhashiri, assistant director for science and engineering education of the NSF. "We are falling behind other industrial nations quite quickly, and this situation is far more critical and consequential than we faced in the post-Sputnik era."

Still another study, conducted by the Educational Testing Service, found that our 13-year-olds were last in math and science skills when compared with students of the same age in Britain, Ireland, South Korea, Spain, and four Canadian provinces. One factor that applied to all of these countries was that math and science scores went down as television watching went up. And that goes back to the family.

"Public education has put this country at a terrible competitive disadvantage," said David Kearns. He said that it should have been a major issue in the 1988 presidential campaign. But if you understand politics, you know why it wasn't. In Disney world it's not a problem.

Reform in the 1990s

In the early 1980s an unusually high number of studies were done on our educational system, and they all called for major reforms. Addressing teachers in 1983, Albert Shanker predicted that the reform movement would fail unless they tried radically different methods of teaching.

He was right. Despite great expectations, nothing really changed. Like the people who ran our industries into the ground, the school administrators continued as they always had. "The 1983 reforms do not change the system at all—just tighten the screws," said David Mandel, Carnegie Forum on Education and the Economy.

Now we see a drive for reform coming from businesses, which are becoming more involved in education. After years of complaining about the system's failure to produce graduates who meet their needs, they're doing something about the problem. "There's a wonderful trend toward business involvement in substantive school reform, and it's developing at a geometric rate every year," said Tom Evans, head of Partnerships in Education.

"I think," said W. E. LaMothe, chairman of Kellogg Co., "in this whole educational area that the level of knowledge and pressure on corporations today is growing to a point where a lot of management people are going to be searching for ways they can get involved." They're finding ways to get involved. NYNEX has been instrumental in creating education coalitions in its business areas. Eastman Kodak participates in a program that encourages minority students in Rochester, New York high schools to pursue science, math, and engineering with the help of mentors from local industries. Xerox, a leader in the reform movement, gives awards to thousands of high school students who excel in the humanities and social sciences. Tandy Corporation offered awards to the top 2 percent of students who completed their junior year in May 1989 and to recommended teachers of science, math, and computer science. Aetna Life & Casualty has established a Saturday Academy for bright seventh graders who have the potential of dropping out. Merrill Lynch pays for the college education of selected second graders who finish high school. The American Bankers

Insurance group has built and maintains a grade school on its premises for employees' children. The list goes on.

In several states, including New Jersey, California, Minnesota, and South Carolina, businesses have formed coalitions to help the schools. In New Jersey the coalition is called "Invest in Children," a name that expresses both the purpose and the motive of business involvement in education. "Business didn't see intervention in education or other programs as its job," said Emerson Ross, a spokesman for Owens-Corning. "But we need people who are equipped to work. Entry level jobs are becoming more sophisticated and high school graduates less so."

South Carolina has enacted a series of educational reforms backed by business, the latest of which created the Business Education Partnership for Excellence in Education. The membership of this task force is required to reflect a balance of business, civic, education, and legislative leaders. Its task is to help implement a program called "Target 2000: School Reform for the Next Decade."

Many corporations have formed partnerships directly with schools to encourage children to stay in school. The number of these partnerships has grown by more than 230 percent over the past six years. There are now more than 140,000. It's a strong trend.

In 1989 about 20 CEOs, including Don Petersen of Ford Motor and Colby Chandler of Kodak, met in Arizona with educators and Albert Shanker to draw attention to the school crisis and develop a plan to deal with it. Lamar Alexander, president of the University of Tennessee and keynote speaker at the meeting, called on Bush to set a goal for education comparable to Kennedy's goal to reach the moon by 1970. The goal would be to make our schools preeminent in math, science, and technology within ten years.

At about the same time, business executives met in New York with Mary Futrell, president of the National Education Association, for the same purpose. "Our schools have not really changed in 50 or 60 years," said Futrell. "We must radically change them to meet the changes in society." Business leaders, who have radically changed their operations to meet the challenge of the global market, agreed with her. "People have finally recognized that productivity comes from people, not machines," said Owen Butler, retired chairman of Procter & Gamble.

It's only logical that businesses should get involved in education, and that they could make a difference. The existing system was de-

signed to meet their needs in an industrial era. But the system is no
longer meeting their needs, it's costing them. They're spending $25
billion a year teaching employees skills that should have been learned
at school. Motorola spends $50 million a year teaching English and
seventh-grade math to its 12,500 factory workers. Kodak is teaching
2,500 how to read and write. So now businesses are working to redesign the system to meet their present and future needs.

That doesn't mean we're going to have more vocational education,
which is already a major part of the curriculum at many schools.
Businesses don't want that, as indicated by a 1989 survey by the Center
for Economic Development. They don't need people with narrow
vocational skills.

What do they need? They need people who can not only read,
write, and do some arithmetic, but who can also think independently
and work in teams. A productive employee must know how to get
information, how to use it, how to develop it, and how to share it.
But students who have been sitting in rows, receiving lectures, and
memorizing unrelated facts can't provide the kind of independent
thinking as well as teamwork that businesses need.

To meet the needs of our society, there will be new approaches
to education, like the plan called "Project 2061: Science for All Americans," which is supported by the leading science and mathematics
organizations. Under this plan, instead of being taught in isolation,
science and mathematics will be related to social, economic, and political developments. In other words, students will be encouraged to
think globally, to make connections between fields.

There will also be a globalization of our school system. In February
1989 a panel of governors urged broad changes in the school system,
including new emphasis on foreign languages and cultures, to prepare
our graduates for the global market. In its April 1989 supplement on
education, the *New York Times* had a feature entitled "The Global
Imperative," which appeared under an enormous headline. "Global
events," the article said, "have always had an effect on educational
institutions at all levels, whether they knew where it came from or
not. But school administrators, whose widest frame of reference has
been a desk in a state education department, are now being sensitized
to the disparate forces from around the world that act on them."

The theme of the article was that as our economy becomes global,
our education system must respond. As Ernest L. Boyer said, our
schools must have an "intellectual understanding of the new global

agenda" and learn to communicate it. Or as Claire Gaudani, president of Connecticut College, put it, our schools must start "meeting the needs of people who will operate in an increasingly internationalized environment even if they never leave Duluth."

A few states have already started. Arkansas requires its high schools to offer a course on global studies that focuses on transnational issues, such as the environment. New York mandates a course in global studies for all high school freshmen and sophomores. At the same time, the study of foreign languages is gaining a stronger position in the schools.

Another trend we see is a lengthening of the school year. With the growth in summer enrollment, the system is moving toward an 11-month school year. Our existing school year, the shortest of any industrialized nation, was designed for a society in which children were needed to help on the family farm. It's obviously no longer relevant, and in fact it now conflicts with the present family structure, in which mothers typically work outside the home.

Projecting these trends, we forecast that there will be meaningful reforms of our school system in the 1990s. The critical factor will be the involvement of businesses, which realize that education is their problem. But they'll have to do more because governments at all levels have started to cut spending on education. So businesses, along with families, will be carrying more of the burden directly. And it's easy to imagine them becoming allies in their efforts to change the system.

= 9 =

Health

We have an illusion about doctors, which the media have helped to create. We believe they can cure us. Whatever the problem, we expect them to have a drug or a surgical procedure for it. We expect them to perform miracles, and when they don't, we sue them for malpractice.

We didn't always have such expectations. Before World War II the doctor was your neighbor, and when you were sick, he came to your house and took your temperature, listened to your heart, and looked at your throat. He also asked about your work, about your family, and about other things that were seemingly unrelated to your health. Without having a word for it, he took a holistic approach to your problem. He would tell you to stay in bed for a day or two, eat simple foods, and drink plenty of liquids.

Then came the war, the wonder drugs, and the miracles of surgery that doctors were able to perform on the wounded. It changed our whole approach to health. With the new mentality, the World War II mentality, we believed that modern medicine would find a cure for every disease, just as we believed that science would find a solution for every problem. Medicine was now a science, so the one belief followed from the other. Since doctors were scientists, their time was too valuable to be spent making house calls. Instead of treating the patient, they were supposed to cure the disease.

This new mentality shifted the responsibility for health from the patient to the doctor. It wasn't your job to take care of yourself, it was the doctor's job to cure you. If you had a problem, he would give you a drug or operate. But one way or another, he would solve the problem.

The media glorified modern medicine and elevated doctors to a high status. They gave us Ben Casey, Marcus Welby, and Dr. Kildare, who performed miracles before our eyes. They helped to create the illusion that we owed our health, our very lives, to these demigods. But in reality the system didn't work. It didn't work because instead of attacking the causes of problems, it only gave us symptom relief. Instead of proacting, it only reacted.

The system was also expensive. In 1989 we spent more than $600 billion on health care, almost 12 percent of our GNP, or as much as we spent for defense and education combined. We spent much more of our GNP on health care than other industrialized nations, yet we ranked lowest in measures of health such as longevity and infant mortality.

Belief in the system, which had been undermined by its inability to find a cure for cancer, was shaken by its complete helplessness against AIDS. Here was a disease for which there were no drugs or surgical procedures. Here was a disease for which there was no symptom relief. Here was a disease that was evidently incurable. So if you were in a high-risk group, you had to assume responsibility for your health, at least until they developed a vaccine. In 1984 the government announced that the AIDS virus had been isolated, and they confidently predicted that there would be a vaccine for AIDS within two years. Five years later, there still isn't one available.

AIDS is a precursor of the New Black Plague, which will come in the 1990s unless we reverse the present trends in the environment. It has already appeared among plants and animals, whose immune systems have been weakened or disabled by pollution of their habitats. When it appears among humans, it will first strike the young, the poor, and the elderly. They'll be especially vulnerable because of age, diet, and life-styles. And just as with AIDS, our medical system will be completely helpless against it.

Even before the AIDS crisis, some people realized the limits of the system and assumed responsibility for their health. They changed their diets, they exercised, they quit smoking, they learned better ways of coping with stress. Instead of relying on symptom relief medicine, they used forms of holistic and preventive medicine, which deserve credit for the biggest medical success story of the past 40 years—the reduction in deaths from heart disease.

Convinced by this success and disillusioned with the system, people are turning to holistic medicine, which treats the whole patient, and to preventive medicine, which attacks causes. They see the connection between diet and health, and they're beginning to see the connection between the environment and health. That's why they eat natural foods, that's why they want to stop pollution. They realize that their health is at stake, and they no longer believe that doctors can cure them. This is a trend, a strong trend, and it could reverse the trends leading to the New Black Plague.

Symptom Relief

Our basic approach to health in this country is symptom relief. We wait until a problem manifests itself, and then we treat its symptoms with drugs.

Look at the drugs they hawk on television. Most of them are for the common cold, which they haven't found a cure for. They offer you Contac, Dristan, and other such products to relieve your symptoms. They show you a diagram of the nasal cavity to demonstrate how the drug clears congestion. It looks scientific, but it's really not. Science is about causes and effects, but these commercials are only about relieving symptoms. If you have a cough, the drug will relieve it. If you have a headache, the drug will relieve it. Whatever you have, the drug will relieve it.

Maybe it will relieve the symptom, but it won't solve the problem, and it will have side effects that are often harmful. For example, some widely used cold remedies contain a decongestant that can elevate blood pressure and lead to strokes. So they not only won't cure your cold, they're bad for your health.

They're also addictive, at least in the sense that every time you have a problem, you're offered a drug. You get into the habit of taking drugs. In fact, taking drugs is part of our culture, from the dropout who takes crack to the executive who takes Valium. We're a nation of addicts.

Under our system of medicine the patient expects the doctor to cure whatever ails him. And the doctor obliges him. Two-thirds of all visits to a doctor end with the writing of a prescription, or seven per year for each adult.

We hear about celebrities, like Elvis Presley, who were victims of the system, but we don't hear about the unknown people who have also been victims. We don't hear about how they get hooked on drugs that doctors have prescribed for them. And we don't hear about side effects. We only hear if they're dramatic, as in the case of thalidomide, which caused horrible deformities in the babies of pregnant women who took it.

Many of the unknown victims are elderly. They account for more than one-half of all deaths from drug reactions, according to a 1989 report by the Department of Health and Human Services. The report cited improper use of drugs by the elderly, misdiagnoses by their doctors, inappropriate dosage levels, and dangerous drug combinations. It estimated that 163,000 elderly Americans have serious mental impairment caused or worsened by drugs, and two million are addicted or are at risk of addiction to tranquilizers or sleeping pills because of daily usage for at least one year.

"Most older people are taking too many drugs, and are taking doses that are dangerously high," said Dr. Sidney Wolfe, director of the Public Citizen Health Research Group. The side effects include depression, confusion, memory loss, delirium, nausea, vomiting, appetite loss, stomach pain, constipation, diarrhea, dizziness, and falls that result in hip fractures. In his 1988 book, *Worst Pills, Best Pills*, Dr. Wolfe said: "The greatest epidemic of drug abuse in American society is among our older people."

In the early 1970s there were shocking revelations about the treatment of inmates in nursing homes. Among other things, they found that drug abuse was common. That was more than 15 years ago. Recent studies have found that more than 40 percent of nursing home inmates are given drugs developed to treat acute mental illness, but that most of the people getting the drugs are not mentally ill. Many of them are given drugs just so nursing home staffs can control them more easily. Some of these drugs can cause serious, even fatal, complications.

This is what our system does to people who can't get away. It forces drugs on them. But this is only an extreme case of what it does to people in general by offering drugs and promising relief, instant relief.

The Diet Connection

Back in the 1960s some people began to talk about the connection between diet and health. They warned us about sugar, salt, animal fats, unbleached flour, and processed foods. They advocated a diet high in fiber, low in fat, and rich in vitamins. They were out of the mainstream, and they were ridiculed as health food nuts.

As usual, the government stuck by its guns, shooting them down and repeating its dogma of the four main food groups. Then in 1988 it issued a massive report on diet and health. It found that diet plays a prominent role in five of the top ten causes of death in this country: heart disease, cancer, strokes, diabetes, and atherosclerosis. After years of dismissing the health food nuts, the government admitted that they were right. Of course, it was too late for a lot of people. This is a lesson in tracking trends: If you wait for the government to confirm something, it may be too late.

Twenty years ago only the nuts talked about the connection between diet and cancer. Now the Center for Disease Control estimates that 35 percent of all cancers are related to diet, and that's probably just the beginning.

"We really need to change the way we eat," said Gladys Bloch, co-author of a study by the National Cancer Institute on the eating habits of Americans. The study found that on a typical day 40 percent don't eat any fruit, 51 percent don't eat any vegetables other than potatoes and salads, and 80 percent don't eat whole grain cereals or breads. In other words, a lot of people aren't eating foods that could prevent cancer.

Another study found that about 25 percent of the caloric intake for American adults, and nearly 50 percent for teenagers, comes from sugar. The author of the study, Harry G. Preuss, professor of medicine and pathology at Georgetown University Medical Center, suggested that our high level of sugar consumption may be a major factor in strokes and heart attacks.

As more and more studies establish the connection between diet and health, the ideas of the health food nuts have been moving into the mainstream. Just look at oat bran, which became a hot commodity because of such a study.

The connection between diet and health isn't a new discovery. In fact, it was a principle of health, and people who had any choice in the matter ate foods that they believed were good for them, whether or not they liked them. If you read an old cookbook, you'll find that the author often included the health benefits of a recipe. And the doctor who came to your house usually prescribed a diet for you. But then after World War II we lost the connection. Instead of eating to maintain our health, we ate what we liked, since health was no longer our responsibility.

As soon as they had wonder drugs to offer, the doctors stopped prescribing diets. They stopped worrying about what people ate. "Medical schools tended to overlook nutrition until recently," said Sohrab Mobrahan, a gastroenterologist at the University of Illinois, "because it was assumed that if a person lived in a wealthy country and had enough money to buy food, he would not have a nutritional problem. Now that attitude is beginning to change."

It's about time, since the problem is right under their noses. Studies have found that 40 percent of the people admitted to hospitals suffer from malnutrition. That may be a coincidence, but I don't think so. It looks like a strong connection between diet and health.

In researching a book on health, we learned that elderly people die of malnutrition. I don't mean people eating dog food, who make the news. I mean people living alone, who can't get to the supermarket or don't feel like cooking for themselves, so they have frozen dinners night after night. Their health declines, but they don't know why. If they go to see a doctor, which isn't easy because his office is probably farther away than the supermarket, he doesn't ask them about their diet, or he doesn't probe, so he doesn't get to the cause of the problem, he only sees its symptoms, which look like the symptoms of other problems. And he prescribes drugs, which don't help.

Our research indicated that the problem of malnutrition among the elderly is widespread. It's not confined to low-income levels, it's also found at the middle- and upper-income levels, wherever people and their doctors fail to make the connection between diet and health.

Government Standards

When you look at the diet the Department of Agriculture (USDA) recommends, you have to conclude that they're influenced by special interests, such as the dairy and meat lobbies, and that they don't appreciate fresh fruits and vegetables. At one point, they tried to pass off ketchup as a vegetable in school lunches. They almost succeeded—

in a 1989 poll, 41 percent of the people identified ketchup as a vegetable.

After issuing their 1988 report on diet and health, the government set guidelines for reducing fats and increasing fiber and complex carbohydrates. But they said they didn't have enough information to recommend specific foods or the proportions of total diet these foods should account for. Evidently, they didn't want to offend special interests by advising people to eat less of their products.

Commenting on the report, the American Heart Association said that the government was not doing enough to promote proper nutrition. The association criticized the slow pace of federal action to require improved labeling of foods, such as detailing the amounts and types of fats included.

At the same time, the government has continued policies that work against its own dietary recommendations. For example, the Public Voice for Food and Health Policy, a public interest group, found that the main course served in school cafeterias often consists of fried foods and other dishes high in saturated fat. The cause of the problem is the surplus food donated by the USDA to the school lunch program, which feeds 27 million children. These commodities, which are high in fat, sugar, or sodium, account for 20 percent of the food used in the program. As a result, the average school lunch contains 39 percent fat, while the National Science Foundation, the National Institute of Health, and the American Heart Association have agreed that fat should not constitute more than 30 percent of a child's entire caloric intake. And that's an upper limit. "Congress has compounded the problem," said Ellen Haas, executive director of the Public Voice, "by bowing to the milk producers lobby and requiring that schools serve whole milk, with low-fat milk optional."

In response to this criticism, Suzanne S. Harris, deputy assistant secretary for food and consumer services of the USDA, said: "There's not significant scientific evidence to justify putting limits on the amount of fat children should get from school lunches." That's the typical government defense when you criticize them—lack of scientific evidence.

By giving children school lunches that are high in fat, sugar, and salt, you not only harm them, but you also teach them bad eating habits. For some children, school may be their only chance to learn what they should eat. And they're learning to eat corn dogs and fried chicken nuggets.

Junk Food

Junk food has a high content of sugar, salt, or fat, all of which have been implicated in our most serious health problems. Some junk food combines all three ingredients and has little nutritional value.

From the time they're old enough to watch television, our children are bombarded with commercials for junk food. They're brainwashed into thinking it's good for them. I saw a commercial for Dunkin' Donuts cereal, with a choice of glazed or chocolate-covered. They described the product as if it had nutritional value. And I'm afraid that kids believed them.

A study by *Consumer Reports* showed that many of the popular cereals are loaded with sugar, salt, and fat. Along with these cereals, many children are now having soft drinks for breakfast. It's the fastest growing breakfast food, not only for school-age children but also for toddlers, with 40 percent of one- to two-year-olds guzzling an average of nine ounces of soft drinks each day. So they start their day with junk food, they have it for lunch, and they often have it for dinner too.

As I said in talking about the family, teenagers do a lot of the food shopping. What do they buy? Snacks, soft drinks, french fries, pizza, cookies, ice cream. When I was a kid, we fantasized about such goodies. We imagined being turned loose in a supermarket with money to buy whatever we wanted. It didn't happen, at least until we were grown up. But now it happens every day. These kids don't have to fantasize about soft drinks, cookies, and ice cream. They can really buy them. They have the money, and they can buy whatever they like.

They also do a lot of the cooking. What do they cook? Something that's quick and easy: a can of chili that you just heat up in a saucepan, or pizza that you just put into a microwave oven for a few minutes. If they actually cook something, they limit it to one pot, skipping the sauce on spaghetti because it means using a second pot. But usually the spaghetti is out of a can, compliments of Chef Boy-Ar-Dee.

Now they have microwave meals for children. George A. Hormel has a line called Kids Kitchen. Another one is My Own Meal. The basic marketing premise is that mothers who work outside the home don't have time to prepare hot nutritious meals for their children. These products will solve that problem. At least, they'll be quicker and easier than canned spaghetti. "They may not taste good to you or me," said Rick Bross, marketing manager for Kids Kitchen, "but our childrens' taste panels and common sense show that these are the foods kids like to eat." Well, they may like them, but will they get what they need from them?

Artificial Food

Artificial food has been produced and processed using man-made chemicals, such as pesticides, hormones, and additives. By this definition, most of our food is artificial, including junk food. Those processed french fries not only have a high content of salt and fat, they've also been adulterated with harmful chemicals.

Our fruits and vegetables are grown with the use of hundreds of pesticides. A 1987 report from the National Academy of Sciences said that nine popular fruits and vegetables, including potatoes, tomatoes, oranges, and apples, may contain levels of pesticide residues that can cause tumors in animals. But they still meet government requirements.

According to a 1988 study, the Environmental Protection Agency (EPA) has established maximum permissible concentration levels in foods for 316 active pesticide ingredients, and tests by the Food and Drug Administration (FDA) can detect only about one-half of them. The study said that except in special cases, tests to detect the other compounds would be too expensive. So they don't know how much of these admittedly harmful chemicals people are ingesting.

In defense of its policies, FDA Commissioner Frank Young said: "The argument goes that pesticide residues are bad and they shouldn't be there. But there is no evidence of what the harm is." There it is again, the typical government response to a problem—lack of scientific evidence.

Once harvested, many fruits and vegetables are treated with chemicals to preserve them or just to make them look better. Those shiny apples you find in the supermarket have been coated with wax, like the one you use on your kitchen floor. Those perfect bananas have been dosed with benomyl, which has caused birth defects in animals. The FDA, which has classified benomyl as a "possible human carcinogen," allows it to be used on apples, apricots, bananas, cherries, citrus fruits, mushrooms, nectarines, peaches, pears, pineapples, and plums.

In processing, about 3,000 nonnutritive substances are added to our foods, and in most cases little or nothing is known about their long-term effects. One of the reasons for the lack of data is that the FDA has only 910 inspectors and investigators nationwide (down from

1,105 in 1977). "There is no way we can touch but a fraction of the vast quantity of foods that Americans buy and eat," an FDA spokesperson said.

Our meat is produced with the use of some 20,000 drugs—that's right, 20,000—most of which haven't been tested for harmful effects. Growth hormones, which increase the weight of animals, are especially popular. The European Community has banned the use of such hormones in raising beef cattle because there's evidence that they cause tumors and genital deformities in children. The American position is that they're not harmful to humans. Well, we've heard this before. For years the government said that the growth hormone DES wasn't harmful, then it turned out to be a dangerous carcinogen. Though the Europeans have other motives for blocking imports of our beef, we suspect they're right about the hormones.

Here's a lesson in tracking trends that shows why you shouldn't wait for the government to admit that something is harmful. In early 1988 we picked up the story about sulfur methazine in the *Wall Street Journal*: "Prices of cattle and hog futures sank amid conflicting reports that a commonly used livestock drug caused cancer in laboratory animals. . . . According to futures traders in Chicago, an item buried in a recent FDA quarterly report says researchers at the National Center for Toxological Research in Arkansas suspect sulfur methazine causes cancer in laboratory mice." They quoted an FDA official, who said: "We haven't concluded anything yet."

A month later the *Journal* reported: "The Agriculture Department's food safety agency, spurred by a new cancer scare, said it plans to crack down on excessive residues of a sulfur drug in hogs being marketed in the U.S." It said that the FDA had "tentatively determined" that sulfur methazine caused tumors in the thyroid glands of mice. It was estimated that at least 70 percent of all hogs slaughtered in this country received some form of sulfur medication.

A few months later the Reuters News Service reported: "Residues of a potentially cancer-causing drug that is used in some animal feed have been found in milk samples collected in ten major American cities, according to the Food and Drug Administration. A survey by the agency in the first week of March showed that the highest residues of the drug, sulfur methazine, were in milk samples in Brooklyn, Boston, and Seattle. Sulfur methazine is outlawed in the raising of milk-producing animals in the U.S., but is commonly used in pork production."

Think about it. The government had evidence that this drug could have harmful effects, at least in milk, so they outlawed it for milk production but allowed it for pork. Meanwhile it was still being used by the dairy industry.

Food Contamination

The problem of food contamination is more serious than people generally realize. According to the FDA, some 33 million Americans are afflicted each year by gastrointestinal illness caused by microorganisms in food. The complications can be fatal, especially to infants, the elderly, and those with weakened immune systems.

One cause of the problem is the consolidation of the food industry, which magnifies the extent of the risk. For example, 30 years ago almost 300 companies sold chickens commercially. Today there are less than 50, and a few giants dominate the market. If the chickens that come from one of these giants have salmonella, then a lot of people will get it. This isn't just hypothetical, since almost four out of ten chickens approved by the Department of Agriculture have salmonella. Two and one-half million Americans get salmonella every year, not only from chickens but also from eggs.

Another cause is the government's failure to enforce standards, under the influence of special interests. In a 1981 report the General Accounting Office said that the Department of Agriculture was enforcing the sanitation laws with less than satisfactory vigor and efficiency. Investigators visited 62 meat and poultry plants and found "high incidence of unacceptable ratings" and a "large number of deficiencies." The report cited instances of filth, flies, rodents, potentially hazardous water supplies, unacceptable inspection practices, and shortages of inspectors in the plants.

Two years later the Associated Press reported: "Millions of Americans are being sold dirty, diseased, and chemically contaminated meat because of breakdowns in the federal inspection system, a former agricultural department employee charged on Monday. John Coplin, a former food safety and inspection supervisor, filed a formal complaint with the merit system's protection board special council that requested an independent investigation of the charges." At a news conference Coplin said: "During my 50 years with the meat industry, I have witnessed all kinds of corruption in the U.S. Department of

Agriculture meat inspection and grading services. But in my judgment, it has never been more corrupt and disgusting than it is today."

In the same year a report by Ralph Nader charged that the food safety inspection service of the Department of Agriculture had reduced the frequency of meat inspections and had done nothing to alleviate the shortage of inspectors. It said the government had speeded up the inspection process and relaxed standards, making it possible for diseased, unsanitary, and improperly graded meat to reach the public.

In 1988 the Gannett News Service wrote: "The agriculture department, in some cases seeking to cooperate with the industry it regulates, hasn't always issued public recall warnings when hazardous foods are distributed. The department at times has failed to warn even supermarket officials that dangerously contaminated products are on the shelves. In deciding not to issue the notices to the public, the department has ignored its own regulations." Rodney Leonard, a former high-ranking USDA food safety official who now heads the Community Nutrition Institute, a public interest group, said of the department: "They rarely notify the public when there's a problem. They work it out in a manner that the company finds most appropriate."

This is how agency officials work hand in glove with the industries they're supposed to regulate. And this is why you shouldn't wait for the government to tell you when there's a problem. If you do, you'll be a victim, like the thousands of people in Pennsylvania and Delaware that got a gastrointestinal disease from contaminated ice, or the people in Tampa who got botulism from tainted coleslaw, or the 29 junior high school students in Minnesota who became ill after eating precooked beef patties. We're seeing more and more of these outbreaks, a clear trend, with a definite, predictable direction.

The New Black Plague

For several years the AIDS story has made headlines, and the public is aware of what can happen when the immune system breaks down. The media talk about an epidemic, but the number of people at risk for AIDS is small compared to the number of people at risk for what I call the New Black Plague. Unlike AIDS, which is caused by a virus and transmitted under certain conditions by bodily fluids, the New Black Plague will be caused by pollution of the environment and transmitted by the air we breathe, the water we drink, and the food we eat. It will drive AIDS off the front page.

It has already appeared among plants and animals. In the northeastern United States the maple trees are dying. They're being attacked by pear thrips, and they're unable to fight back against these insects because their immune systems have been weakened by air pollution. In the St. Lawrence River the beluga whales are dying. They're getting diseases such as septicemia, bronchial pneumonia, hepatitis, gastric ulcers, pulmonary abscesses, and bladder cancer, and they're succumbing because their immune systems have been disabled by water contamination.

We were tracking this trend in late 1988 when we saw a story in the back pages of the *Wall Street Journal*, which said: "Scientists have known for years that pollution can magnify the vulnerability of plants and animals to natural threats, but proving the pollution is the main culprit in specific cases is notoriously tricky. Recently, however, examples that may reflect a kind of environmental AIDS, in which the weakening effects of pollution have opened the door for sudden massive damage from other problems, are appearing with disturbing frequency. This year a virus wiped out more than half of the harbor seals along the North Sea coast. A still-spreading plague, many researchers speculate, is killing animals whose immune systems have been weakened by toxic chemicals."

We were surprised to see the story, since we hadn't expected the media to pick up the trend so early. We went to our files, and after rereading all the stories about dying plants and animals that we had clipped from newspapers, we concluded that the plague was coming sooner than we had thought.

The stories only focus on plants and animals, they don't speculate about what will happen next. But if toxic substances in the environment are breaking down the immune systems of maples and whales, they're doing the same to us. And before long we'll see people dying because their immune systems have been weakened or disabled.

Everyone will be at risk, since we've all been exposed to toxic substances in the air, in the water, and in artificial foods. But the young, the poor, and the elderly will be most at risk. The young live on junk foods, the poor and many of the elderly suffer from malnutrition, as well as stress. These groups will have the least resistance to the New Black Plague. Also, children who are in day-care centers, who are almost five times more likely to be hospitalized for an illness than children cared for in other settings, will be greatly exposed to it.

If we use the Globalnomic system, we can make connections between the breakdown of the family and the diet of the young, the plight of the elderly. We can make connections between education and poverty, between the environment and health. We can see how these fields are interrelated, and how trends in one affect the others.

Natural Foods

Natural foods have been produced and processed without using man-made chemicals. Of course, they're not new, they're the oldest kind of food, and before World War II people ate them without thinking about it. They ate chickens that were raised without the use of hormones. They ate beef that was produced without the use of drugs. They ate vegetables that were grown without the use of pesticides. But with the rise of the World War II mentality, these natural foods were replaced by artificial foods. And people ate them without thinking about it.

Now that they have more information, people are returning to natural foods. It's a strong trend, especially among the baby boomers, and we see the evidence in the supermarkets. We see natural beef, free-range chickens, and organic vegetables. We see sulfite-free salad bars. We see processed foods without additives. We see products in supermarkets that a few years ago we only saw in health food stores.

Americans spent $4.2 billion on natural foods in 1990, more than 30 percent above what they spent in 1987 and more than double what they spent in 1979. The figures include sales at the nation's 7,253 health food stores and in the health food sections of supermarkets. Sales of health foods in supermarkets increased by 10 percent to $679 million, compared with an increase of only 3 percent in 1986. "Clearly it's a boom industry," said John C. McMillin, a food industry analyst with Prudential Bache Securities. "It's no longer the college hippie who's eating health food. It's everybody."

It isn't just a fad, it has social, economic, and political significance. As I said, our concern for health is driven by the knowledge that when we get old, we'll have no one to take care of us, an effect of the breakdown of the family. Our demand for natural foods is changing the way foods are produced, processed, and marketed, an effect on the economy. And it's going to have political effects, not only on agricultural policies but also on environmental policies.

The large corporations have already begun to exploit the trend. If you look at the boxes of cereal on the supermarket shelves, you'll see the word "natural" on many of them. If you read the lists of ingredients of processed foods, you'll see the phrase "natural flavors" on many of them. At times this may be misleading, as in the case of Circus Fun cereal, from General Mills, which proclaims "all-natural fruit flavors," while the list of ingredients reveals artificial flavors as well. The problem is, the FDA hasn't defined what "natural" means. Well, it means food produced and processed without using man-made chemicals. That's common sense, but it's beyond the grasp of bureaucrats (or within the grasp of special interests).

Back in the 1960s, when people began to talk about natural foods, they sounded radical, since they were challenging the establishment. But if anyone was radical, it was the people who gave us artificial foods, since they changed our traditional diet. They could claim that they increased productivity, but they didn't take into account the long-term costs of damage to the environment, of damage to our health.

If you want natural foods, you have to pay more. But you're investing in your health, and what you can save by not buying junk foods will make up the difference. Look what you pay for a bag of potato chips, or a liter of soft drinks. For that you could buy a free-range chicken, instead of one that has been fattened with hormones. For that you could buy a head of organic lettuce, instead of one that has been sprayed with pesticides. For that you could buy a bottle of natural fruit juice, instead of one that has been laced with additives.

I'm not saying that everybody will switch to natural foods. A lot of people, especially the young, the poor, and the elderly, will continue to eat artificial foods. So we're going to have a bimodal market, with natural foods at the high end and artificial foods at the low end.

Alternative Medicine

As I said earlier, our image of doctors has been fabricated by the media, which gave us Ben Casey, Marcus Welby, and Dr. Kildare, among others. They have all the answers, and whether or not they save the patient, they always know what to do. But that's Disney world. In the real world doctors don't have all the answers, and they often don't know what to do. If they don't have a drug or a surgical procedure for your malady, they're at a loss.

As people have realized the deficiencies of symptom relief medicine, they've become more interested in preventive medicine. Not long ago the idea of preventing disease through diet and exercise was something you read about only in specialized magazines. Now it's in the mainstream, as is holistic medicine. Other approaches, like chiropractic, homeopathy, acupuncture, massage therapy, rolfing, shiatsu, hypnotherapy, and polarity therapy have also gained followers.

Of course, they haven't been accepted by the medical establishment, who oppose alternatives as a matter of principle. Look what they did to Linus Pauling, who had the nerve to suggest that vitamin C might be useful in treating cancer. They brought out the guns of the Mayo Clinic and shot him down. He had won two Nobel Prizes, and they still wouldn't seriously consider his approach. But many people are trying it because they're unhappy with the establishment. This is a trend. At one time, people wouldn't question their doctors. They wouldn't even think about it. Now we have commercials telling us to get more than one opinion.

People are not only questioning their doctors, they're questioning our whole system. In a 1989 poll conducted by Louis Harris, 89 percent of the people said our health care system is fundamentally flawed. A big problem is that many people simply cannot afford health care. In the late 1970s, more than 75 percent of the people living below the poverty level were eligible for Medicaid. In 1989 only 38 percent of them were eligible. About 37 million Americans are not covered by any form of health insurance.

With the cost of health care escalating, the issue has become a serious concern for working people. In fact, health care was the main issue in every major strike last year. So it's also a serious concern for management.

In the same Harris poll cited above, almost two-thirds of the people said they would swap our system for the Canadian national health care system. We forecast that this will be a major issue of the 1990s and that before the turn of the century we'll have some form of national health care system.

10

The Environment

They emerged in the 1960s, riding the wave of the protest movement, but instead of marching against the war, they marched for the earth. They were visionaries, inspired by the work of researchers in the little-known field of ecology, and they were concerned about the future. They saw that life on earth was threatened not only by nuclear war but also by damage to the environment. They raised the issues that led to some major legislation in the 1970s, including the creation of the Environmental Protection Agency. But they were opposed by developers and other special interest groups, who accused them of obstructing progress. They were labeled by the media as "environmentalists," a term with negative implications. They were blamed for inflation, for unemployment, and for our lack of competitiveness in world markets.

By the early 1980s they no longer had much influence on government policy. Reviving the economy and building up the military became priorities, while the issue of the environment languished. The EPA budget was cut, personnel were reduced, and career officers were replaced by political appointees. Like other agencies, the EPA was co-opted by special interests, and its positions reflected their views. The agency relaxed its standards on air and water quality, permitted the dumping of toxic waste in landfills, approved the use of known carcinogens in pesticides, and ignored the evidence of global problems such as acid rain, the warming trend, and damage to the ozone layer. Its role of protecting the environment was subverted by the Reagan administration, who had other priorities.

Again, our political leaders weren't thinking globally. The purpose of reviving the economy was to raise our standard of living. Our standard of living is measured not only by our wealth but also by our health, and our health is affected by the environment. So an economic policy that ignores the environment won't raise our standard of living. It may enable us to buy a few more consumer goods, but meanwhile it increases our risk of getting cancer. If you make the connection between the environment and health, you can see the effect of such a policy. But politicians don't make the connection. They let farmers spray their fields with a chemical that has been shown to cause tumors in animals, and they defend their position by citing a lack of scientific evidence. They wait and see how many people die, and then—maybe—they do something about it. They don't proact, they only react.

After years of ignoring environmental problems, the government will soon have to face them because of the growing public concern. The problems are visible, the causes are known, and the effects are being felt. We're running out of places to dump our garbage, we're unable to deal with our toxic waste, we're polluting our air, we're contaminating our water, we're changing our climate, we're exposing ourselves to deadly radiation. More and more people are realizing that these problems threaten their health as well as the future of life on earth, and they're demanding that the government do something before it's too late.

Projecting this trend, we forecast that the environment will be a major issue in the 1990s, and that in response to public concern, the government will attack the causes of the problems. The only question is whether they and the governments of other nations will do enough to reverse trends that could turn the earth into just another dead planet.

Garbage

In this country we generate about 180 million tons of garbage every year. We produce more garbage per capita than any other country in the world, far more than developing countries, and about twice as much as Japan. Also, our garbage differs from that of most other countries. Unlike theirs, which is mostly biodegradable food waste, ours is full of materials that are not biodegradable, as well as materials that are toxic or carcinogenic.

How do we dispose of our garbage? Mainly, we dump it. We haul it away and dump it in landfills, 80 percent of it. But existing landfills are filling up. The EPA estimates that by 1995 about one-half of the existing landfills will have to be closed. And we're running out of places for new ones. One-half of our cities have already run out of landfill space.

We can see the effects. In some communities disposal costs are so high that people dump trash illegally. In New Jersey shopkeepers come to work in the morning and find their trash bins filled with household garbage that has been dumped overnight. In other areas bags of garbage are left along the roads by people who are unable or unwilling to pay the hauling costs.

One response to this problem is the growing use of so-called resource recovery plants. They're really incinerators with a new name, and they burn garbage, reducing it to about 30 percent of its raw weight. In the process they produce emissions that pollute the air, so while they relieve the problem of landfill space, they contribute to another problem. And they create a new problem—how to dispose of the ash. People don't want the ash buried in their backyards because it contains dioxins, furans, and heavy metals. Remember the barge from Philadelphia that roamed around the world for almost two years, looking for a place to dump its ash? Well, that shows the extent of the problem.

At the beginning of 1991 about 130 resource recovery plants were in operation around the country, with about 90 more planned. If they were all built, they could process 29 percent of our garbage. But they probably won't all be built, since with the loss of tax incentives and the decline in energy prices they've become less profitable. So these incinerators aren't going to solve the problem.

Of particular concern is the large quantity of plastic products that we use and throw away. Since most of this garbage isn't biodegradable, it's accumulating on land and sea. On the land it lies around for up to 400 years before it disintegrates, and on the sea it floats around for no one knows how long. According to the General Accounting Office, 46,000 pieces of plastic garbage are floating in every square mile of ocean. And it's killing the fish that swallow it.

Toxic Waste

In addition to garbage, we generate about 250 million tons of industrial waste every year, which includes toxic or hazardous waste. We produce more toxic waste per capita than any other country in the world.

How do we dispose of it? Again, we dump it, which causes problems, since after a while the toxins and carcinogens are released into the soil and the water. The General Accounting Office estimates that there are as many as 425,000 hazardous waste sites in the country. Since 1980 the EPA has started cleanups of 257 and has completed 48. The original $1.6 billion Superfund was enough to clean up about 170. Based on those figures, it would cost a total of $4 trillion to clean up all the sites, and if we did it over ten years, the annual outlay for the cleanup would be more than we're now spending on defense.

Meanwhile, these sites have harmful effects. A 1989 study by the Department of Health showed that people living within one kilometer of the Lipari landfill in Pennsylvania are more likely to contract adult leukemia or produce babies with low birth weights than people living beyond that range. Many carcinogens, including benzene, methylene chloride, and arsenic, have been found at the site.

We also dispose of toxic waste through the sewage system. About 12 percent of the waste flowing through the sewers and into the sewage treatment plants is industrial waste containing toxic chemicals. According to federal law, when toxic waste is mixed with domestic sewage, it's no longer considered hazardous. But it has been estimated that only about 60 percent of the toxic chemicals are neutralized through biodegradation in the most efficient plants. Where does the active residue go? Into the rivers, into the oceans.

In 1980 a public opinion survey showed that the majority of people would accept toxic waste facilities only if they were located at least 100 miles away from their homes. This attitude has been called NIMBY, not in my backyard. It developed in response to problems like Love Canal, New York, and Times Beach, Missouri, which made us realize the dangers of dumping toxic wastes in our backyards. But as the poll showed, we were willing to dump these wastes in somebody else's backyard.

We tried dumping them in western states, but they didn't want them, and we tried dumping them in Third World countries, but they didn't want them either. We're beginning to realize that we can't solve the problem by dumping it on somebody else. In the 1990s our attitude is going to change from not in my backyard to not in anybody's backyard.

Routine Emissions

Our use of fossil fuels for energy releases 5.4 billion tons of carbon into the atmosphere every year. It's raising the level of carbon dioxide, which causes the earth to retain more heat. It's a primary cause of the warming trend. And carbon is only one of the many substances released into the atmosphere by routine emissions from motor vehicles, power plants, chemical plants, and other sources.

In the 1970s we implemented measures to conserve energy and reduce emissions, but in the 1980s, with cheaper oil and less concern about the environment, we relaxed our efforts. We now spend about 11 percent of our GNP on energy, while Japan spends only about 5 percent. This shows that we have room for improvement. If we used less energy, we would lower the volume of emissions. But our government policies aren't encouraging further conservation. Nor are they encouraging the development of alternative sources of energy, with the budget for this activity having been cut by 70 percent between 1981 and 1988.

In fact, the fuel efficiency of our cars has fallen since 1988, with the trend toward bigger engines. The auto companies say this is what America wants. Well, it's what the auto companies want, because they can make bigger profits on such cars. So they don't care about mileage. And when they face the next crisis, they'll say that no one could have foreseen it.

Our power plants rely on fossil fuels as much as ever. We were going to use more nuclear energy, but the utilities weren't able to convince people that it was safe, for reasons that I can understand. How would you like to live near a nuclear plant? How would you like to have nuclear waste dumped in your neighborhood?

Our industrial plants routinely release toxic materials into the air, into the water, and into the ground. A 1988 survey found that 22.5 billion pounds of toxic chemicals—some of them linked to cancer and birth defects—are released each year by industrial plants. The EPA said the amount was "startling and unacceptably high." What's startling is that this was the first such survey ever done, and that of the nine cancer-causing chemicals listed in the EPA report, none are federally regulated.

Whether they're coming from motor vehicles, power plants, industrial plants, or other sources, routine emissions are primary causes of environmental problems—air pollution, water contamination, acid rain, the greenhouse effect, the destruction of the ozone layer. At existing levels they're threatening our health, they're destroying our habitat. Yet in the 1980s the government did almost nothing to control them.

Leaks and Spills

It's estimated that 75 percent of our population lives close to a chemical plant, exposing them to leaks and spills of toxic chemicals. This risk was dramatized by the Bhopal incident, but every day the people who live near chemical plants are affected by them.

Here's a story from our files about Poca City, Oklahoma, where residents protested against the brown, oily water seeping into their basements, yards, and streets from the nearby Conoco refinery. But nothing was done about the problem, since government tests showed that the contamination was "within safe limits." They always show that. Whatever the problem, it's within safe limits. But who sets these limits? Political appointees, who represent special interests.

Here's another. "Thousands Who Fled Toxic Cloud Return to Homes in Massachusetts. Up to 25,000 people were evacuated in Springfield and Chicopee because of a series of fires that began Friday at the Advanced Laboratories Factory, which manufactures chlorine pellets for swimming pools." I know we're used to large numbers, but think about 25,000 people fleeing from a cloud of chlorine gas. That's a lot of people.

These accidents not only happen at the plants, they also happen while chemicals are being transported. An enormous volume of toxic chemicals, about four billion tons annually, is being carried by railroads. According to an Illinois public action council, the number of railroad accidents involving toxic chemicals has been increasing. And the number of accidents requiring evacuation in 1987 was double the number five years earlier. So they've been getting worse.

Barges also have accidents. From our file on the subject, I pulled out a clipping that reads: "Acid Spill on Mississippi Barge. A section of the Mississippi River was sealed off for several hours Thursday after hydrochloric acid leaked from a tank on a barge about 15 miles north of St. Louis." There are others like it, mounting evidence of the problem.

In January 1988 there was a major oil spill on the Monongahela River, involving over one million gallons of diesel fuel. It affected communities from Pittsburgh to West Virginia and Ohio, which get their drinking water from this river. But that was nothing compared to the 1989 oil spill in Alaska, the effects of which are beyond comprehension. In one accident a whole region has been destroyed. Who's at fault? The media and the politicians found a scapegoat in the captain of the tanker. But the people really at fault are the ones who let such an accident be possible.

Then there are the underground tanks. Of the 1.4 million underground tanks in this country, it's estimated that as many as 10 percent of them are leaking. These tanks store gasoline or chemicals that can contaminate the soil and the water. About 85 percent of them are made of bare steel, which is vulnerable to corrosion. So more of them are going to leak.

In October 1988 the leaks from a nuclear fuel plant made the headlines. "Last week the government admitted that for many years it had concealed major safety violations at a nuclear fuel plant in Ohio," ABC News reported. "There's a rising sense of anger of people who live near it."

While the plant released tons of radioactive waste into the environment, the government assured people that its emissions were within safe limits.

"The government was lying to us," a resident said.

"We found them lying so much, we didn't know if they knew how to tell the truth," another resident said.

The story grew as leaks at other plants were exposed, and the public became aware of the problem. Here we see how the government covers up problems, and how the public only becomes aware of them when they make headlines.

Chemical Warfare

In the Vietnam War we tried to uncover the Vietcong by defoliating the jungle, using a herbicide called Agent Orange. The whole idea now seems crazy, and we wonder why the geniuses who thought of it didn't suspect that if Agent Orange killed plants, it would kill people.

But what about the idea of using chemical warfare here? What about the idea of using thousands of pesticides to protect our crops, to beautify our yards, and to make our lives more comfortable? Isn't that just as crazy? If those chemicals kill plants and other animals, they'll kill us, just as Agent Orange did. It's common sense.

They're already killing us, and every year they're killing more of us. In the early 1980s researchers said that every year pesticides killed about 1,000 people. By 1987 they said that every year pesticides killed about 20,000 people. You can be sure that as they discover more about the link between pesticides and cancer, the numbers will get higher and higher. This is a trend, a clear trend.

Every year about 2.6 billion pounds of pesticides are used in this country, mostly in food production. In 1972 Congress passed a law requiring pesticide manufacturers to test their products for health effects. The law gave them four years to complete the tests, but the deadline was extended. In 1978 Congress decided that the 50,000 products already on the market didn't have to be tested, only the 600 active ingredients had to be tested. They still haven't all been tested, but of those that have been tested the EPA has said that at least 66 are "probable carcinogens," and dozens of others are known to cause birth defects, nervous system disorders, and other chronic illnesses. Yet the agency has banned only three of them and seriously restricted only a few others.

A study by the Natural Resources Defense Council, released in March 1989, concluded that exposure to toxic residues from pesticides used on fruits and vegetables was especially high in children under the age of six. It found that relative to their body weight, children eat six times more fruit than adults and therefore ingest toxic residues at levels far above those considered "safe" by the EPA. It singled out daminozide (Alar), a suspected carcinogen, which is used to regulate the ripening of apples, and it roused the public. The problem made headlines, it was on the talkshows, and it became a cover story for both *Time* and *Newsweek*. From coast to coast, supermarkets immediately stopped carrying apples treated with daminozide—which shows the power of public concern.

Then there's the story of dioxin, the active ingredient of Agent Orange. For years the government and the timber industry sprayed forests with herbicides containing dioxin, until the EPA restricted its use in 1979. Until then, they claimed it was safe. Now, with evidence showing that it causes birth defects and breaks down the immune system, the government still allows dioxin to be used on rice paddies, range lands, sugarcane fields, and fruit orchards, as well as on buildings, industrial sites, and parking lots. It's also formed in the process of bleaching paper pulp, so it's found in many paper products, including milk cartons, cereal boxes, frozen food packaging, coffee filters, paper plates, paper towels, facial tissues, disposable diapers, tampons, and pads.

Dioxin is only one of the thousands of man-made chemicals being used in our war against nature, and many of them could be just as harmful. In September 1987 AP reported: "Dow Chemical is recalling its pesticide cyhezatin, because of the risk of birth defects." That's nice—after when it may have been too late, they recall the product. This is what happens with such products. The ingredients are assumed to be harmless until proven otherwise, at our expense.

Some chemicals were banned after long and extensive use. For example, EDB was used for years. EDB is ethylene dibromide, and studies have demonstrated that it's highly carcinogenic. At one time we used 21 million pounds of EDB every year as a pesticide. There's a lot of EDB still around, contaminating water.

In recent tests of farmland, analysts found DDT, DDE, lindane, hexchlorobenzene, and endrin in the soil. They found these chemicals, many of which had been banned for years, in the bodies of dead wildlife. If they had looked, they probably would have found the same chemicals in the bodies of dead people. If they're in the soil and in other animals, they're moving up the food chain and into our stomachs.

Chemical warfare is being waged not only on farmland but also in our houses and yards, where we're directly exposed to its harmful effects. A 1987 study by the Consumers' Union said that 28 percent of the active ingredients in household pesticides had been found to cause cancer in animals, but because the EPA lacked data on the effects of exposure, these chemicals were still being used. There it is, a lack of evidence, the old excuse to do nothing.

One reason why the EPA lacks data is that their budget for reviewing products never was very large, and it was cut from $13.4 million in 1980 to only $9.5 million in 1988. Adjusted for inflation, their present review budget is less than half of what it was eight years ago. That's an indication of government priorities. While they were building up the military to protect us from the Soviet Union, they were cutting back on expenses to protect us from internal chemical warfare, which every year kills more and more of us.

Air Pollution

In 1983, when the astronauts in the space shuttle looked at the earth, they were shocked by the air pollution they saw. "It was appalling to me to see how dirty our atmosphere is getting," said Paul J. Weitz, commander of the flight. "Unfortunately, the world is rapidly becoming a gray planet."

Now, you might think that statements like this would rouse Congress into action, unless you understand politicians. In 1970 they passed the Clean Air Act, which mandated standards of air quality. When the deadline for compliance arrived in 1979, they extended it to 1982. They extended it again in 1982. And then again. Instead of enforcing it, they made deals, appeased special interests, and offered political solutions.

While they procrastinated, air pollution was getting worse. According to the EPA, 110 million Americans were breathing bad air in 1988, about 30 million more than in 1986. The major pollutants were particulates (dust, soot, smoke, and water droplets), sulfur dioxide, carbon monoxide, nitrogen dioxide, ozone, and lead. The most pervasive pollutant was ozone, which is formed at ground level when emissions from motor vehicles, factories, and power plants react under the influence of sunlight and change chemically. The average levels of ozone, a major component of urban smog, were 5 percent higher than in 1983. More than one-third of Americans live in areas where ozone regularly exceeds acceptable levels. In a 1989 hearing on the subject of air pollution, Richard E. Ayres, chairman of the National Clean Air Coalition, told Congress: "We believe that the declining air quality of our cities can fairly be characterized as a public health crisis."

For years it was believed that urban smog was a problem only for people suffering from asthma, emphysema, and other respiratory diseases. But there's mounting evidence that it can affect healthy adults, and that repeated exposure can cause permanent lung damage. There's also evidence that it causes cancer. If you think globally, you can see the connection between the environment and health, the cause and effect.

Opponents of stricter controls on air pollution claim that they would cost too much. But what are the costs of not having stricter controls? In 1989 a Senate subcommittee estimated that air pollution causes $60 to $100 billion in environmental damage each year. The American Lung Association estimated that taxpayers and consumers spend about $40 billion for health care and other costs of illness and death resulting from air pollution.

Meanwhile, the government has failed to enforce its standards for air quality. Many cities, especially New York and Los Angeles, have pollutant levels far above the maximum safe levels. And unless there's a change in policy, the problem will get worse.

Water Contamination

Half of the drinking water in this country is provided by underground water, and the other half, by public water systems. Recent studies have shown that both of these sources are widely contaminated.

A study by the EPA found that underground water in 38 states was contaminated by pesticides and other chemicals. They said that the concentrations were generally below safe levels. We've heard that before, and we also remember being told that pesticides would never get into the ground water but would bind to the soil or break down into harmless substances. So we can predict the conclusion of the next study.

Another study, by the National Wildlife Federation, found that thousands of public water systems failed to meet government safety standards. The report, which cited more than 100,000 violations, said that excessive amounts of bacteria, lead, arsenic, and pesticides were present in our public drinking water. It blamed the EPA for not enforcing laws to protect us.

Almost every week we read a story about the problem of water contamination. Here's one from our files: "Toxic chemicals dumped in the Great Lakes are combining to form new poisons so quickly, scientists can't even catalog them, much less agree on how dangerous they are. The number of toxic substances detected in the lakes, source of drinking water for more than 20 million people, has doubled in two years to more than 800."

Here's another: "Millions of gallons of toxic waste from the Stringfellow Acid Pits, 50 miles east of Los Angeles, are flowing towards the Chino Basin aquifer, a major source of drinking water for communities such as Ontario, Rancho, Cucamonga, Upland and Riverside, according to the Office of Technology Assessment. The acid pits were a dumping ground for more than 30 million gallons of liquid waste between 1956 and 1972 when chemicals were discovered leaking through what was thought to be impermeable bedrock." There it is again. The government assured us that something was safe, and then we found out that it really wasn't. And they wonder why we don't trust them.

Our file is growing, and the trend is clear. Our water supply is being contaminated by toxic waste, by leaks and spills, by chemical warfare, by sewage, and by nuclear waste. We're seeing the problem not only in underground water, but in lakes, rivers, and now the oceans. It's killing fish in the Great Lakes, in the Hudson River, in Chesapeake Bay, and even in the Atlantic Ocean. In the summer of 1988 the New Jersey beaches were strewn with thousands of eels, flounders, bass, shrimp, and crabs that were killed by contamination. "The environment is trying to say something," said Stuart J. Wilk, a researcher with the National Marine Fishery Service in Sandy Hook.

According to a 1989 report by the Natural Resources Defense Council, each year 5 trillion gallons of industrial waste and 2.3 trillion gallons of untreated sewage are dumped into our coastal waters. Years ago we never imagined that we could contaminate the oceans. But now we're doing it, and unless we stop, we're going to kill them, as we killed Lake Erie.

The Water Shortage

Even without contamination, we would still face a water shortage in some regions of this country. Demand for water has increased in these regions, while supply has been reduced by climatic changes.

Over the past 15 years the regions with the fastest population growth have been those with limited water resources: the West, the Southwest, and the Southeast. Many people were attracted to these regions because of climate. But the climate is changing. It's getting warmer everywhere, and this affects the water supply. Rivers, which are the main source of water for the West and Southwest, are lower than they've been since the years of the dust bowl. And the warmer it gets, the lower they'll fall.

Demand for water comes from agriculture, industry, utilities, offices, and residences. The heaviest demand comes from agriculture that relies on irrigation. So we're going to see a shortage in the West and Southwest, in states like Texas, Arizona, and California, where arid or semiarid lands are being farmed intensively. And we're going to see a shortage in Florida, where the water supply has been overburdened by rapid development. The water table there has already fallen to critical levels.

The Midwest will also have shortages, as we saw with the drought of 1988. We don't expect this to happen every year, but we do expect it to happen more often as a result of climatic changes. We won't be able to depend on this region to produce as much food as it has in the past.

With lower supply in relation to demand, the price of water will increase. We're going to see rationing, as we already have in San Francisco. And we're going to see recycling, especially by industry.

As with most problems, the media talk a lot about the water shortage during a crisis, as they did during the summer of 1988. We saw pictures of dusty fields in Iowa, of barges stuck in the Mississippi. But when the immediate crisis is over, they forget about the problem, as they did the following winter, and we get the impression that it's gone away.

But it hasn't gone away, it's still with us. What's gone are the days of cheap, plentiful water.

Acid Rain

Acid rain is caused by sulfur and nitrogen oxides emitted by coal-burning power plants, auto exhaust, and other sources. These emissions move through the atmosphere, where they undergo chemical change, and they fall back to earth in the form of acid rain.

In July 1988 the New York State environmental agency released the results of a three-year study on acid rain. It found that 25 percent of the lakes in the Adirondack region were so acidic that they could no longer support fish. In addition, 20 percent of the lakes in the region were considered endangered from high acidity. So almost one-half of the lakes in the region had been severely affected by acid rain.

The commissioner of the state's Environmental Conservation Department, Thomas E. Jorling, said the study "confirms beyond a doubt that the adverse effects of acid rain on aquatic systems are real." The study, he said, "gives documentation that the skeptics out there said they needed."

Well, there were a lot of skeptics, especially in the federal government. Christian Rice, a spokesperson for the EPA, said that the New York study was unlikely to influence the administration's position and that more data were still needed. "The question is," Rice said, "what is the trend? And neither our study nor New York State's study gives us that."

What is the trend? It's obvious. Look at what's happening around the world. Here, and in Canada, and over in Europe, acid rain is killing lakes, forests, and wildlife. If you use your eyes, you can see this. But federal officials refuse to see it. They say there's a lack of evidence.

Not only that, they tried to convince us that acid rain was good. "I think we need to do more research before we run off and worry about acid rain falling from the sky," said James B. Edwards, secretary of energy under Reagan. "I don't want to stop acid rain, because 99.9 percent of all rain is of acid nature. In some areas it's good for crops because the fields are alkaline. A little acid helps neutralize the soil." There it is, the rosy scenario. Acid rain is good for the crops.

Is it also good for people? In 1986 the Brookhaven National Laboratory estimated that acid rain kills 50,000 Americans and 5,000 to 11,000 Canadians annually. Yet in 1987 a federal government study concluded that there was little evidence of an immediate threat to the environment or public health from acid rain. It said that damage to lakes was limited to a few areas, mostly in the Northeast, and that even in those areas, only a small percentage were affected. The study said there was probably no damage to forests. Canada's environment minister, Tom McMillan, dismissed this report as voodoo science. And many scientists complained that its executive summary was inaccurate and misleading. They said it was tailored to support the government's opposition to more controls.

Where is this opposition coming from? Special interests, such as the auto industry, the utilities, and the coal producers. In April 1987 Senator Robert C. Byrd said acid rain wasn't an emergency, and he denounced legislation proposed to control the sources of pollution that cause it. Byrd, of course, represents West Virginia, a coal-producing state that would be affected by such legislation.

The Greenhouse Effect

The story of the greenhouse effect illustrates the typical stages of public awareness of a problem and government reaction to it. We're given a warning, but it's dismissed for lack of evidence, and nothing is done about the problem. Then when it begins to affect us, the media start talking about it. When it becomes headline news, the government reacts. But instead of attacking the cause of the problem, they look for ways to relieve the symptoms.

The greenhouse effect, or warming trend, was first predicted in 1896 by a Swedish chemist, Svante Arrhenius. As his country industrialized, he said that emissions from factories would increase the levels of carbon dioxide in the atmosphere, and that this would result in a warming trend. But he was regarded as a kook.

In the early 1970s a few scientists warned us about the effect, predicting that the earth would begin to heat up by the late 1980s. But their warning was dismissed for lack of evidence. Anyway, why should they have worried about something that might occur in the future?

As recently as October 1983 the National Academy of Sciences, which represents the establishment, said that the greenhouse effect wouldn't come soon, and that it wouldn't pose as much of a threat as some scientists said.

The public became aware of the problem during the heat wave of 1988. Until then, you didn't hear much about the greenhouse effect. There was only an occasional story in the newspapers, usually buried in the back pages. Then suddenly the media were talking about it. The problem became headline news. But the politicians were right in the middle of an election campaign, which isn't a time to address issues, so they ignored it.

Now, one hot summer doesn't make a warming trend. But it hasn't been just one hot summer. In fact, the 1980s accounted for the six warmest years in the history of global measurements.

In June 1988 James E. Hansen of NASA told a Senate committee: "There is no disputing some facts. Atmospheric levels of carbon dioxide have increased 25 percent since preindustrial times, and they are rising at a rapid clip. The earth's temperature has jumped nearly one degree in the past 30 years, leaving the planet warmer today than it has been since measurements began 130 years ago."

According to Hansen, if the present trend continues for another 20 years, it will be warmer than it has been in the last 100,000 years.

Other climatologists agree that it will get warmer. John Firror, director of Advanced Studies for Atmospheric Research in Boulder, Colorado, said: "There is no disagreement that we're in for rapid heating. The only question is how rapid."

How will this affect us? Well, for one thing, we're going to have more summers like the one of 1988. It was not only uncomfortable, but thousands of people died from the heat. In August 1988 W. Moulton Avery, executive director of the Center for Environmental Physiology in Washington, D.C., said that the summer probably killed more people than the heat wave of 1980, which he estimated killed about 15,000 Americans.

How else will the warming trend affect us? The farm belt will become less productive, with more and more crop losses. At some point, Iowa will become a dust bowl, and Canada will become a breadbasket. The polar ice caps will melt, causing the oceans to rise and flood the coastlines. Lakes will dry up, forests will shrink, and wildlife will be decimated. Now, we're not talking about something that might happen in the distant future. We're talking about something that *will* happen in the next 20 to 50 years unless we reverse the present trend.

In October 1988 the EPA released a report on the warming trend and its probable impact. It made headline news, since it came from the government. This is typical. If other people say it, they're dismissed as kooks. But when it finally comes from the government, then it's official. Yet this same government ignored the warnings of scientists who years ago identified the cause and predicted the effect. This same government relaxed standards and thereby accelerated the trend.

In the report, they recommended that we adapt to the changes, since the trend might be irreversible. In other words, it was too late to do anything. And using this as an excuse not to attack the causes of the problem, they offered to relieve the symptoms. "Major changes will be here by the years 1990 and 2000," said John Hoffman, an EPA official, "and we have to learn how to live with them."

More recently, they recommended some policy options that would slow the warming trend, including improving energy efficiency, switching to biomass fuels, taxing the use of fossil fuels, and developing solar energy technology. Good ideas, and all of them were recommended by forward-looking people years ago. Instead of proacting, the government is reacting, now that the problem has made the headlines. But will they follow through when the story is no longer on the front page?

The Ozone Layer

In the early 1970s a few scientists warned that chlorine gases then used in aerosol cans and still used in refrigerators, insulating foams, and industrial solvents would act as a powerful catalyst in the upper atmosphere to break down the ozone layer that protects us from harmful ultraviolet radiation. As usual, their warning was dismissed for lack of evidence, and nothing was done about the problem.

We eventually stopped using chlorofluorocarbons (CFCs) in aerosol cans, but we continued using them for other purposes, since manufacturers insisted that no substitutes were available. And the government waited while the scientific establishment studied the problem.

Then when dramatic evidence was found, it made the front page. In March 1988 the *New York Times* wrote: "The destruction of the earth's protective ozone layer set in motion by the release of industrial gases into the atmosphere will continue for decades, despite best efforts of governments and industries to control it, scientists now agree. Society appears to have ignited a sequence of atmospheric processes that cannot be quickly reversed. A surprisingly rapid depletion of ozone now seen by satellites—confirmed last week by a government panel of 100 atmospheric scientists—has prompted widespread rethinking of forecasts that the changes would be gradual."

Now it's official. Now that it's been confirmed by a government panel of 100 scientists, we can believe it. But what about the scientists who warned us about it 15 years ago? What about the damage that's been done since then? And what about the future?

A treaty signed by 47 countries would reduce production of CFCs by 50 percent over the next ten years (the Montreal Protocol), and the 12 countries of the European Community have gone a step further, agreeing to ban the use of CFCs by the end of the century. Still, the atmospheric levels of chlorine would rise, since CFCs take as long as a century to break down, and the loss of ozone would continue. Data collected by NASA indicate that the amount of ozone over the Northern Hemisphere declined by as much as 3 percent from 1969 to 1986. It's estimated that each 1 percent reduction in ozone may cause a 6 percent increase in skin cancer, and that the odds of getting malignant melanoma, the most serious form of skin cancer, will almost triple in the 1990s. The number of cases of melanoma has already jumped by 93 percent in the past eight years. It's also estimated that for every 10 percent increase in ultraviolet radiation, there will be a 6 percent increase in cataracts. With greater exposure to ultraviolet radiation, the number of cataracts has grown sharply in recent years.

Further, some scientists have concluded that the greater exposure to ultraviolet radiation would damage our immune systems. The effect would be an increase in immune system diseases like AIDS and the New Black Plague.

For a while our government backed away from the idea of reducing world production and use of CFCs. Instead, they considered a public relations campaign to encourage the use of hats, sunglasses, and skin lotions. Once again, they offered to relieve the symptoms, while refusing to attack the causes of a problem.

A Major Issue

"We can't afford to have clean air. It costs too much." You often hear this type of argument. It comes from applying the standard technique of cost-benefit analysis to environmental problems. In fact, the EPA uses this technique to determine the value of a regulation. What will it cost, and how much will it benefit the public?

Well, measuring the cost is easy. But if you don't think globally, measuring the benefits is difficult. That's why our leaders buy the argument that we can't afford to have clean air. They don't make connections between the environment and health, between the environment and the economy. If they did, they would see that the deterioration of the environment is a primary cause of our rising health costs and our declining economy. And maybe then they would do something about the problems.

As you must have gathered by now, I don't have a lot of faith in our leaders. I believe that unless they're pressured by an informed, concerned, and aroused public, they'll continue to ignore the problems or give us only symptom relief. But I do have a lot of faith in people. I believe that if they can get information about the real world, they can make connections, and they can change policies.

We're seeing it happen. We're seeing the formation of a major trend. We're seeing the growth of public concern for the environment, and we're seeing the responses of the federal, state, and local governments.

We're seeing new laws on the generation and disposal of garbage. In Florida, which has an especially severe problem, they're attacking the causes. As of January 1, 1990, plastic shopping bags used by retailers will have to be biodegradable. There will be disposal fees on newsprint to encourage recycling. Motorists who litter will get black marks on their driving records. Unauthorized dumping of 500 or more pounds of trash will be a felony.

We're seeing more laws that mandate recycling. Such laws have been passed in ten states and are pending in 24 states. A bill has been proposed in the House that would mandate recycling in every state by 1994. We're also seeing more laws that require products to be biodegradable. Such laws have been passed in 16 states and are pending in as many others.

We're seeing a wave of "green" products—the word "green" is now being used by marketing people for products that might appeal to environmentally conscious shoppers. In a 1989 poll 77 percent of the people said they would pay extra for a product packaged with recyclable or biodegradable materials, and 53 percent said they had declined to buy a product in the past year because they were concerned about its effect on the environment. Wal-Mart, the nation's third largest retailer, announced last August that it would push its suppliers to develop environmentally friendly products. Major consumer products companies, such as Proctor & Gamble and Coca-Cola, are responding to the trend.

We're seeing more regulations on the use of toxic chemicals. In California, under a law passed in 1988, no business in the state may expose people to chemicals that cause cancer or birth defects without giving a clear and reasonable warning. So even when you pull up to a gas station, you'll be warned of the risks.

We're seeing more restrictions on sewage treatment. In the summer of 1988 the Senate passed a law that will ban the dumping of sewage sludge into the ocean by 1992. The law was enacted in response to pressure from the public, which had been aroused by contamination of beaches. This shows that if people demand action, they'll get it.

We're going to see tighter emission controls, not only for motor vehicles but also for factories and power plants. In his first budget message, Bush said he is "committed to ending the long debate on acid rain," and in Ottawa he pledged to reduce acid rain, a problem that has strained our relations with Canada. As I write this, Congress is preparing to amend the Clean Air Act, and after hearing evidence on the health hazards of air pollution, they'll make the law tougher.

We're going to see less chemical warfare. Supermarkets are responding to public concern and refusing to carry certain foods that have been sprayed with pesticides. And this is only the beginning of a trend.

We're going to see more limits on the use of ozone-destroying chemicals. In May 1989, at a meeting in Helsinki, 81 nations adopted a declaration calling for a complete phaseout of chlorofluorocarbons (CFCs) by the end of the century, and for a ban on the use of halons as soon as possible. This goes far beyond the provisions of the Montreal Protocol.

But will we reverse air pollution? Will we reverse water contamination? Will we reverse acid rain, the greenhouse effect, the damage to the ozone layer? Will we reverse the trends of the past 200 years?

The answer depends on all of us, as consumers, as voters, and as members of the global community. As trend trackers, we have to recognize that environmental policies will depend on the state of the economy—in times of slow growth there's less willingness to bear the costs of caring for the environment. So demand for clean air, pure water, and environmentally safe products won't increase at a steady rate.

At the same time, we have to recognize that politics will affect this trend. For example, the Administration's proposed national energy policy emphasizes increases in domestic oil production over efficiency and conservation. The philosophy behind such policies was aptly expressed by Budget Director Richard Darman when he said: "Americans did not fight and win the wars of the 20th century to make the world safe for green vegetables."

= 11 =

The Military

Until the Cold War the military played a minor role in this country. When we had a war, we would mobilize, but always with some opposition, reflecting our heritage of isolationism, antimilitarism, and pacifism. When the war was over, we would demobilize.

Even after World War II we followed this pattern, until we felt threatened by the Soviet Union, and then we broke with our tradition. We maintained our armed forces at a level far above the prewar level, and when we got into the Korean War we built them up again. When that war was over, we demobilized less than after World War II, and for the rest of the 1950s and into the 1960s we spent almost 10 percent of our GNP on defense.

Now, I'm not questioning our decision to contain the expansion of the Soviet Union. Someone had to do it, and we were the only people who could. But we paid a heavy price for it, and we played the role of superpower longer than necessary. What happened was, it went to our heads, and we couldn't see how the world was changing, how the real power was shifting to countries that spent less on defense.

In the 1970s we reduced military spending after pulling out of Vietnam and directed more of our resources to the domestic programs launched in the 1960s. But the trend was reversed late in the decade in reaction to the Soviet invasion of Afghanistan and the hostage crisis in Iran. By 1980 we were committed to the largest peacetime military buildup in our history. How did the government finance this buildup? It borrowed the money, and it cut expenditures for domestic programs. At a time when we were losing ground to our competitors in the global market, the government invested our savings in the military. At a time when people needed help, it used scarce resources to develop, produce, and test weapons.

The buildup made us look stronger, but this was only an illusion. By pushing us deeper into debt, it undermined the health of our economy. By taking a bigger share of our research, it further impaired our competitiveness. By crowding out domestic programs, it compromised our values. By absorbing funds that might have gone into education, it limited our future. So after eight years of building up the military, we were really much weaker.

For a while the government had public support for the military buildup. Then, alarmed by the budget deficits, people began to have doubts about it. Finally, angered by the Pentagon scandals, they turned against it. By early 1989 they favored sharp cuts in defense spending. But our political leaders insisted that we should continue to build up the military.

Then came the changes in Eastern Europe, and after the opening of the Berlin Wall our leaders finally proposed "cuts" in defense spending. But they still weren't prepared to make real cuts, they were only proposing to spend less than they would have before. So even though the Cold War is over, they haven't begun to demobilize, and they haven't begun to reverse its effects.

We forecast that unless the public puts very strong pressure on the politicians to make drastic cuts in the military, they'll continue to find reasons—and uses—for it. They've already shifted the battleground to Latin America.

The Military Buildup

In the early 1980s the government implemented a policy to build up the military. In fact, they increased the annual defense budget by more than 50 percent.

Why did they do it? They did it because they had a World War II mentality, which equates military power with success. They remembered how we defeated Germany and Japan, and how we contained the Soviet Union, and they believed that we could regain our dominant position in the world by building up our military. They forgot, or never understood, that military power wasn't the reason for our success.

Also, they were bound by their ideology, which divided the world into good guys and bad guys. We, and the countries that went along with us, were good guys. The Soviet Union was an "evil empire," and the countries that experimented with its ideas were bad guys. In their minds, the only competition that mattered was between us and the Soviet Union.

Twenty years earlier, this might have been the case. But the world had changed, and other issues were more important than the contest between the superpowers. While we continued to slug it out, like two fighters in a blind alley trying to settle an old score, the real action was somewhere else. The Reagan people couldn't see this. All they could see was an arms race, and they wanted to win it. They wanted to show the rest of the world that we weren't wimps like Jimmy Carter, we were tough, we were macho, we were standing tall like John Wayne. And boy, did we ever show them in Grenada.

Living in Disney world, the government created a fantasy. If it had been a low-budget movie, we could have just written it off. But it was an extravaganza that cost us $2 trillion. That's right, $2 trillion. Think what we could have done with that money. We could have invested it in the civilian economy. We could have used it for research, for education, for housing, for transportation, for maintenance of our infrastructure, and for the environment. Instead, we blew it, and what's worse, we borrowed it. So now we have an enormous debt and virtually nothing to show for it.

Steroid Strength

In 1988 I noticed a body-building craze among teenagers. They were lifting weights and taking steroids. They were developing strong-looking bodies, but neglecting their brains and damaging their health.

I interviewed a few, and I pointed out the harmful effects of taking steroids—including impotency, liver cancer, and mental problems. They didn't listen, they just wanted to build their muscles so they could strut around and show off their strength. But that strength was only an illusion, since they were ruining their bodies, and after a while they wouldn't look so strong.

If you think about it, our country did the same thing. We built up the military but neglected education and damaged our economic health. We strutted around and showed off our strength, but it was only an illusion, since we were wasting our resources. And now, compared with Europe and Japan, we don't look so strong.

Like those kids, we had the wrong priorities. We put our money into defense while cutting other programs and using debt to finance our muscle building. When later asked about the deficit, Reagan reminded reporters that during his 1980 campaign he had told them: "If it came to a choice between deficit spending, balancing the budget, and defense spending, which side would I come down on—and I said, dealing with the situation at the time, I would have to come down on the side of defense." So his top priority was defense.

Studies have found that defense spending retards economic growth. The higher a nation's defense spending, the lower its investment spending. Economic growth depends on investment spending, which increases productivity. Among the industrialized nations of the West, we've spent the highest percentage of our GNP on defense, and we've had the lowest growth in manufacturing productivity.

Defense spending creates jobs, but it generates fewer jobs than other types of public or private spending. A 1983 study found that every $1 billion spent on military procurement created 28,000 jobs, while the same $1 billion could have funded 71,000 jobs in education or 57,000 jobs if left with taxpayers for personal consumption. And the jobs created by defense spending offer little hope for the unemployed, since most of them are filled by scientists, engineers, and professionals.

Defense spending also leads to commercial spin-offs, but the benefits are less than proponents claim. For example, the Reagan administration claimed that the space-based missile defense system known as Star Wars would have significant economic benefits. A 1988 report by the Council on Economic Priorities challenged this argument. It found that whatever commercial spinoffs might result from Star Wars, they were unlikely to be substantial in relation to the cost of the program, which from 1983 to 1988 absorbed 11 percent of national research and development spending. The report said that instead of hoping for illusory spin-offs, we would benefit more by spending research funds directly on civilian technologies, as our competitors were doing.

In a March 1989 interview, Arno Penzias, the Nobel laureate physicist who runs Bell Laboratories, said he had yet to find a factual basis for the "legends" about commercial spin-offs from military spending. "What the economy gets when you spend, say, $18 billion on an aircraft carrier is an aircraft carrier. Period," he said. "Now, if you want an aircraft carrier, fine. But don't pretend it's going to give you some pots and pans, or a TV set, or a better lathe."

On top of our defense spending, we have the space program, which in recent years has become more oriented toward military purposes. Under our current space policy, the primary objective of the space program is to strengthen our national security. The Department of Defense has first access to shuttle flights, and 34 percent of the payloads through 1994 will be military. This wasn't the original intent of the program. The legislation specified a civilian space program, separate from the military. But the program has been diverted by the military, so whatever benefits from commercial spin-offs might have resulted, they're going to be diminished.

It has been argued that defense spending stimulates the economy, and to some extent, it does. But the waste factor is extremely high, and the benefits are distributed unevenly. As weapons have accounted for a greater share of the defense budget, spending has become more concentrated. Most of the defense contracts go to California, New York, and New England, while other regions get few benefits.

We spend more than 6 percent of our GNP on defense, and if you include military research and the space program, the percentage is considerably higher. West Germany spends 3 percent of its GNP on defense and Japan only 1 percent. While we have steroid strength, they have healthy economies.

Waste, Fraud, and Abuse

With the military buildup of the 1980s, there was a lot of waste, fraud, and abuse in defense spending. It made you wonder if they were really building up the military, or if they were just spending more money.

We began to keep a file on the subject in 1983. Stories were appearing in the back pages of newspapers about the problem of waste in the Pentagon. But there wasn't too much concern about it. When a commission headed by J. Peter Grace reported that the government could save billions of dollars with better management of defense spending, it didn't make headlines. It didn't even make the front page.

Then, in a report from the Pentagon's inspector general, the media found something that the public could relate to. The government had paid $435 for a claw hammer that you could buy in the hardware store for no more than $15. This wasn't a cost overrun on a highly sophisticated weapon that only an expert could understand. It was a gross overpayment for a household tool, and it made people angry.

In February 1984 another report from the inspector general said that the Pentagon had wasted millions of dollars on new weapons because of lax supervision of pricing by subcontractors. In one case, the auditors found that the army paid as much as $41 million "more than necessary" for the UH-60A Black Hawk helicopter "because the prime contractor negotiated better prices with its subcontractors after it had completed negotiations with the government."

Trying to head off a political issue, Defense Secretary Caspar W. Weinberger insisted that he had undertaken a full-scale reform of defense procurement. "This administration," he said, "has taken on the problems that have been part of the procurement system for many years. We have identified them, analyzed them, and are now fixing them."

Since it was an election year, the government mounted a publicity campaign to show that they were fixing the problems. They announced refunds they had received from contractors and cost savings they had obtained. But the refunds represented only a small fraction of the abuses uncovered by auditors, and the cost savings were overstated. Again we can see how politicians use the media to create illusions.

They kept the problems from becoming an issue in the election, but they did almost nothing to solve them. Now and then they would throw a bone to the public, as they did in early 1985 when an audit revealed that General Dynamics had overcharged the government by $244 million on defense contracts. Weinberger announced that he was suspending all overhead payments to the contractor for at least 30 days and ordering "a complete and comprehensive review of billing procedures."

If you follow these cases, you can see the pattern. An audit finds that some contractor has ripped off the government for a large amount of money. The discovery is highly publicized to reassure us that the government is doing something about the problem. For a while, congressmen talk about it, using it to make headlines. But then they stop, it fades from the news, and you almost never find out what happened.

In 1986, reacting to more horror stories, the administration formed a commission to study the problem of waste and abuse in defense spending. The commission was headed by David Packard, one of the founders of Hewlett-Packard, and it recommended sweeping reforms of the military procurement system. A few of its recommendations were adopted, but most were ignored. As usual, the real purpose of forming the commission was to buy time and hope that the problem would go away or fade from the news.

In July they threw a bone to the public. Litton Industries pleaded guilty to defrauding the Pentagon of $6.3 million on electronics contracts. Litton agreed to pay $15 million in restitution and penalties. Of course, it was an election year, and nailing Litton made it look as if the government was doing something about the problem of waste and abuse.

Later that year we read about the Bradley fighting vehicle. Experts warned that the vehicle might sink if it tried to cross deep rivers in combat, but the Pentagon went ahead with the $12.2 billion project. It accepted certifications from FMC, the contractor, that the Bradley was capable of crossing deep water. Troops who used the vehicle in training wore life preservers.

In February 1987 we read about the B-1 bomber, which wouldn't fly. The Pentagon requested $802 million to fix it, but critics said that the final cost of fixing it would be more than $3 billion. Weinberger insisted that with the additional funds the bomber could perform all its missions.

In June they threw another bone to the public. Textron pleaded guilty to making false statements in billing the Pentagon on arms contracts. Textron agreed to pay $4.6 million in penalties. Speaking as if the government had won a major victory, Attorney General Edwin Meese said: "Contractors are on notice that the nation's buildup of its defenses is not an invitation to plunder the public purse."

In August we read that defective bolts had forced the military to make repairs on tanks, howitzers, and other weapons. The problem had crippled more than 10 percent of our M-60 tanks, which cost $1.6 million each.

At the same time, a report from the House Armed Services Committee raised questions about the accuracy of the MX missile. It presented new data on test flights and suggested that there were problems with the missile's guidance system. It said that Northrop, which supplied a vital component of the system, hadn't met specifications on parts.

Toward the end of the year we read that the cost of fixing the B-1 bomber would be $6.2 billion, bringing the total cost of the program to $28 billion, or $280 million per plane. And we still didn't know if it would fly.

Meanwhile, the air force brought back the leather "wild blue yonder" jackets. "We're talking image," a spokesman said. "We're trying to remind everyone that the air force mission is to fly and fight if we have to." In other words, they were trying to maintain an illusion. But if our planes won't fly, what good is a flight jacket?

In March 1988 they threw another bone to the public. Motorola pleaded guilty to criminal charges of overcharging on military contracts and agreed to repay $16 million to the Pentagon. The contracts, which went back to 1983, were for elements of a satellite communications system and for missile guidance devices. The Justice Department prosecutor said it was "one of the largest criminal settlements we have had in the military procurement area."

A few months later we read that the Justice Department was investigating fraud and bribery in military procurement. The prosecutor alleged that consultants had obtained confidential information from Pentagon officials and had sold it to defense contractors. The probe involved as many as 100 contracts worth billions of dollars. The story made headlines, and it became known as the Pentagon scandals.

For a while it drew a lot of attention from the media and from congressmen, but then it got crowded off of the front page by other news, especially the election campaign. And it was hardly mentioned by the candidates.

In October Sundstrand pleaded guilty to overcharging the government on military contracts and agreed to pay $115 million in fines and penalties. This was another bone to the public, and coming just before the election its timing was perfect. By golly, they were nailing the rascals.

But we didn't know what happened in the other cases. In fact, according to a report by the General Accounting Office, even the government didn't know what happened in almost half of them. Apparently, those cases had fallen into limbo.

In late 1988 a committee of experts concluded that the Defense Department had failed to improve the procurement system. "Scandals, cost overruns, mismanagement on a vast scale, inefficiency and incompetence have justifiably and understandably shaken public support for defense spending," said Patrick J. Leahy, senator from Vermont. "Something must be done to get the Pentagon's house in order."

The politicians have been saying this for years. But meanwhile they've been accepting large contributions from PACs that are sponsored by defense contractors. They've also been collecting honoraria to tour the plants of these contractors. So it's easy to see why they just talk.

Senior military officers have testified repeatedly that they're not ready for sustained combat. After spending more than $2 trillion, they're not ready. Yet they don't want to throw away money on education.

Pentagon, Inc.

When Eisenhower warned us about the "military-industrial complex," most of us didn't know what he was talking about. We were a country in which the military had always played a minor role, so it was hard for us to imagine how they could have a lot of influence.

But when we began to maintain our armed forces at a high level during peacetime, the role of the military changed. It built a constituency among those who benefited from defense spending, especially among the industries that supplied weapons and materials. Instead of producing such items only during wartime, these industries supplied them all the time. They depended on the military, and the military depended on them. The military and industry developed a symbiotic relationship.

The military now plays a major role in our country. About 30 percent of our federal budget goes to defense. About 40 percent of our scientists, engineers, and technical professionals work in the defense sector. About two-thirds of our computer research is funded by the Department of Defense. Up to 90 percent of departmental budgets at some of our top universities, such as Stanford, MIT, and Carnegie Mellon, come from the Pentagon. A little-known arm of the military, the Defense Advanced Research Projects Agency (Darpa), has a major impact on the selection and development of new technology.

In the fall of 1988 an advisory panel urged the military to play an even greater role. The panel, which was drawn from industry and universities, recommended that the Pentagon be more involved in setting economic policy. These and other experts argued that the Pentagon should exert more influence over such matters as taxes, trade, the environment, and education in order to head off "an increasing loss of technological leadership to both our allies and adversaries." In other words, they wanted to respond to Japan, Inc. by creating Pentagon, Inc.

Some people favor the idea, but it would do the opposite of what they claim. Our loss of technological leadership has been in the civilian economy, and a primary cause of this loss has been our diversion of resources to the military. To give the Pentagon even more influence over economic policy would be the fulfillment of Eisenhower's warning.

Cutting Defense

While public opinion in this country was turning against defense spending, Gorbachev realized that the arms race was destroying the Soviet economy, and that someone had to make the first move. In December 1988, in a speech at the United Nations, he announced unilateral cuts in the Soviet military forces.

Our leaders reacted with caution, and they pointed out that the Soviets still had superior strength in conventional arms, so it would be premature for us to consider cutting our own forces. They were taken by surprise, and they really didn't know what to do. Unable to accept the change in Soviet policy, they clung to the World War II mentality.

Meanwhile, Poland was dismantling the system that the Soviet Union had imposed on it, and people were waiting to see if Gorbachev would send in the tanks, as his predecessors had done when Hungary and Czechoslovakia tried to change their systems. When he let Poland form a government that wasn't dominated by the Communist party, it became clear that there really had been a change in Soviet policy.

The developments in Hungary and other countries in Eastern Europe confirmed the change. But the diehards in Washington still resisted the idea. In late August 1989 Secretary of Defense Dick Cheney was still against cutting defense, and when his former House colleagues trimmed the military budget, he said they acted on the mistaken assumption that the Soviet threat was diminishing. He argued that on the contrary we faced "a more formidable, offensive strategic arsenal today" than before Mr. Gorbachev came to power in 1985.

Now, bear in mind that about 60 percent of our defense budget is allocated to Europe, and that the rationale for the budget had been our fear of the Warsaw Pact armies rolling into Western Europe. While

Cheney was speaking, the Warsaw Pact was falling apart, and it was already hard to imagine the countries of Eastern Europe joining the Soviet Union in an invasion of France. But the Cold Warriors still saw the world as it had been 40 years ago. They couldn't see that it was changing.

They were finally overtaken by the events of November 1989. A little more than a week after the opening of the Berlin Wall, Cheney sang a different song. On November 17 he proposed cutting $180 billion in defense spending over the next three years. Again, he was reacting, and he was trying to create the impression that this was a major change in policy. When I heard the amount of the proposed cuts, it sounded convincing. But then I read that he was proposing to spend $180 billion less than we would have spent if we had increased defense spending as he had wanted. In other words, they weren't cuts in the sense that you or I understand the word, which means to spend less. They were "cuts" in the political sense. And they would hardly make a dent in the budget deficit.

Here we've been offered a golden opportunity to solve a major economic problem, but instead of taking it, our leaders are balking. Why? Because they were used to the status quo, they were comfortable with the Cold War. "For all its risks and uncertainties," said Under Secretary of State Lawrence Eagleburger, "the Cold War was characterized by a remarkably stable and predictable set of relations among the great powers."

That's why our leaders are balking. They want to hold on to the world they knew, the world in which they could go to bed at night feeling secure because either we or the Soviet Union could press a button and destroy it. They want to hold on to the world in which we were the good guys and the Soviets were the bad guys. They want to hold on to the world in which we and the Soviet Union were dominant. But that world was already changing when they decided to build up the military in the 1980s, and it was gone by the end of the decade.

The Cold War is over, and we should follow our tradition of demobilizing when a war is over. It has been a long war, and even though few of the battles were fought on our soil, it has been a costly one. We had more casualties in this war than in all our other wars put together. As casualties, I count not only the thousands who were killed, wounded, or otherwise disabled in Korea and Vietnam, but also the millions who suffered because of our high priority on defense spending. Our cities weren't bombed by the Soviets, but parts of them look as if they had been. And they're full of refugees.

I remember after World War II displaced persons came here from Europe, victims of the war. They were known as DPs, and they were everywhere. Well, we have them now, but they're not from Europe, they're from North Dakota, Detroit, Texas, and the Bronx. They're the children below the poverty level, the elderly without care, the homeless, the high school dropouts, the drug addicts, the hard core unemployed, and the working poor. These and others are the victims of the Cold War, the DPs of the 1990s.

When we saw the suffering in Europe after World War II, we gave them economic aid. We should give no less to our own people who have been displaced by the Cold War. We should launch a domestic Marshall Plan to rebuild our country. But we have to make real cuts in defense spending and reallocate our resources. As long as we just make the "cuts" that Cheney proposed, we'll continue to feel the effects of the war, and we'll continue to decline economically, socially, and politically.

With limited resources, we have to choose between fighter planes and education, tanks and health care, aircraft carriers and mass transportation, missiles and global competitiveness. As Eisenhower said: "Every gun that is made, every warship launched, every rocket fired signifies in the final sense a theft from those who hunger and are not fed, those who are cold and are not clothed. This world in arms is not spending money alone. It's spending the sweat of laborers, the genius of its scientists, the hopes of its children. This is not a way of life at all in any true sense. Under the cloud of threatening war, it is humanity hanging from a cross of iron."

= 12 =

The Economy

Our economic policies are like the drugs we take for our health problems—instead of attacking the causes, they only relieve the symptoms, and they have harmful side effects. If we have a headache, we take a pill. If we have inflation, we take a dose of tight money.

Our policymakers have a one-dimensional approach to the problems—instead of viewing the whole patient, they only look at the complaint. If we have unemployment, they stimulate the economy with deficit spending, ignoring the fact that people who lack the required skills won't get jobs no matter how much you spend, unless you educate them.

If you think globally, you can see that the causes of our economic problems are in other fields. You can see that a cause of our poverty is the breakdown of the family. You can see that a cause of our low productivity is the failure of the school system. You can see that a cause of our loss of technological leadership is the buildup of the military. But our policymakers don't think globally.

When the Reagan administration came into office, it inherited some major economic problems: high inflation, high unemployment, low growth, a budget deficit, and a trade deficit. It fought inflation with monetary policy, which caused a recession and increased the rate of unemployment. It fought unemployment with fiscal policy, which increased the budget deficit. It created an illusion of prosperity with the excess spending generated by the deficit and financed by foreign debt. When its policies increased the trade deficit, it tried to solve the problem by devaluing the dollar, but this made our assets less expensive for foreigners to buy. So its one-dimensional solutions compounded the problems.

The present economic trends are unfavorable. We have a slowing growth rate. We have low productivity. We have a crumbling infrastructure. We have enormous debts. We have an intractable trade deficit. We have a growing underclass and a shrinking middle class. We have a declining standard of living.

The government can reverse these trends by attacking the causes of our problems. One of these causes is the budget deficit, which absorbs funds that might otherwise be available to the private sector. Another is defense spending, which diverts resources from other areas. Another is our low rate of saving, which fails to provide the capital we need. These causes are interrelated. If we cut defense spending, we could reduce the budget deficit and allocate more resources to other areas. If we increased our rate of saving, we would have more capital for both the private and public sectors.

But unless the politicians are forced by public awareness, public concern, and public pressure into attacking the causes of our problems, they'll only try to relieve the symptoms, and they'll lead us downward in the 1990s.

Fighting Inflation

According to the monetarist theory, inflation is caused by excessive growth of the money supply. In other words, if there's too much money chasing too few goods, prices will go up. So you can prevent inflation by controlling the growth of the money supply, and you can cure it by slowing, stopping, or reversing this growth, a policy called "tight money."

Beginning in 1979, the Federal Reserve applied this theory to fight inflation. They tightened money, and after Reagan was elected they tightened it further. The policy drove up interest rates, since it lowered the supply of loanable funds. The higher rates discouraged businesses as well as consumers from borrowing and spending, and the economy plunged into the worst recession since the 1930s.

Here you can see how global thinking might have led to another policy. The high inflation wasn't caused by too much money chasing too few goods, it was caused by supply shocks (sudden shortages of vital materials such as food and oil as a result of drought, war, or other catastrophe). And the rate of inflation didn't fall to acceptable levels until the price of oil went down. So a dose of tight money, with its harmful side effects, wasn't called for.

Since it was an election year, and since there was also concern about a worldwide financial collapse triggered by defaults on Third World debt, the government reversed its policy in 1982, and we recovered from the recession. But we haven't recovered from the side effects. As the tight money drove up interest rates, lenders from countries that had lower rates were attracted here. To lend dollars, they had to buy them, and with Germans, Japanese, and others buying dollars so that they could lend them and earn higher interest rates, demand for the dollar was very strong. This drove up the value of the dollar in relation to other currencies.

The revaluation of the dollar made imports less expensive for us, and it made our exports more expensive for foreigners, so we bought more from other countries and sold less to them. We already had a trade deficit, but the stronger dollar made things worse. It opened our market to competition in almost every industry, and it knocked us out of foreign markets. For a while it raised our purchasing power, without our having done anything to earn such a windfall. It made us feel richer, while covering up the fact that we were getting poorer. And the government, which had unintentionally produced this effect, pointed to the strong dollar as evidence of the success of its economic policy.

Fiscal Stimulus

Fiscal policy involves taxes and government spending. Since the 1930s, the government has used fiscal policy to stimulate the economy. The theory is if businesses don't spend enough to keep the economy at full employment, then the government should compensate by spending more than its revenues, a policy called "deficit spending."

The low growth and high inflation of the 1970s, a period of regular budget deficits, led some economists to question the theory. They argued that when the government borrows from the public to finance the deficits, it drives up interest rates and crowds businesses out of the market for loanable funds. As a result, businesses invest less in new technology and equipment, and this affects productivity. So deficit spending wasn't the solution, it was the problem.

Buying this argument, the policymakers of the Reagan administration developed a plan to balance the budget. Instead of cutting government spending, they started the process by cutting taxes. They believed that the immediate prospect of lower revenues would force Congress to cut spending, and that the effect of lower tax rates on revenues would eventually be offset by higher taxable incomes resulting from economic growth. Before long, with expenditures falling and revenues rising, the budget would be balanced.

What went wrong? For one thing, it's always harder for politicians to cut spending than to cut taxes. Also, Reagan wanted to increase defense spending, which meant that the full brunt of the cuts had to be absorbed by other programs. This made it even harder for Congress to cut spending. In fact, as a result of the military buildup, government spending rose to the highest level since World War II.

The irony is, under an administration that was going to balance the budget, we had deficits that set peacetime records. This is what stimulated the economy, the spending generated by these huge deficits.

The Trade Deficit

When a country spends more for imports than it earns from exports, it has a trade deficit. It finances this deficit by borrowing from other countries. Borrowing makes it possible for a country to spend more for imports than it earns from exports, just as borrowing makes it possible for individuals to spend more than they earn. So borrowing is the cause of trade deficits, not the effect.

Now, a trade deficit isn't necessarily bad. If you're importing machinery to produce goods that you can later export, then a deficit isn't bad, because this kind of import will generate income and enable you to repay your debt. But if you're importing consumer goods, then a deficit is bad, because this kind of import won't generate any income. Sooner or later you'll exhaust your capacity to borrow and you'll have to stop. At that point your income from exports will be absorbed by debt repayments, and your standard of living will be reduced.

Before that happens, a trade deficit has bad effects. The worst effect is that it eliminates jobs. For every car we import, we have fewer jobs in our auto industry. For every VCR we import, we have fewer jobs in our electronics industry. For every sweater we import, we have fewer jobs in our textile industry. It has been estimated that in 1987 our trade deficit cost us 5.1 million jobs.

The politicians, as well as some economists, tell us not to worry about our trade deficits. They remind us that we've had them before. We did have them, back when we were a developing country, but then we were importing goods that generated income, made us wealthy, and enabled us to repay our debt. Now we're importing goods that won't generate any income. When you buy a car that was made in Japan, it's not going to breed and produce more cars that we can sell back to them. So don't listen to people who tell you we've had trade deficits before, or to people who tell you Japan had trade deficits until 1963. They're ignoring the important fact that we didn't have them, nor did Japan, as a result of consumer spending.

In 1980 the trade deficit was $36.4 billion, and by 1984 it had grown to $123.3 billion. By then the problem was too big to ignore, and the politicians reacted to it. But as usual they didn't attack the causes, they only offered symptom relief. Some of them urged quotas and tariffs to protect our industries, while others prescribed devaluation of the dollar to make us more competitive. And there was a struggle between the proponents of these solutions.

Devaluation

Reagan, who believed in free trade, strongly opposed the protectionists, though he did accept quotas for the automobile, steel, and textile industries. He favored devaluation, and in September 1985 he implemented a plan to reduce the trade deficit. The reasoning was if the stronger dollar had caused the problem, then a weaker dollar would solve it by making imports more expensive and our exports less expensive.

How would they devalue the dollar? By doing the opposite of what they had done to fight inflation. Now, instead of tightening the money supply, they would ease it, which would bring down interest rates. As rates came down, lenders from other countries would be less attracted here. And knowing that the policy of our government was to devalue the dollar, they wouldn't want to hold dollars. So Germans, Japanese, and others would sell more dollars than they bought, and its value would fall.

The plan worked, at least to weaken the dollar. From early 1985 to the end of 1986, the dollar fell 47 percent against the German mark and 42 percent against the Japanese yen. But the devaluation didn't reduce the trade deficit. In fact, the deficit for 1986 was $156 billion, another record. And it was still getting larger.

Some economists questioned the policy. Paul Volcker, then chairman of the Federal Reserve, said: "Economic history is littered with examples of countries that have acted as if currency depreciation alone could substitute for other action to restore balance and competitiveness to their economies." But still hoping for a quick fix, the administration insisted that a weaker dollar would solve the problem.

Meanwhile, foreign companies that had gained important shares of our market weren't about to give them up. In theory, they should have raised the prices on their products as the dollar weakened. In reality, they were willing to accept lower profit margins to hold their market shares. This strategy gave them time to reduce their costs and eventually regain some of those margins. It also gave them time to upgrade their products and raise prices accordingly. By offering quality and good service, they had established brand loyalty, and their customers stayed with them. By then some of them no longer had any American competition, and if they did lose market share at the low end, they lost it to the Koreans and the Taiwanese, which obviously didn't reduce our imports.

On the other hand, devaluing the dollar was supposed to help our exports. But who could we sell our products to? The Latin American countries, which had been our best customers, were so deeply in debt that they could no longer buy anything. And since our companies weren't oriented toward selling products in the more competitive European and Japanese markets, they couldn't penetrate those markets overnight.

As the deficits grew worse, the sentiment for protectionism grew. In a poll conducted in April 1987, 69 percent of the people supported new tariffs on Japanese products. Congress considered legislation that would have set targets for reducing the trade surpluses of our trading partners. Throwing a bone to the public, Reagan slapped a tariff on Japanese electronic products in retaliation for alleged dumping of computer chips. But he continued to insist that his policy was working. In a radio address on June 27, 1987, he declared: "The improvement in the trade deficit which we've been talking about for several months is now being certified on the front pages of many of our nation's newspapers."

The May trade deficit, announced a few weeks later, jumped to $14.4 billion. The June deficit was $15.7 billion.

Commenting on the figures, Marlin Fitzwater, White House spokesperson, said: "We are concerned that the trade deficit is not coming down as fast as expected. Nevertheless, the value of the dollar and other factors should have a positive impact in the months ahead."

The July deficit surged to $16.5 billion.

By then the markets no longer believed that the policy of devaluation would work. Instead, they began to believe what Paul Volcker had been saying all along, that the cause of the problem was the budget deficit.

The Budget Deficit

When the government borrows from the public to finance budget deficits, it draws funds from our pool of savings. This pool also provides the funds invested by businesses to expand operations or increase productivity.

Now, if the government borrows significantly more, as it did in the early 1980s, only three things can happen. One is that the pool of savings will grow to accommodate the greater demand for loanable funds. Another is that businesses will be crowded out by the government. And the other is that the needs of both the government and businesses will be met by lenders from outside the country.

Our pool of savings didn't grow. In fact, it shrunk in relative terms, since our rate of saving continued to decline. So interest rates were higher than they would have been if the government hadn't borrowed so much, and businesses were crowded out to some extent. But what stopped interest rates from going any higher was the willingness, the eagerness, of foreigners to lend us money.

Why were they willing? Why were they eager? For one thing, we offered them higher rates than they could earn in their own countries. But more important, by lending us money they enabled us to buy their products, just as General Motors lends us money to enable us to buy their cars. By lending us money they stimulated their economies, they created jobs for their people. And by borrowing from them we could spend more for imports than we earned from exports.

That's the connection between the budget deficit and the trade deficit. Given a certain rate of saving and a certain rate of business spending, a budget deficit will inevitably cause a trade deficit because it generates excess spending, which is financed by foreign debt. This excess spending, which represents the difference between what we consume and what we produce, is the trade deficit.

Apologists for the government have pointed out that some countries have trade deficits without having budget deficits, and that other countries have budget deficits without having trade deficits. They claim that this disproves the connection between the budget deficit and the trade deficit. But they ignore the other variable. Yes, a country with a low rate of saving can have a trade deficit even though its budget is balanced (Britain), and a country with a high rate of saving can have a trade surplus even though it has a budget deficit (Italy). The point is, with our low rate of saving, we're going to have trade deficits as long as we have budget deficits, unless we reduce our business spending, which would make things even worse.

If you understand the causes of the problem, you can see why devaluation didn't solve it. Devaluation didn't change the relationship between the rate of saving, the rate of business spending, and the budget deficit, it only gave us a temporary advantage in the terms of trade. It didn't attack the causes, it only gave us symptom relief.

A Debtor Nation

When a country borrows, it has to pay interest and principal to foreign creditors. To make these payments, it has to earn money from trade surpluses and overseas investments. But if it doesn't earn enough, then it's in trouble. Sooner or later it reaches a point where its creditors won't lend it any more money.

Until 1971 we were earning money from trade surpluses as well as from overseas investments. Then we were earning money only from overseas investments. We were still lending more to other countries than we were borrowing from them, so we were a net creditor. But by 1985, as a result of our mounting foreign debt, we were borrowing more from other countries than we were lending to them, so we had became a net debtor.

This worried some economists, but it didn't worry our political leaders. In June 1987 the *New York Times* wrote: "President Reagan contends that this country's debtor status is a sign of strength, showing the eagerness with which foreigners want to invest in the United States. The administration notes that the United States was a net debtor for most of the 19th century with no bad effects while European capital helped build railroads and factories in this country." But we're not borrowing to build railroads and factories, we're borrowing to buy cars, sweaters, and TV sets.

Whatever the politicians say, the burden of our foreign debt will reduce our standard of living. If you owe money, you have to repay it, which means that you have less to spend on other things. So you have to defer the purchase of a new car, a new appliance, or new clothes. You have to make sacrifices. It has been estimated that the average family will have to forgo $2,600 in consumption just to repay the foreign debt incurred in 1987 alone. Think about it. That's where a lot of your future paycheck will be going—to repay our foreign debt.

Meanwhile, foreign investors are taking advantage of the weak dollar and buying our assets. They're buying our companies, our real estate, and our natural resources. They're buying America. They already own such well-known companies as A&P, Standard Oil, Tropicana, Doubleday, Mack Truck, Bloomingdale's, Smith-Corona, Firestone, Pillsbury, and Helena Rubenstein. They own hotels and office buildings and shopping centers.

What's happening is, our creditors are converting their debt to equity. They don't want to take the risk of holding debt, which loses its value when the dollar falls, so they're switching to assets, which at least have the possibility of increasing in value. They're hedging their risk, and at the same time they're gaining access to our market, our technology, and our natural resources.

The politicians say it's wonderful that all these people want to invest here. They say it's the solution to the problem of our foreign debt. But they're ignoring the fact that instead of paying interest to foreign lenders, we'll have to pay dividends, rent, and royalties to foreign owners. And since owners get a higher return than lenders, the burden will be heavier.

The Crash of 1987

We follow the stock market as an indicator of public opinion. It's better than a poll because here people aren't just talking, they're putting money on the line, so it tells you what they really think. In 1984 the market was telling us that people believed the rosy scenario, ignoring the contrary evidence of the real world.

Why did they believe it? Because they had a leader with strong convictions and the ability to communicate them. Because they liked him and trusted him. Because after the cheerless years under Carter they were ready to believe that things were looking up. So they bought the illusion of prosperity, they bet on it, and they drove the market to record heights. They finally began to regard the market, which only reflected their optimism, as evidence that they were right. It was a classic case of a speculative bubble that had to burst.

In 1984, as we followed the market, we were getting news from two different worlds. The leading role in one of them was played by Reagan, joined by a chorus of media hypesters and Wall Street hucksters, who kept telling us that everything was just fine. The leading role in the other was played by Paul Volcker, joined by some other economists, who kept telling us that there were serious problems.

As the market rebounded from a low in July, we looked for reasons, but we didn't see any fundamental improvements in the economy. We only saw falling interest rates, the result of the inflow of foreign money, and we were wary. On August 3, 1984, the Dow closed above 1200, overcoming the expected resistance at that level, and the bull market was under way.

For 1985, the government projected a strong economy, with a healthy growth rate of 4 percent. But the economy proved to be weaker than expected. In June 1985 the *Wall Street Journal* wrote: "The only remaining strength in the economy is coming from consumer spending, and from the housing industry, which is getting a boost from the drop in mortgage interest rates during recent months. Some analysts fear that manufacturers' problems will eventually slow growth in personal income, which could slow consumer spending as well."

This was the pattern: optimistic projections from Disney world, which the market believed, and the actual results from the real world, which the market ignored.

By the end of the year proponents of the rosy scenario were talking about the "wealth effect" from the rise in stock prices: "Reaganites argue that the recent surge in stock and bond prices has made consumers feel so wealthy that they will keep spending despite their debt burdens." That concept explained the behavior of consumers: borrow and spend in relation to the value of your assets, not in relation to your income. So if stock and bond prices were higher, you could borrow and spend more, even though you weren't earning any more income. If you had trouble paying your debts, you could sell your assets. But what would happen to the value of these assets if a lot of other people were in the same position?

The boom continued, since most people weren't asking such questions. According to a Harris poll taken at the end of 1985, consumer optimism was high. When asked about business conditions in their home area, 34 percent of the people said that conditions were good, while only 26 percent said they were bad. When asked about the future, 52 percent said they expected business conditions to remain the same, while only 18 percent believed they would get worse.

Instead of growing by 4 percent as projected, the economy grew by only 3 percent in 1985. But this didn't trouble the market. By February 1986 the Dow was up to 1600, which meant that stock prices were about 45 percent higher than they had been just three years earlier. What was the basis? Were the companies earning that much more?

In February 1986 the *Wall Street Journal* wrote: "The economy is off to an unexpectedly favorable start this year, and many economists now see the momentum being maintained for most of 1986. Only late this year or early next year do they see any signs of a slowdown. Among the reasons being given for this very bright forecast was the sharp decline in oil prices, a lower inflation and stable interest rates."

"The good times heralded by a new era of low lending rates seem here to stay awhile," wrote the *New York Times* in March 1986. It talked about how lower interest rates had lured home buyers back into the market, eased the pressure on automakers, and encouraged business spending.

The market reacted positively to the lower interest rates, and on March 20 the Dow broke 1800.

"Lines formed ten deep in front of the stock quotation machine at the Merrill Lynch kiosk in Grand Central Station last week," the *Times* reported. "Brokers all around the country heard from long-forgotten customers, and mutual fund managers were buttonholed in restaurants for stock tips. From cocktail parties to subway platforms to suburban golf courses and country stores, conversations kept erupting about the most powerful rally to hit Wall Street in years."

In April a new Gallup poll found that most people were optimistic about the economy. But what was happening in the real world? Industrial production, factory orders, retail sales, and personal income were all down. The rosy view of the economy, which people had bought from the government, wasn't supported by the facts. It was only an illusion.

By summer it was obvious that the economy wasn't doing as well as the government had projected. Industrial production was still falling. Retail sales were still sluggish. Housing starts were slipping. And the use of industrial capacity was dropping. But the market ignored these facts.

At that point we started a "Stock Market Crash" file, and we began to mark newspaper stories that showed the views from the two different worlds. We could see that the bull market would last only as long as people believed the rosy view of the economy from Disney world, and that if for any reason Reagan lost his credibility, the bears would come out.

On September 4, 1986, the Dow hit a high of 1919.71. But a week later it lost 87 points in one day, or 4.9 percent of market value. By the end of that week, the Dow had lost 161 points, or 7.4 percent of market value.

"No one expected this," said Douglas Loudon, the chief of equity investment at Scudder, Stevens & Clark. "When I got out of a meeting and saw the market was down 70 points at three o'clock, I kicked my Quotron a couple of times. I figured it couldn't be right." That was how most people in the market reacted to the sell-off, they were taken by surprise, since they had been ignoring the facts from the real world.

How did the government react? "White House Unruffled by Stock Plunge," the *Wall Street Journal* reported. "Reagan administration officials, shrugging off last week's stock market plunge, said they don't plan to respond with new economic initiatives and added that West Germany and Japan will probably stimulate their economies before long." Donald Regan, White House chief of staff and former chairman of Merrill Lynch, said: "We're taking this very calmly."

On the same day AP wrote a story that began: "It was a nasty experience for investors, but many analysts contend the severe sell-off on Wall Street over the past few days is no cause for grave concern about the economic outlook."

In the real world there were many causes for concern. Factory orders declined in August, foreclosures were up, and businesses planned to cut their spending. Across the country you could see a glut in commercial office space, with vacancy rates at an all-time high of 18.3 percent.

As we moved into fall, things got worse. Factory orders declined 3.6 percent in October, and machine tool orders fell a whopping 23 percent. The farm belt was suffering, and the oil belt was in deep recession. But Reagan maintained: "Our economy is solid and accelerating again. Sure, there are ups and downs, and some sectors of the economy are not yet sharing in the expansion. The indications are that the economy is gathering momentum for even more growth, more job creation, a narrowing trade deficit and continued low inflation in the months ahead. We're going to keep the good times rolling until they extend to every corner of the country." And the market believed him.

On January 8, 1987, the Dow broke 2000.

The next day the *New York Times* wrote: "Most economic forecasters kicked off 1987 with a promise that it would be another year of decidedly unexciting economic growth. It has turned out to be a promise that the stock market, so far at least, seems to be irreverently ignoring."

"With the stock market soaring and bulls stampeding," the *Wall Street Journal* wrote, "remaining a bear isn't easy. Some nervous individuals say there may be short-lived, choppy times, small corrections or indigestion ahead, but they're not bears. In fact, there are so few bears around that many market analysts are unable to name a single one. Why the scarcity? The answer seems to be in the psychology of the herd, which even some of the holdouts are finding hard to resist."

They did find some bears. John Mendelson, head of market analysis of Dean Witter Reynolds, said: "My position is that the music stopped playing last summer, but the dancers are still dancing." Charles Allmon, editor and publisher of *Grove's Stock Outlook*, said: "This market is disconnected from reality. It's a speculator's market, not an investor's market and sooner or later it's going to come to an ignominious end." But the vast majority of people on Wall Street were optimistic. They had to be, since it's their business.

With the Dow above 2000, Malcolm Forbes said: "The market is still undervalued. Look for the Dow at 3000 in 18 months if Congress doesn't erect any roadblocks—new taxes, protectionist trade measures, or takeover bans—and the foreign governments prod their own economies."

We didn't believe it. We were looking at the facts and charting reality. We were tracking trends. On January 20 we issued a press release, predicting that before the end of 1987, the market would crash.

On January 22 the *New York Times* wrote: "A Perplexing Rally Has Wall Street Jittery. Rarely has the stock market been the source of so much concentration and befuddlement as it is today. Yesterday, after a 13-straight-day advance that piled $200 billion onto the value of investor portfolios, the stock market rally of 1987 finally suffered a down day. Investors from Maine to California wondered whether the spectacular advance, just the latest leg of one of the longest and most powerful bull markets in Wall Street history, had come to an end. Or whether the market was just taking a breather before charging ahead once again." Well, it charged ahead.

In the first three months of 1987, the Dow gained 25 percent.

"Raging Bull Conjures Up Roaring '20s," wrote *USA TODAY*. "Increasingly, experts are drawing parallels between the current four-and-a-half-year-old bull market and the roaring bull market of the '20s. The big question for investors: If it's the 1920s all over again, is this 1926 or 1929?"

On March 31 the Dow plunged in reaction to a decline in the dollar. Investors were afraid that the Fed would have to raise interest rates to keep the dollar from going into a free-fall. So every time the dollar fell the market reacted negatively.

The market recovered, surging ahead by 70 points in early April. By now the Dow was over 2200, and despite a few setbacks along the way it broke 2700 in August. On August 25 it closed at 2722.42. That was the peak. The unfounded optimism had driven the market as high as it would go. Meanwhile, it had become so volatile that a rise or fall of 50 points in one day was nothing unusual. But when it fell by 92 points on October 6, and then by 95 points on October 14 in reaction to the August trade figures, and by 108 points on October 15, it made an impression.

Showing concern, the government tried to talk down interest rates, which had been increasing. At a White House briefing Secretary of the Treasury James A. Baker III told reporters: "We don't want to see interest rates increase on the basis of unjustified inflationary fears. We recognize some market nervousness but it is clear to me that conditions do not warrant *Apocalypse Now* scenarios."

But by then the market had begun to pay attention to what was happening in the real world. At the time we were trying to get the Germans and the Japanese to lower their interest rates, not only to stimulate their economies but also to give us room to lower our interest rates without causing the dollar to fall. They were resisting, especially the Germans, for fear of inflation. So Baker warned them that if they didn't cooperate, he would let the dollar fall. On October 18, the day before the crash, he said in a television interview: "We will not sit back in this country and watch surplus countries jack up their interest rates and squeeze growth worldwide on the expectation that the United States somehow will follow by raising its interest rates." This statement was directed mainly at the Germans, but it was unsettling for all investors.

On October 19, before the market opened, the *Wall Street Journal* wrote: "Although no one is forecasting a crash like that in 1929–30, there's a growing consensus that the bull market is seriously, if not mortally, wounded. Nevertheless, some see the next 300 point move in the industrial average taking the market back up to the 2500 level rather than down to the 1900."

That morning the lead story of the money section of *USA TODAY* was headlined: "Is It a Bear or a Bargain? Value Hunters Prowl for Hard-Hit Stocks." The story said that the recent drop in the Dow might mean a chance for individual investors to buy at prices they thought they would never see again. It quoted Bill Miller, director of investment management at Legg, Mason, Wood, Walker, Inc., who said: "I'm encouraged. We are finding many more stocks to buy now than we did a month or two ago."

And they were still finding people to sell them to—like my dentist, whose broker called him that morning and talked him into buying $200,000 worth of stocks on margin, so that he would be positioned for the recovery.

That day the Dow plunged 508 points, a drop of 22.6 percent, wiping out more than $500 billion of wealth. It was the worst crash in our history.

Maintaining the Illusion

The government's reaction was typical. Before getting into his helicopter, Reagan said: "There is nothing wrong with the economy. All the business indices are up."

He was joined by a chorus of politicians and business leaders insisting that the economy was perfectly sound. Walter B. Wriston, former chairman of Citicorp, said: "We learned what we always knew. That is, when markets reach an all-time high, there's always a correction. This correction was sharper and deeper than had been anticipated, but it was not the end of the world. There is nothing fundamentally the matter with our economy." This is the man who promoted massive, indiscriminate lending to Third World countries on the theory that a sovereign nation would never default.

To convince us that nothing was wrong, almost 300 companies announced that they would repurchase their shares. They committed a total of $23.2 billion for this purpose. But think about what they did. They borrowed money, and they didn't spend it to develop new technologies or new products, they spent it to prop up their stocks. In fact, they manipulated the market.

Meanwhile, the government found an explanation for the crash—they blamed it on program trading, as we had predicted months earlier. Program trading was a perfect scapegoat, since few people understood it. If you don't understand what they're talking about, how can you question their explanation? It's like blaming witches or other practitioners of black magic. So nothing was wrong with the economy, the crash was just something that happened on Wall Street for technical reasons.

We found an equally plausible explanation for the crash in the following story, which appeared that week in the *Poughkeepsie Journal*: "The cause of Monday's historic stock market crash lurked unnoticed Tuesday at the foot of Wall Street among decaying tombstones in the Trinity Cemetery. Joan Berkowitz, a 1982 Vassar graduate, who now preserves historic monuments, lugged the water bucket to the crumbling headstone of Mary Louis Four who died in 1791. Berkowitz smiled and noted the connection between her work and Wall Street's collapse. 'We took that tombstone out of the ground on Friday and since then all hell broke loose.'"

At that point the politicians did what they often do when there's a problem—they formed a commission to study it. Their action got headlines: "Never Again? Stock Plunge Brings Calls for the Overhaul of Financial Markets. Changes Now Appear Likely." This headline appeared on October 26, 1987, more than two years ago, and nothing has happened. But nothing was supposed to happen. Once the market calmed down, the commission had served its purpose.

When the commission issued its report, it blamed program trading for the crash, but it also pointed to the trade deficit and the budget deficit as contributing factors. When asked about it, Reagan said: "I don't believe that the dollar or anything outside Wall Street had anything to do with the great debacle in October. And that is borne out in the report that has been presented to me by the commission that I appointed, the Brady Commission." So the last word from the government was that the crash had been a technical aberration.

To placate those who believed that something was wrong with the economy, Reagan announced on October 22 that he would meet with congressional leaders to find ways of reducing the budget deficit. He said that "everything was on the table," including possible tax increases. It looked as if the government would attack the cause of the problem. But after all the talk they came up with a package of bits and pieces that cut the deficit by $30 billion, only $7 billion more than Gramm-Rudman would have done automatically.

By then the crash was yesterday's news, and as time passed the media said that it hadn't been significant. "It was the doomsday that didn't happen," AP wrote. "The October stock market collapse, instead of ushering in a recession or worse, has been almost a nonevent as far as the U.S. economy is concerned." Well, the government put off the recession with its policy of deficit spending. But even though it took a while, the crash signaled the end of the boom.

Why did it happen? It happened because our political leaders ignored the problems. It happened because they did virtually nothing about the budget deficit. It happened because after all their promises, their policy of devaluation failed to have any meaningful impact on the trade deficit. It happened because they lost credibility.

What did it mean? It meant that we had reached a turning point, the end of an era. It meant that we no longer believed the rosy scenario. It meant that we had lost the World War II mentality, which Reagan personified. It meant that we were ready for a new era, a new mentality.

Of course, people on Wall Street avoid mentioning the "C" word. They call the crash a "market break," "market pause," or even "intermediate-term market correction." Some of the media have picked up these euphemisms, accepting Wall Street's revision of history. But history, when distorted this way, has a habit of repeating itself.

We saw what looked like a repeat on October 13, 1989, when the Dow plunged 190 points. We weren't surprised, since we were tracking trends, and the facts in the real world contradicted the rosy scenario presented by the government. Car sales in the first two weeks of October were down 13 percent from the year earlier. Housing starts, down 5 percent, were at the lowest level since the 1982 recession. After improving for a while, the trade deficit was again getting worse. Yet Treasury Secretary Nicholas Brady said that the stock market decline "doesn't signal any fundamental change in the condition of the economy."

That sounded like what Reagan said after the 1987 crash. It also sounded like what Herbert Hoover said after the 1929 crash: "The fundamental business of the country . . . is on a sound and prosperous basis." Well, maybe they have to say things like that. But they don't have to set policy as if they believe them.

Facing Reality

In the presidential election of 1988, people were asked if they were better off than they were eight years ago. Evidently, most people felt they were, since Bush won. But it was an illusion. In reality most people are worse off.

The average family's real income is lower than it was in 1973, even though more members are now working. The average worker's real income is also lower, reflecting the fact that most of the new jobs created during the 1980s were service jobs, while manufacturing jobs were being destroyed. The average person entering the work force earns a lower real starting salary than he or she would have 15 years ago.

With lower real incomes, people have tried to maintain their standard of living by borrowing. Encouraged by the government, they've raised the level of consumer debt to 65 percent of the GNP. They've also raised the level of mortgage debt in relation to income. Back in the 1970s, the bank limit on mortgage payments was 25 percent of family income, now it's 33 percent or higher. On top of that, people have taken out second mortgages, euphemistically called "home equity loans." So they've borrowed beyond the limit, and now they're exposed to the risk of recession.

At the same time, more and more people have slipped below the poverty level, which is defined as an income of $12,100 for a family of four. By this measure, about 32 million people live below the poverty level. With the increasing number of single-parent families, children have the highest poverty rate. In the 1960s they were no worse off than the population as a whole. Now they're 50 percent more likely to be poor. In fact, one child out of four is living in poverty.

While more and more people have joined the ranks of the poor, the gap between rich and poor has widened. From 1979 to 1987 the standard of living for the poorest fifth of the population fell by 9 percent, and the standard of living for the richest fifth rose by 19 percent. In fact, the gap between rich and poor is the widest it has been since World War II. The causes can be found in the breakdown of the family, in the decline of education, and in government policies.

It has been said that under Reagan the rich got richer and the poor got poorer, but that's not exactly what happened. The whole country got poorer, since the devaluation of the dollar reduced our purchasing power in the global market, and the rich got more of our declining wealth. The tide that lifts all boats hasn't been rising, it has been falling.

With the shift in wealth and income, the middle class has been shrinking. This trend is especially clear among people under 30, who for the first time in our history don't expect to have a higher standard of living than their parents. Between 1973 and 1986 the real income of families headed by people under 30 fell by 26 percent, as much as personal income fell between 1929 and 1933, the deepest year of the depression. Another measure is home ownership among people age 25 to 29, which fell from 43 percent in 1980 to 36 percent in 1988. People in this age group have been caught in a double bind, as higher home prices and higher interest rates have made it harder for them to qualify for a mortgage, and higher rents have made it harder for them to save for a down payment. Whether they rent or own their homes, they're paying about twice as much of their incomes for housing as the previous generation did, so they have less income available for other things.

While we were getting poorer, the government created an illusion of prosperity with excess spending generated by the budget deficit and financed by foreign debt. They're still trying to maintain that illusion. They keep the economy going by borrowing and spending. They put on a show of trying to reduce the budget deficit, and they cover up the size of the problem by not including the cost of bailing out the savings and loans, while consolidating the temporary surplus of the Social Security fund with the general budget. They use smoke and mirrors to make the situation look better. But if they looked beyond the next election, they would see that they won't be able to maintain the illusion much longer.

Unless the politicians face reality, they're going to lead us downward. We're now in a recession, and their options are limited. Normally, they would try to get us out of a recession through deficit spending. But they were already resorting to that during the 1980s to create an illusion of prosperity. So the deficit is getting even bigger.

The politicians are calling this recession a "lull," a "temporary interruption." They're not admitting that we have problems, and of course they're not doing anything about them. At best, we're going to have a period of slow growth in the 1990s as we work off the excesses of the 1980s. But if our political leaders keep playing the rosy scenario, we're going to have a disaster. As usual, they'll attempt to stimulate the economy in time for the 1992 election, but that will only give us symptom relief while masking the fundamental problems. And it could be the last gasp of borrow-and-spend economics.

= 13 =

The World

When people look back at the 1980s, they'll conclude that its most important world trend was globalization. This trend didn't start in the 1980s, but it accelerated and brought changes that weren't imagined ten years earlier.

Despite the pressures for international cooperation, the world in 1980 was sharply divided by ideology. What emerged during the decade was a trend away from ideology, which removed the biggest obstacle to globalization. Around the world, political leaders became more pragmatic. Their focus shifted from military conflict to economic competition, from mission control to the marketplace.

The most dramatic events occurred in Eastern Europe, starting in the Soviet Union, where a new leader questioned its economic system and decided to change it. He recognized that to achieve the goal of a better life for his people, he would not only have to attract foreign capital and technology, he would also have to shift resources from the military to the civilian sector. So he made changes in Soviet policy that led to the end of the Cold War.

As we and the Soviet Union moved toward demilitarization, the rest of the world followed the trend. The regional conflicts that had flared up in the 1970s gradually died down. By 1988 the arms business was no longer a growth industry.

Meanwhile, another obstacle to globalization was removed—our economic dominance of the world. It had been eroded in the 1970s, and it crumbled in the 1980s, clearing the way for three powerful blocs to compete: Western Europe, North America, and the Pacific Rim. Europe will be the main event of the 1990s. Twelve countries there have agreed on a plan of economic unification that by the end of 1992 will create the largest single market in the world. This agreement, together with the rise of Japan and our loss of dominance, will speed the process of globalization.

We have strong ties with both Europe and the Pacific Rim. We're the common ground between them, which gives us an extraordinary opportunity in the global market of the 1990s. So instead of looking back at the short, exceptional period in which we dominated the world, we should look ahead to a long, normal period in which we'll be one of three main players.

While competition has intensified, all countries have become more dependent on one another. We all have to think globally about the economy.

At the same time, we all have to think globally about the environment. We have to see that economic development and the maintenance of the earth are related issues that concern us wherever we live. The ultimate issue is whether the earth will still be habitable by the end of the next century, and the outcome will probably be determined by what we do within the next 10 to 20 years.

Away from Ideology

Ideology is based on illusion—the illusion that you know all the answers, without having to look at the facts. Not only that, you deny the facts to maintain your illusion. You deny reality.

When they look back on this century, future historians will call it the Age of Ideology. It has been dominated by ideologies: communism, fascism, nazism, fundamentalism, not to mention the less extreme forms of party politics. But in the late 1980s we saw a trend away from ideology, and we expect it to accelerate in the 1990s.

In this country a strongly ideological president was succeeded by a pragmatic one in 1988. When all is said and done, that's the most significant fact about the election. The candidates with ideologies got nowhere in the primaries, and one big reason why Dukakis lost was that Bush successfully pinned the liberal label on him. People have had enough of ideologies. They want pragmatic leaders.

We saw the media pick this up. "President-elect George Bush asked Nicholas Brady to remain treasury secretary," the *Wall Street Journal* wrote shortly after the election, "providing further evidence that the Bush administration will be pragmatic, without strong ideological leanings." That's the word you kept hearing—pragmatic—as Bush made appointments.

We saw a change from ideological to pragmatic leadership in the Soviet Union. Instead of trying to maintain the illusion of supremacy through military exploits, Gorbachev confronted the fact that the Soviet Union is a second-rate economic power.

We also saw this trend in Great Britain, where Margaret Thatcher, who has a very strong ideology, was replaced by someone who is regarded as more pragmatic.

So around the world we see a trend away from ideology and toward pragmatism.

Demilitarization

A major world trend that emerged in the 1980s was demilitarization. After the way the decade began, it caught a lot of people by surprise.

We've always had people who were against war, whether for religious or personal reasons. We've had treaties and arms agreements before. What's new is the recognition that military strength is debilitating and that war is an economic disaster. If you were against war in the 1960s, you were an idealist. Now you're a realist. The proponents of the antiwar movement are no longer folksingers, they're businesspeople.

Where did it begin? Well, it should have begun in this country after our experience in Vietnam, but other countries weren't ready for it. Roused by the seizure of our embassy in Iran, we began to rebuild our military. With regional conflicts in Afghanistan, Angola, and Nicaragua, we were still engaged in the Cold War. And it might have gone on if there hadn't been a change of mentality in the Soviet Union.

We've talked about the World War II mentality and how it locked us into the past. It also existed in the Soviet Union, and it did the same there. It prevented them from seeing any alternative to military competition, and it kept them from moving into the present.

Gorbachev is the first postwar Soviet leader to break with that mentality. I mentioned earlier that when you see him, he isn't wearing medals on his chest. He isn't living in the past, he's living in the present and looking at the future. And he sees that if his country continues to spend more than 15 percent of its GNP on defense, it will decline economically.

That's where the trend of demilitarization began, in the Soviet Union. People there had gone through an experience similar to ours in Vietnam—their failure in Afghanistan—and when Gorbachev came along, they were ready for him. At least some of them were. The hard-liners cling to the old mentality, as they do here, and resist his new policies. But they're dying off, as they are here, and in the 1990s he'll be able to do more.

One of his new policies is to support the United Nations in its role as peacekeeper. In September 1987 he said that wider use should be made of UN forces "in disengaging the troops of warring sides and observing cease fire and armistice agreements." This was a complete reversal of Soviet policy. For decades the Soviets objected whenever UN troops were sent to keep peace in trouble spots, and they refused to contribute money for this purpose. But in October 1987 they volunteered to pay $197 million in arrears toward the cost of UN peacekeeping operations. With this and other developments, we expect the United Nations to assume the role for which it was designed—to keep the peace.

Gorbachev also suggested that the United States, the Soviet Union, Britain, China, and France work to strengthen the World Court, which was established in 1945 as part of the United Nations. Britain is now the only permanent member of the UN Security Council that regards the World Court as an authority on international legal disputes.

The European response to Gorbachev's initiatives has been positive. Europe, where the Cold War started, was ready to end it before either the Soviet Union or we were, partly because they were most directly threatened by it, and partly because they saw the opportunities that would follow it.

Our position hasn't been so clear. In fact, in this trend we're following the rest of the world. As we look around, we suddenly see an ending of wars. In his campaign Bush could point out rightly that the world was more at peace in 1988 than it had been within anyone's memory. But the cause wasn't our buildup of arms, it was economic pressure on the countries at war. It wasn't our fleet in the Persian Gulf that ended the war between Iran and Iraq, it was their ruined economies.

As the threat of war diminishes, the countries where we have military bases have been turning against them. You see this in the Philippines, in Korea, in Spain, in Greece. You also see it in Germany, where opposition was heightened in 1989 by a series of military plane crashes. At the same time, we're realizing that we simply cannot afford to play the role of world peacekeeper. Like the Soviet Union, we have economic problems, and we know that a reduction in defense spending would help solve them. As I said earlier, it's the only way of eliminating the budget deficit without causing other problems. Beyond that, the shift in resources from military to civilian use would increase our competitiveness and enhance our quality of life. So we have ample motive to join the trend.

The End of the Cold War

"There are certain periods in history where the course of events depends very much on a particular personality," said Alexander N. Yakovlev, the Soviet political theorist. "Do you think the changes in the Soviet Union wouldn't have happened if someone else were in the post? I think they would happen, but later. I think that Gorbachev's personality just speeded up events. Thanks to his personal qualities, his political acumen, his education, and a surprising ability to understand the rhythm and demands of the times."

Here's a leader who looked at his country and decided to change it. That's what *perestroika* was, a restructuring. And though people both inside and outside of the Soviet Union have been disappointed by the results, he has made changes in the system. The fact that he is being openly challenged by someone who has different views is evidence of these changes. Before Gorbachev, such a debate was unthinkable.

From a world perspective, his most important change was in the mentality that led to the arms race. He evidently realized that the Soviet economy was losing ground because of its huge allocation of resources to the military. He also evidently realized that as long as the Cold War persisted, the Soviet Union would never be able to attract foreign capital and technology, which it badly needs. So he changed its foreign policy.

In his first meeting with Helmut Kohl, the West German chancellor, Gorbachev said: "We Europeans should at last behave in accordance with the logic of the new times. Not to get ready for war, not to intimidate one another, not to compete in perfecting weaponry, and not simply to try to prevent war. But to learn to make peace."

Led by West Germany, the Europeans reacted positively to Gorbachev's initiatives, which offered a chance not only to make peace but also to do business. They realized that if Gorbachev succeeded, the Soviet Union would become less of a military threat and more of an economic partner, and they decided to back his reforms by expanding trade with the Soviet Union.

At first Americans were suspicious, but gradually our attitude changed. The president who had called the Soviet Union an "evil empire" concluded an arms agreement with them, and for the last three years of his administration exchanged televised New Year's greetings with Gorbachev. Then came the Armenian earthquake of 1988. It occurred while Gorbachev was visiting here, while we were focused on him, so it had a far greater impact than it otherwise would have. It pushed us beyond the existing limits of global cooperation. For the first time since World War II we offered aid to the Soviet Union, and—just as important—they accepted it.

The events in Eastern Europe that made headlines during 1989 were the logical outcome of Gorbachev's changes in policy. He set the trend, and the peoples of Poland, Hungary, East Germany, Czechoslovakia, Bulgaria and finally Romania followed it. The result was the opening of the Berlin Wall, the end of the Cold War. This was a turning point in history, since it was the end of the division of Europe between the two superpowers. From then on the countries of Europe, both East and West, would be able to seek their own destinies.

"None of this would have happened without the vision and courage of Mr. Gorbachev, who started to enlarge liberty in the Soviet Union." It wasn't a Soviet political theorist who said that, it was Margaret Thatcher.

Our Loss of Dominance

In the 1980s, as foreign products invaded our markets and foreign investors took over our companies, many Americans were surprised. They didn't anticipate this development because their vision was blurred by the World War II mentality. At the end of the war we were the dominant economic power in the world, and they thought we would always be in this position. But we were in this position only because the other industrialized countries had been devastated. So for a while we didn't have any economic competition, we just had military competition from the Soviet Union. This period was an exception, and it lasted only until Europe and Japan recovered from the war.

People with a World War II mentality can't accept our loss of dominance. They forget that before the war we didn't dominate the world and that during the war Germany and Japan were serious threats. They also assume that if we don't dominate the world, some other country will, and they worry that Japan will take our place. Well, they can relax, because Japan won't take our place. Japan will be a strong economic power, but it won't dominate the world. With all the competition, no country will. When people talk about the next century being dominated by Japan, they're forgetting us, they're forgetting Europe.

Instead of one dominant country, we're going to see three major regional blocs: Western Europe, North America, and the Pacific Rim. Twelve countries in Europe have agreed on the timing to merge their markets. And we've signed a treaty with Canada that will remove virtually all trade barriers between us. So the trend is clear.

The regional blocs will be consolidated in the early 1990s and extended in the late 1990s. By the turn of the century, they will at least to some extent include Eastern Europe, Latin America, and Southeast Asia.

This process of regionalization won't divide up the world, it will advance the trend toward globalization. And it will happen faster than most people think.

1992

If you ask Americans the significance of 1992, they'll probably say it's the 500th anniversary of the discovery of America. But if you ask Europeans, they'll say it's the year when Europe becomes a single market.

When I first read about 1992 in the newspaper it caught my attention, and the more I read about it the more I realized that this was going to be a major event. That's what happens when you track trends, when you read the paper with a purpose. You pick up things that other people don't. According to a Commerce Department survey in late 1988, four out of five American senior executives didn't know about 1992. As of June 1989, three out of four American industrial companies didn't have a strategic plan to deal with it.

The first step toward a European market was taken in 1957 with the treaty of Rome. Tariff barriers were removed in 1968, but there were still nontariff barriers—border controls, different standards, and indirect taxes—that hinder the free flow of goods, people, and money. There was also the problem of agricultural subsidies.

In early 1988 the members of the European Community agreed to cut these subsidies, which removed the biggest obstacle. In June they adopted measures to end all restrictions on the flow of money within the bloc, and they formed a committee of central bankers and other experts to draw up a plan for a European central bank. And they approved the free flow of people between countries, so you'll be able to drive through Europe without stopping for customs.

By the end of 1992 the European Commission will have approved some 300 directives eliminating the last obstacles to a single market, which will include Portugal, Spain, France, Belgium, Luxembourg, West Germany, Italy, Greece, Denmark, the Netherlands, Britain, and Ireland. With 320 million people, it will be the largest market in the world.

Within this market, the countries will have their specialities. Each country will have a comparative advantage, and by uniting they'll be able to produce and market on a larger scale. To appreciate the change, imagine what our economy would have been like if each state had been a country, and then imagine them uniting. Of course, we're only talking about an economic union, not a full political union, but they're already coordinating policies.

Combined, the 12 countries have a GNP of $4.6 trillion, which is comparable to ours, and they account for 20 percent of world trade. In 1987 their exports were 60 percent more than ours and almost double Japan's. Their imports were about equal to ours and more than triple Japan's. Without question, they'll be the most important trading bloc in the world.

This will surprise a lot of people. They might have been worried about Japan, but when they looked at Europe they saw only the individual countries. When they compared us to West Germany, they could still feel we were superior. In the 1990s they'll see a united Europe, which has suddenly become larger than we are, and then they'll realize what has happened. But if you track trends, it won't surprise you.

How will it affect the world? It will give us a balance of economic power, which we really haven't had since the Middle Ages. It will bring about the end of an era in which individual countries struggled for dominance. It will be a giant step in the process of globalization.

Of those Americans who know what's happening, some are afraid that a "fortress Europe" will emerge, with new barriers between them and us. But Willy Declercq, the European Community's top official, stated: "There will be no fortress Europe." And Roy Denman, its ambassador to the United States, said: "For the Community to go protectionist in 1992 would mean shooting itself in the foot, because of the risk of retaliation from other countries." He called such worries "unjustified hoo-ha."

I agree. Remember, they export a lot to us, and they want to keep a good customer. They also have a lot of money invested here, and they want to earn a good return on it. So it's in their interest to keep their market open to us.

But a united Europe will present a challenge to us. For the first time, European companies will have the advantage that ours have always had, a large internal market, and they'll become stronger competitors. They're already merging to position themselves for 1992. Nestlé has acquired Roundtree, a British chocolate maker. Asea, the Swedish engineering group, has merged with Brown Boveri, its Swiss competitor. Grand Metropolitan, a British food conglomerate, has bought Irish Distillers, and of course it has also bought Pillsbury, becoming one of the world's largest food and drink companies. Pechiney, a French metals group, has picked up Triangle Industries of the United States, becoming the world's largest packaging company. Siemans, a giant German electronics company, is taking over IBM's Rolm division. General Electric of Britain (no relation to the United States company of the same name) is forming a joint venture with Cie. Générale d'Electricité of France to create one of the world's largest manufacturers of power-generating equipment.

A united Europe will also offer an opportunity to us, but to take advantage of it, we'll have to change our mentality. Our companies, which have a large internal market, generally haven't looked for exports. They've been content to sell their products domestically. In recent years they've been aroused by the competition from imports, and they've fought back. But they still have a negative attitude. They're still more interested in defending their market than in attacking other markets. And you can't win with that strategy.

I know a lot of companies that in the past considered doing business in Europe, but decided that it wasn't worth the time, money, or trouble. Well, they should look again, because it's going to be a new situation. It's going to be more like doing business in this country, with all the advantages of a large market.

American companies that have a positive attitude are getting ready for 1992. They're looking ahead, and they're proacting. Ford Motor sees the development of European standards that will enable it to cut costs and push into new markets. "It will enormously simplify our business," said Jan Caneris, director of European affairs in Brussels. "We're already one of the lowest cost automobile producers in Europe, including the Japanese. We have 11 percent of the market now. After 1992, we'll considerably increase our share."

General Electric has committed $1.7 billion to a new plant in Spain that will have the advantage of low-cost labor within a united Europe. AT&T has set up its first major European office in Brussels. Kraft has targeted Spain and Italy for expansion. Maytag bought into the European market by acquiring Hoover, which gets 65 percent of its income from overseas sales. "With 1992 on the horizon," said Paul Pilkauskas, a commercial officer at the American embassy in Bonn, "we're suddenly seeing a lot of new ventures."

Like these companies, others will have to begin thinking globally. They'll have to follow global trends, because they no longer have a domestic market. They now have a global market, which is both a challenge and an opportunity.

The Global Market

When I talk about the global market, I mean the flow across international borders of money, goods, services, jobs, and technology. It has been going on for a long time, ever since the beginning of civilization. But in the 1980s it accelerated to a point where something new was happening. The world was becoming one market.

It happened first in the financial markets, since money is so easy to move—you only have to transmit information. With advances in data processing and communications, the financial markets around the world became one market. The Crash of 1987 provided dramatic evidence of this trend. It didn't just happen in New York. It happened in Tokyo, in London, and in other cities. It was a global crash.

With the globalization of financial markets, the relative importance of the dollar as an international currency and of the United States as a financial power has declined. As recently as 1983 the dollar accounted for 72 percent of international lending by major banks. By 1988 it accounted for only 53 percent of such lending. When a large multinational company needs money, it goes into a market where the lenders could be Americans, British, Dutch, Swiss, Germans, or Japanese. Of the world's ten largest banks, only one is American.

"We are now talking about an integrated world market," said William Brodsky, president of the Chicago Mercantile Exchange. "We're in a learning period as to what the impact of one market is on the other." At the leading edge of the trend toward a global market, the futures and options markets have begun using a computer network, called Globex, that enables them to trade 24 hours a day.

You can see the same trend in the market for goods. It's especially obvious with automobiles. This industry no longer thinks only of domestic markets, it thinks of the global market. It makes "world" cars, and wherever it makes them it uses materials and components from a number of countries. In fact, you would have trouble finding a car produced with materials and components from only one country.

Other industries are thinking globally. When Hamish Maxwell, chairman of Philip Morris, was planning to take over Kraft, he said one of the reasons for the merger was to create a giant that could sell Cheese Whiz and Jello around the globe (though this could make you want to reverse the globalization trend). "The $13 billion takeover," wrote the *New York Times*, "is the latest and most ambitious move in the food industry's drive to build the global supermarket, to sell the same products in grocery stores, bodegas, marchés, and supermercados." You can see this happening in your local supermarket, where many of the branded goods are produced by British, Swiss, Dutch, and French as well as American companies. If you travel, you can see it happening around the world.

It's also happening in the media and entertainment industry. One of the reasons given for the merger of Time Inc. and Warner Communications was to increase their ability to compete in the global market. J. Richard Munro, chairman of Time, said: "We believe that by the mid-1990s the media and entertainment industry will be composed of a limited number of global giants. Time intends to be one of these companies." Other potential global giants are foreign, or of foreign origin. Rupert Murdoch, originally an Australian and now a United States citizen, has built a media and entertainment empire. Maxwell Communications, a British company, has acquired Macmillan. Bertelsmann, a German company, has acquired Doubleday, Bantam Books, and RCA Records. Sony has bought CBS Records and Columbia Pictures.

As the markets for goods and services have become global, the market for jobs has naturally followed. In the 1980s manufacturing jobs moved to countries with low labor costs. Now service jobs are moving to countries with low labor costs but relatively high levels of education. New York Life, which had trouble finding enough skilled workers to process claims in the United States, has set up an operation in Ireland that is linked by computer to its processing center in New Jersey. This trend has been called the development of the global office, and it will accelerate in the 1990s.

We're also seeing a transfer of technology, though it has been impeded by political barriers. As more of the large corporations become transnational, the barriers will break down, and there will be a global market for technology just as there is for money, goods, services, and jobs.

The Ultimate Issue

As far back as I can remember, the world has been threatened by nuclear war. For the baby boomers, this has been the most immediate global issue. They grew up with the knowledge that at any moment someone could press a button and destroy all life on earth.

The threat still exists, and it will continue to exist as long as any country has nuclear weapons. But at least now, with arms reductions, we're heading in the right direction. So we can address the ultimate issue.

There are five billion people in the world. If the population continues to increase at the present rate, it will double in about 25 years. At the same time, the people in developing countries, where most of the increase will occur, will aspire to a higher standard living. Whatever the earth's capacity to support human life, it will be strained by these two trends.

I'm not only talking about the resources required to feed, clothe, and shelter five billion additional people, I'm also talking about the effect on the environment: air pollution, water contamination, acid rain, the greenhouse effect, the ozone layer. It's not only an economic problem, it's also an environmental problem.

As I say in my talks, the winds of Chernobyl didn't stop at the Soviet border. A nuclear accident is a global problem. Air pollution is a global problem. Water contamination is a global problem. Acid rain is a global problem. The greenhouse effect is a global problem. The destruction of the ozone layer is a global problem. But poverty and hunger are also global problems, and unless we make connections among them, our attempted solutions will lead to conflicts. They may even lead to environmental wars. In the future I can see a conflict over the environment escalating into a crisis, with the offending country branded as "aggressor," as if it had invaded another country.

One such conflict is over the Amazon rain forest, which is now being sacrificed for economic development. We need the rain forest because it removes carbon dioxide from the air and supplies oxygen— it has been called the "lungs of the world." But Brazil, which is burdened by a huge foreign debt, needs economic development to support its population. So the government has sent people into the Amazon to create farms and ranches out of the rain forest. To clear the land, they burn the trees. In 1988 they burned 120,000 square miles of forest, almost one-half the size of Texas, releasing about two billion tons of carbon dioxide into the air. By clearing the trees, they removed a means of absorbing carbon dioxide from the air. To make things worse, the rain forest topsoil won't support a farm or ranch for very long. When it has been exhausted or eroded away, the people have to move on and burn again. At the rate they're going, the forest will be completely destroyed within 20 years. We'll not only lose the source of half of the world's oxygen, we'll also lose thousands of species of plants and animals that can never be replaced.

Brazil has been criticized for its policy of exploiting the Amazon, but its options have been limited by the burden of its foreign debt. As one of its presidential candidates said: "If the Amazon forests are the lungs of the world, the foreign debt is the pneumonia of Brazil." As a solution, he has proposed converting the foreign debt obligations into local currency for environmental projects. It's a good idea, and a few such debt-for-nature swaps have already been done in Ecuador and Costa Rica. But Brazil's creditors will be slow to accept the inevitable reduction of debt, and meanwhile the destruction of the rain forest will continue.

This isn't a Brazilian problem, it's a global problem. Because of its major contribution to the warming trend, the burning of trees to create a marginal farm out of the rain forest in Brazil will end up destroying a highly productive farm in Iowa. If you think globally, you can see that. But we're not in the habit of thinking globally, since until recently we weren't aware of the ultimate issue.

The ultimate issue, which includes the issues of nuclear war, population growth, and economic development, is the maintenance of the earth. In the 1990s this issue will expand our field of vision, it will make us think globally. We saw evidence of this process in the 1989 Paris summit meeting of the Group of Seven, which devoted a lot of attention to the environment. For the first time, we saw the leaders of the industrialized nations making connections between economic development, debt reduction, and the environment. If their global thinking leads to actions without delay, we still have time to keep the earth from becoming unfit for human life.

III

STRATEGIES
FOR PROFIT

= 14 =

Corporate Strategies

Now that we've looked at the major trends shaping the future, let's look at some corporate strategies to profit from them. But first let's review the Globalnomic system.

Trends are formed by current events, so if you want to identify them, you have to follow these events. You can get the necessary information mainly from newspapers, by reading for a purpose. When you spot an apparent trend, you should look for its causes and effects, which you'll often find in other fields. If the direction or sequence of events has social, political, and economic significance, then it's a trend, and you should track it. By projecting the trend, you can make forecasts. You can anticipate the future and act accordingly, instead of being taken by surprise and then looking for a solution or a way out. Instead of reacting, you can proact. Instead of losing, you can profit. The important thing, which distinguishes our method of forecasting, is to make connections between fields. If you do this, you can see how a trend in a seemingly unrelated field will affect your business. So you have to keep making connections.

Of course, as I said at the beginning, if you want to see what's coming, you have to look ahead. The other day I was talking with a marketing executive from a large corporation, and when I asked him to describe their market, he told me what it was at the present. When

I asked him what it would be in the future, he said he didn't know. I told him that if he didn't look ahead, he would never hit his market, because it was a moving target. If he aimed where it was at the present, he would miss it. He had to lead it. The point is, your market is always a moving target, and you always have to lead it. You always have to look ahead.

Most large companies do forecasting, and some of them have market researchers who study trends. But I've yet to find a company that has people tracking trends in different fields the way we do. So if their market researchers look ahead, they take a one-dimensional view, and they not only miss things, they often give misleading directions. This is a problem you can overcome by setting up a department to track trends, using our system. Then your market researchers will have the benefit of a global view.

The Media

If you're a manager, you have the problem of getting the information you need to make decisions. Basically, you need information about your business (internal) and information about the outside world (external). Without much difficulty, you can set up a system that will give you the necessary internal information. But getting the necessary external information is another matter. As I said earlier, there are two main obstacles: the illusions created by the media, which blur your vision of current events, and the sheer quantity of information, which overloads your capacity to absorb it. And these two obstacles are getting bigger.

With our system, you can surmount them. You can gain access to the real world by using newspapers such as the *New York Times*, *USA TODAY*, and the *Wall Street Journal* as your primary sources of information and by using the alternatives listed in the back of this book as your secondary sources. You can avoid overload by reading for a purpose and screening out the information that has no social, political, or economic significance. The advantage of reading (or using a computer) to get information is that you have control and you can direct your attention to the matters that concern you, instead of just sitting there and letting a television news programmer determine what you get. Relying on television for information is like going to a restaurant and not only letting the waiter select your meal but also letting him predigest it.

The trends we've been tracking in the media—concentration of ownership, government control, news as entertainment—make your task of getting real information much more difficult. But fortunately the niches left open by these trends are being filled by alternative media, and these have become necessary supplements for people who want to be well informed. So don't rely entirely on the major newspapers, use other media to balance your diet of information.

You also have the problem of getting information about your products or services to people who might buy them. You must remember that they have the same two obstacles: they're being subjected to a lot of hype, and they're being bombarded by too many ads. With remote control of their TV sets, they can escape your commercials by muting them or by changing channels. If you want to reach them, you have to hold them.

It used to be easier. Network television had an enormous share of the audience, and you could be sure to reach the middle and upper middle class. But as we've seen, network television is steadily losing its share of the audience, especially the more educated and more affluent segment. If you want to reach the high end, you have to devise new advertising strategies. You have to appeal to their intelligence, their taste, their status. You have to use media such as cable TV, FM radio, newspapers, and magazines. You have to regard the high end as a separate class—they're no longer upper-middle class, they're simply upper. They're a result of trends in our country that are creating a self-perpetuating upper class and a permanent lower class, with a widening gap between them.

At the same time, the middle class is shrinking, and the audience of network television is increasingly lower class. If that's your market, then this is still a good medium for your advertising. But if not, then you should consider other media, because many of the people you're trying to reach with your commercials have tuned out.

One new medium is rental video. We've already seen ads, as well as previews, before you get to the movie. We're going to see more of them, since video is a medium with a lot of potential for advertising. With a movie that has already been proven at the box office, you can be sure of an audience. Also, you can choose the movie that will reach your market. But if your ads are dull or obnoxious, people will respond by pressing the fast forward button.

If you're trying to sell your product to different market segments, then you should consider the strategy of market niche advertising.

That is, use different media and different ads for specific markets, rather than the broad approach you may have used in the past. The evolution of the media will force you to do this eventually, but before it does you should proact and take advantage of media trends.

Whatever media you use, you should apply the Globalnomic system to your advertising. You should recognize how your market is affected by trends and pitch your ads accordingly. One thing that amazes me about TV commercials for food and household products is that they frequently show women in the role of housewife, as if the nuclear family were still the norm. For daytime TV, when the audience includes housewives, along with retired people, the unemployed, and people who work flexible hours, this may not be so bad. But for nighttime TV, when the audience includes women who work outside the home, it makes me wonder what world the advertisers are living in.

Politics

The most important lesson you can learn from studying politics is not to trust politicians and not to rely on political solutions. Politicians don't attack the causes of problems, they only offer symptom relief. So you should plan accordingly.

By tracking trends you can see through the illusions that politicians create and maintain. If you had been tracking trends in the 1980s, you would have realized that the government's pronouncements about the economy were coming straight from Disney world. In general, when a politician tells you something, you can assume that the opposite is true. When he gives you evidence that a situation is getting better, you can be sure that it's getting worse. When the Coast Guard seizes a ship full of cocaine, the government claims a major victory in its war against drugs. But this only relieves the symptom, it does nothing about the underlying causes of the problem. No matter how many ships full of cocaine they seize, the drug problem will continue to grow unless we do something about its causes. So don't be lulled by the government's claims that it's winning the war against drugs.

If you want to understand politicians, you have to remember that they're living in another world. They may have lived in the real world before they became politicians, but once they enter politics, they lose touch with what's happening. They have one goal—to get elected—and they rely on handlers, pollsters, and spin doctors to help them achieve it. Whatever their view of reality, it gets distorted in the process. They come out with slogans like: "Just say no to drugs." Now, who do they think they're talking to? Real people who can see no other escape from their bounded lives? Or Disney world people who never thought of just saying no and only needed this simple advice to become upstanding citizens?

If you don't trust politicians, you won't rely on political solutions, either for your own industry or for others. I want to stress the former, since it's always easier to see how political solutions don't work for other industries, and it's tempting to accept them for your own. With the trend toward government by special interests, you might think you can profit by influencing elected or appointed officials in your favor. But I don't recommend it. Just look at what happened to the thrift industry, which over the years has had a lot of influence on government officials. This industry is a disaster, despite—or because of—its special treatment from the government. I would even go so far as to say that the worst thing that can happen to an industry is to get special treatment from the government.

Also, there are countertrends that make the currying of governmental favor a bad strategy. For one thing, the level of public tolerance for government by special interests is getting lower. For another thing, the pendulum is swinging back from deregulation to reregulation, especially in areas where the public has become concerned about safety, such as the airlines industry. And finally, the ability of the government to help you is becoming more and more limited, if only because it has run out of money.

Instead of supporting candidates who represent your special interests, you would do better to support those who represent common interests. Measures that seem to work in your favor are likely to work against you someday. Just look at our automakers, who got measures that seemed to work in their favor. But if they had listened to Ralph Nader, who represented the common interests of consumers, they wouldn't have lost so much of their market to the Japanese.

Speaking of the Japanese, you can see how they're being hurt by politics. A year ago, you might have wondered if anything could stop them from dominating the world. Well, you're seeing it now—politics. You're seeing that they're not immune to the diseases of government by special interests, influence peddling, and corruption. We had one president resign because he got caught in Watergate, but they've had three prime ministers in a row resign because they got caught in scandals. And this will have its effect on them.

In the long run you can profit by taking a stand for better government and calling for real solutions to the chronic problems of our society. I'm not saying that government should provide the solutions. I'm saying that it should present the problems instead of hiding them, and it should get the solutions from the public. That's how our government is supposed to work, and at times that's how it really does work. You can see how it's working with environmental problems. In response to public pressure, the government is finally acting. It's not doing much, but it's doing something.

If you're wondering how you can profit from this kind of action, you only have to apply the Globalnomic system. The effect of cleaner air is better health, the effect of better health is higher productivity and lower insurance costs. So you can profit by influencing government policies not on behalf of your special interests but on behalf of common interests.

The Family

Trends in the family can affect your business in two main ways: they affect your employees, and they affect your markets. If you track the trends, you can profit in both areas.

With the rise of two-income and single-parent families, working mothers have become the norm rather than the exception. No matter what business you're in, you're relying on women more than you would have a generation ago. This is a trend that won't be reversed. In fact, it's a trend that can give you—and our country—a decided advantage in the competition of the global market. You only have to look at Japan to see how far behind us some of our competitors are in moving toward a society that releases the potential of women.

We still have a long way to go, and if you're a corporate manager you can profit by adopting policies that will attract and keep the best women as employees. One such policy is equal pay, which by now should be universal. Another important policy is to recognize the needs of women during pregnancy and the early years of motherhood. Leaves of absence, flexible hours, child care assistance, and other benefits should be provided. Yes, they'll cost you in the short run, but they'll pay dividends in the long run. If you value the employee, you want to keep her, and you want to enable her to develop her full potential—

while working for you. It's common sense, it's business sense, to provide good benefits in this area.

Beyond the direct profit to your company, you'll realize an indirect profit from policies that help your employees in their family roles. Remember that the breakdown of the family has been a primary cause of the decline in education and related problems, including unemployment, poverty, homelessness, crime, and drugs. These problems cost you money, they make it harder for you to run a business, and they affect your competitiveness. So if you think globally, you'll see the broader potential returns from such policies.

Another way you can accommodate your employees is by choosing a location for your business that will minimize their commuting time. In recent years a number of large corporations have moved their offices to places that are convenient for the top executives but not for the employees, whose commuting time has been greatly lengthened. This puts further strains on the family, which for other reasons is already overextended. It affects the productivity of employees, subjecting them to the wear and tear of unnecessary commuting. The burden falls most heavily on the working mother, who loses an hour or two in a day that's never long enough. So if you're a large corporation, you should think about your employees when you plan to relocate. You should also decentralize the work place to minimize commuting time, just as your financial managers have decentralized collections to minimize float time. An extra benefit of decentralization is that the fewer people you have in one place, the more work they'll get done.

One way you can decentralize the work place is to use electronic systems—computers, modems, and the like—that will enable your employees to do at least some of their work at home. This cuts down on commuting time and makes the workday more flexible. I don't mean that they would work at home every day, but they would work at home some days and come to the office other days, in a way that would maximize their productivity. We already see a trend toward working at home among professionals, and with advances in computer networking and telecommunications it will spread to office employees.

Turning to your markets, you should always be conscious of trends in the family. Earlier, I mentioned how advertisers of food and household products seem to ignore the critical fact that most women are no longer housewives. They're still consumers, but if you want to reach them you have to address them in their present roles. You also have to recognize that men have become consumers of products other than beer, razors, and cars, though you would never know it to watch the commercials for a sporting event. Teenagers, who are no longer closely supervised by parents and have been given new family responsibilities, have become very important consumers. And the elderly, who are no longer part of an extended family or even attached to a nuclear family, have become an independent market. So trends in the family affect your markets in significant ways.

The market of working women, including working mothers, has grown tremendously in the past 20 years. Among the companies that proacted to this trend, especially in apparel, there have been some spectacular successes. But on the whole, companies haven't addressed this market, as if the people making decisions still see the world as it was in the 1950s. There are a lot of needs to be met by new products and services, a lot of opportunities for profit. This market is relatively undeveloped, it's still growing, and it's going to evolve into a variety of niches.

The market of men in their expanding role as consumers is also something to look at closely. If you go into the supermarket, you see more men shopping than you did 20 years ago. They're husbands whose wives work outside the home. They're single, they're divorced. Or maybe they're gay. Whatever the reason, they're buying food and household products. You'll find them in other stores as well, and not just hardware stores. They may not like shopping, but they're doing it. They have no choice.

The market of teenagers, which has been created by the two-income and single-parent families, is surprisingly large. They're not only buying soda, candy, and ice cream, but also food and household products. We see them in stores with lists, and though their mothers might have indicated what brand they should buy, they have some discretionary power. And they have the money.

The market of the elderly, which has been affected by family trends, is a group marketing people talk about. But many of them don't act as if they really believe in it. Yet the figures are convincing: the elderly are not only increasing in number, they're also getting a bigger per capita share of income and wealth. With the breakdown of the family, more of them live on their own and make their own consumer decisions. They're a distinct market, and they have needs that can be met by special products (housing, furniture, appliances, fixtures, and hardware) and services (home delivery, home care, and so on).

While their number will continue to grow, their per capita share of income and wealth won't continue to grow as it has. In the 1990s they'll have smaller adjustments in Social Security, less appreciation in the value of their homes, and higher medical costs.

Education

The decline in the quality of our public education is the biggest problem that our corporate managers face. But many of them act as if they believe that education is the responsibility of the school system. It is, up to a point, but it's also the responsibility of the business sector, as some enlightened corporate leaders have recognized. If you want the educational system to meet your needs, then you have to get involved in it. You have to invest time and money in it.

This may sound like a strategy that won't pay off for a long time. But whether intentionally or not, you're already spending a lot of money on education. You're spending money to teach your employees how to read and write and do arithmetic. You're giving them remedial education on the job, which is probably the most expensive way of doing it. Every time your employees misspell a word in a letter or miscalculate an amount in an order and you have to correct it, you're teaching them something they should have learned in school. It's costing you time, and it's costing you money. There's also an opportunity cost, since the less education people have, the less they earn, the less they spend, the less market you have for your product. So why not invest in the school system?

The place to start is the public schools in your area. You can help reform the curriculum and improve the quality of teaching. You can give incentives to students not to drop out. You can encourage them to pursue subjects that are useful to your business, such as chemistry or math. You can offer scholarships for college. You can emulate the models of Xerox, Eastman Kodak, NYNEX, and other corporations who have gotten involved in education.

The community colleges have also become a focus of corporate involvement. Here you can participate in programs that educate and train people before or after you employ them. You can have some input into what they learn. You can help these colleges serve their communities, as they were intended to.

At the four-year college level you can provide tuition assistance to your employees. This is nothing new, but in recent years I've noticed that some corporations have reduced or eliminated tuition assistance as part of a general effort to cut costs. It's a shortsighted policy, it's as bad as cutting research and development expenditures. Your employees are your most valuable resource, and unless they continue their education, they'll become depleted. That's something I really want to stress, and it's one of the main themes of this book: education is a continuing process, and the minute you stop learning, you're dead. So one of the basic strategies for profit, especially in this age of drastic change, is to make sure your employees keep learning.

If you're a manager, one of your most important jobs is to identify and train future managers. What will they be like? They'll be information generalists and precision specialists. They'll have a liberal arts background, with a lot of exposure to foreign cultures and languages. On top of that, they may also have professional degrees. But the key to success will be their ability to think globally, in the sense that we've been using the phrase—to make connections. For this, a liberal arts education with a global perspective is the best preparation.

To an admissions director at a college where enrollment has been declining, it may seem optimistic to talk about a boom in education. But in the 1990s we're going to have one, stimulated by the recognition that we've fallen behind our economic competitors. Though there hasn't been a dramatic event like the launching of Sputnik to awaken us, more and more people are realizing that the failure of our educational system has put us at risk. And starting with the public schools, we're going to see efforts to catch up. We're also going to see the process of education extended well beyond college. For those of you whose business is educational products and services, it's time to proact and take advantage of this trend.

Health

When I talk with corporate managers, I often hear them complain about the high cost of health benefits. They say that this is one of the reasons why they can't compete with foreign products, at least on price, and they have a point. But what are they doing about the problem? They're cutting health benefits, they're making employees bear more of the costs.

If you take a narrow view, this approach may seem logical. It saves money, but only in the short run, and it does nothing about the real problem—the health of your employees. In fact, it's only symptom relief, and it will have harmful side effects. It will hurt morale, it will lower productivity, and it will eventually affect the quality of the people you're able to attract and keep as employees.

What other approach could you take? You could implement a health and fitness program for your employees. Again, it would cost you in the short run, but it would pay off in the long run not only in lower health insurance costs but also in higher productivity. The program should include nutrition, exercise, and stress reduction. Ideally, it should be integrated into the work environment, instead of being separated and unrelated. It should be part of the workday, and it should create a feeling in employees that exercising is as important for the success of the company as market analysis.

Recently, I had lunch with a manager in his company's cafeteria. I didn't expect much, but I was shocked by the wide array of junk food offered there. It was really hard to find anything that didn't pose a risk to my health. I finally settled for a roast beef sandwich as the least of many evils. I made no comment, since I was a guest, but if I had asked my host why his company offered junk food to its employees, I'm sure he would have said because that was what they liked. Of course, a company can't make its employees eat health food, but it can give them the opportunity—and encourage them—to eat such food instead of limiting its menu to junk.

Many employees spend a large part of their day sitting at desks or workstations. In the short run their lack of physical activity will lower their productivity, and in the long run it will impair their health. So exercise is necessary, and it doesn't require expensive machines. It only requires a space for people to move around freely and an instructor who can lead them in a number of different techniques. Moderate forms of exercise are also good for stress reduction, and both objectives can be achieved at the same time. Another way to reduce stress is meditation, which some companies are now using with positive results.

Work space and office furniture designs are important elements of any health and fitness program. If your employees have back problems because of their chairs, or if they have eyestrain because of their video display terminals, you probably weren't thinking globally when you bought them. And now you're paying doctor bills and losing productivity.

If you're in the food business, trends in health will affect your markets. The trend toward natural foods is strong, and it will get stronger. More and more consumers will insist on knowing how the food was grown or raised, and how it was processed. These demands will bring stricter regulations on labeling. A product that now claims to be "all natural" may actually contain artificial flavors and colors, chemical preservatives, or monosodium glutamate, but in the 1990s food processors won't be able to get away with this. So if you want to take advantage of the trend, it's time to proact.

The trend away from foods that are high in saturated fat and cholesterol is also strong. Producers of beef, pork, and chicken will respond by offering leaner meats. This will suit them, because grain will be less available for use as feed. Demand for fish will rise, while supply will fall due to pollution and overexploitation. The lower supply will drive the price of fish to a level that will encourage more fish farming.

Consumption of soda and alcoholic beverages will decline, giving way to fruit drinks, seltzer, and mineral water. The fastest growing beverage will be water. Within the soda market, cola drinks will suffer the most. To see this trend, just look at the proliferation of the "caffeine free" label on beverages. I even saw it on a bottle of water.

The restaurant business will be affected by these trends. Seafood restaurants will be more popular, as will Italian and other Mediterranean cuisines that use olive oil, which has recently become a hot product.

Though the baby boomers will be aging, they'll still want to exercise. Instead of running, they'll be walking. Instead of downhill skiing, they'll be going cross-country. Instead of playing tennis and other racket games, they'll be playing golf. And they'll be swimming.

Demand for prescription drugs will be strong, but within this market the most exciting opportunities will be in drugs that help the body fight disease. The immune system will be the center of attention, not only because of AIDS but also because so many other diseases (including the New Black Plague) will be linked to failures in this system. The most profitable drugs will be those that are preventive, or curative, rather than those that simply give relief. While a vaccine for AIDS is still far away, someone will make a lot of money in the near future with a vaccine for Lyme disease.

Hospitals will have trouble making money. Under the prospective payment system, their income is strictly regulated while their costs are subject to market factors, like the current shortage of nurses. At the same time, certain procedures are increasingly performed in clinics.

So there will be fewer reasons to go to a hospital, which will cause a shakeout in the industry. Private hospitals will be more specialized, and public hospitals will be places where the poor go to die.

The Environment

Trends in the environment are creating many opportunities for profit. They're also raising many challenges. In fact, we're entering a period in which the changes will be no less sweeping than what happened during the Industrial Revolution. Whether you win or lose will depend on whether you proact or react to these changes.

You might think they'll affect only products like automobiles or chemicals, but they'll affect all products and services. The public is becoming conscious of environmental problems. It's internalizing a new set of values by which your products and services will be judged. What you're selling, how you package it, how you market it—these will be weighed against the environmental standards that are now forming in the public mind. The quality and price of your product will still be important, but all other things being equal, the balance could be tipped for or against you by this new factor, the environmental factor.

Eventually, you'll be required by a new set of laws to conform to environmental standards. But in the meantime you have an opportunity to get the jump on your competitors by developing new products or modifying existing ones to meet the changing public demand. The wave is rising, you can see it coming, and if you position yourself for it, you can profit from it. You can ride it all the way to the shore.

Let's look at the environmental problems that I talked about earlier. Let's look at the garbage problem, where a lot has happened just since I started writing this book—it shows how fast these trends are moving. Source reduction is catching on. People are beginning to feel that less is more when it comes to packaging. Whatever type of packaging you use, people are beginning to expect it to be recyclable or biodegradable. By now recycling is a civic virtue, and you should appeal to it. You should identify your product with it, right on the label. Your product should be designed for recycling, and you should convey that idea to the public. You can also profit by using recycled materials, provided you make the necessary changes in your manufacturing process. Again, if you proact, you'll be in a position to use such materials, the cost of which will get lower and lower as recycling expands.

Let's look at the chemical warfare problem. The public is demanding that agriculture and industry find other ways to control pests and to kill weeds. The laws still permit the present approach, but they will be changed, and in the meantime you have an opportunity to get the jump on your competitors. If you make pesticides or herbicides, you should be developing safer approaches, like products that use pheromones to control insects. If you use any of the chemicals that have become suspect, you should look for substitutes. You shouldn't wait until the EPA has gathered sufficient evidence to prove that they're harmful, because long before then the public will have become aroused, as it did over Alar, and the product will be banned, leaving you without an immediate alternative. So it's not only in the common interest for you to stop using such products, it's in your own interest. In the long run you'll profit from it.

Routine emissions from industrial plants, power plants, autos, trucks, and other sources have been implicated in a number of problems: air pollution, water contamination, acid rain, the greenhouse effect, and the destruction of the ozone layer. These are global problems, and the governments of the industrialized nations are beginning to cooperate in measures to attack the causes. The measures will have three main thrusts: they'll require greater energy efficiency, they'll impose stricter controls on emissions, and they'll discourage the use of fossil fuels. But even without these measures the cost of energy would increase significantly in the 1990s, for reasons that have both short-term and long-term effects. The oil-exporting countries will be more united than they were in the 1980s, creating a short-term rise in prices. The consumption of oil will be greater than the discovery of new reserves, affecting prices over the long-term. So there will be a strong economic motive to achieve greater efficiency and to look for alternative fuels. There will also be a strong environmental factor, and this will make a difference. If you're using energy, you can profit by working on greater efficiency and finding better ways to control emissions. Again, you should proact, instead of waiting for the government to make you do it.

For companies in the energy business and companies that make equipment to increase efficiency or control emissions, there are special opportunities. If you're running an oil company, you should look at alternative sources of energy, like solar. If you're making autos, now is the time to get moving on the electric car, which eventually will be the norm for urban driving. To meet the clean air standards in New York and Los Angeles, they'll either have to limit cars or change them, and they're more likely to change them.

If you're storing or transporting oil, chemicals, or other hazardous materials, you can be sure that your activities will be more strictly regulated in the 1990s. The Exxon oil spill in Alaska raised the public consciousness of the inherent potential for disaster in our present techniques. There will be more spills in the future. It may take a spill in the Chesapeake Bay, but at some point the government will act, and before they do you should proact by finding safer ways to store and transport these materials.

Whatever your business, you should think about water. It's going to be a vital resource in the next century. It always has been a vital resource, but in this county we've lost sight of the fact, and we've developed agriculture and industry without regard for it. In the 1990s, as we begin to have water shortages, we'll suffer the consequences. So if your business relies on water, you should worry about it, you should plan how to get it. You may have to relocate, but now is the time to make the decision, instead of waiting and then reacting. By then you'll have to pay top dollar for a location with an adequate supply of water, and you'll have to accept a low price for your present location.

When you look at trends in the environment, it's important to realize that to some extent the damage has already been done and may never be repaired, or at least not during your lifetime. To adjust to the changing situation, you need adaptive strategies. A trend that calls for an adaptive strategy, since it wouldn't be reversed for a long time even if the causes were eliminated, is the warming trend. At this point, whatever we do, you can be sure that the climate will get warmer in the future. If your business will be affected, you should proact to the change. You shouldn't wait until the government makes it official that there's a warming trend.

Adaptive strategies should be used for other trends that won't be reversed in the near future, such as the destruction of the ozone layer. I distinguish them from the strategies that stop or reverse environmental trends, which are corrective strategies. Both can be profitable, and both may be called for, since none of the problems can be solved overnight. But corrective strategies will get a more positive response from the public, now that its consciousness has been raised, and in the long run they'll be more profitable for everyone. So they should be your primary strategies.

The Military

It's been more than 40 years since we built up our military in response to the threat of Soviet expansion following World War II, and during that period defense contractors as well as their suppliers have prospered. But the good times are over for these companies. If you're one of them, you should turn your attention to civilian products and services, because in the years ahead the government's expenditures for defense will steadily decline.

As I said earlier, there has been a change in mentality among the leaders of the Soviet Union—it's not just Gorbachev, or by now he would have been sent to Siberia. They no longer believe that we intend to attack them, and they realize that the military power they've achieved for defense against the West is not necessary. If it's not necessary, then it's a luxury they can't afford. So they're going to reduce their military to a level necessary to maintain their internal security, which is threatened by the rise of nationalism among their many ethnic groups.

Our present leaders have been so conditioned by the Cold War to regard the Soviet Union as a threat that they'll have trouble accepting the new reality. But they will accept it, because after all they're politicians, and when they see that the public is against spending so much on defense, they'll discover that it's not necessary. Remember that the only justification for our present level of defense spending was the threat of Communist aggression. Now that this ideology is in retreat, the public is beginning to have less use for the military.

Whether or not you're a defense contractor, you'll be affected by this trend, if only because our defense spending is such a big percentage of the GNP. At a recent conference I was asked if a major reduction in defense spending would lead to unemployment. I said it wouldn't, because the resources that we're using for defense would be reallocated for other purposes. But it will be a massive reallocation. Instead of spending all that money on developing and procuring weapons, we'll spend more and more of it on such tasks as reforming our school system, restoring our environment, rebuilding our infrastructure, and reclaiming our homeless. So if you're involved in the defense sector, now is the time to start applying your technology to civilian products and services. You have a lot of knowledge and experience, and if you proact, you can profit from the trend. If you only react to it, you'll lose, and this time the government won't bail you out, because you'll no longer be vital to our national security.

The Economy

Trends in the economy can be the most difficult to identify, especially if you only look at economic data. As you know, these data can be interpreted in many ways, and they can be used to mislead you, as they were in the 1980s. So whatever you do, you should heavily discount any politician's interpretation of the data, and you should be wary of any economist who sees the world through the narrow eyes of his profession.

Taking a global view of the data and making connections between the economy and other fields, you can clearly see the present trends: the growing problem of our twin deficits, the mounting debt, the weakening dollar, the declining standard of living, the shrinking middle class, the widening gap between the rich and poor, the loss of upward mobility, the looming prospect of social unrest. These are the trends in the real world, as opposed to the rosy scenario you get from Disney world. These are the trends that will affect you.

The truth is, our economy deteriorated in the 1980s, despite claims by politicians that these were boom years. The apparent prosperity that some—but not most—people enjoyed was based on the illusion that unlike every other country we have an unlimited capacity to borrow. So we're borrowing and spending as if there were no tomorrow. At the rate we're going, there won't be much of a tomorrow for our children, who will have to service all the debt we're piling up. In a sense, we've done to our economy what we've done to our environment—we've damaged it, and we've set in motion trends that will continue to damage it, even if we reverse them now. It's no coincidence, since our behavior in both cases stems from our habit of looking behind us and failing to see the future effects of our present actions.

Given the trends in the economy, you have two types of strategies that you can pursue, as you do with the environment: corrective and adaptive. For example, as a corrective strategy, you could pressure the government to reduce the budget deficit, an ultimate cause of many of our problems. Back in 1983 the Grace Commission recommended specific ways to eliminate wasteful government spending. These measures would have saved $424 billion over three years. But not enough business leaders supported the commission, and feeling little pressure the government did virtually nothing about the problem. That was six years ago, and Peter Grace is still trying to get them to do something.

As I pointed out earlier, a reduction in the budget deficit together with an increase in the savings rate would eliminate the trade deficit. In other words, it would eliminate our need for foreign debt, which is the cause of the trade deficit. Here you could pursue another corrective strategy by encouraging your employees to participate in company savings plans. Of course, it would help if the government provided meaningful tax incentives for saving, instead of doing the opposite. But again you could pressure them to act in the common interest.

The elimination of the trade deficit would halt the long slide of the dollar, not for technical reasons (which account for its recent upsurge), but for fundamental reasons. This, in turn, would help to stop the decline in our standard of living, which is partly due to the loss of purchasing power of our currency. By reducing the budget deficit and increasing the savings rate, we could do a lot for our economic health. If the government adopts policies to achieve these objectives, you'll profit from them. If not, you'll suffer.

In calling for such policies, remember to think globally. You don't want the government to balance the budget by cutting spending for education. You want them to eliminate waste, fraud, and abuse. The Grace Commission's report gave ample evidence that this would be enough to solve the problem.

You should also pursue adaptive strategies, realizing that to some extent the damage has already been done. Whatever we do, we'll have less disposable income than we otherwise would have, if only because of our debt burden. Having less money to spend, we'll be more careful about how we spend it. This means quality, value, and service will be more important. The product itself will be more important. People have been given so much hype by advertisers that they're not inclined to believe anything about a product. They want to see it, they want to try it, they want to get their money's worth. So if you want them to buy your product, you have to give them quality, value, and service. You can't sell it on marketing alone, as our companies who are competing with the Japanese have learned.

Also, the middle class will continue to shrink, and not only that, it will continue to break into segments. The mass market of middle-class consumers with similar tastes no longer exists as it did 20 years ago. It's being replaced by a bimodal market of high-end and low-end consumers, with niches between them. So a mass market strategy, with the middle as the target, is becoming less and less effective. In fact, the retail infrastructure of department stores and specialty stores located in shopping malls, which were built to sell to the middle class, is already becoming obsolete. Profit margins are being eroded by dis-counters, hypermarkets, low-price clubs, and generics. Some branded products are being pushed aside by upscaled house brands. Some man-ufacturers will have to develop their own outlets. Most will have to find new channels of distribution.

What strategies should you pursue? Well, the obvious ones are high-end or low-end strategies. With a high-end strategy, you take advantage of the fact that real income of the top fifth of the population has grown faster than that of any other group, and you appeal to the factors that induce a person in this group to buy a Mercedes. With a low-end strategy, you recognize that real income of the bottom fifth of the population has declined, and you sell to them mainly on price. Of course, the low end extends beyond the bottom fifth and toward the middle, since real income has declined for many of these people as well.

Between these two strategies are a variety of niches to be developed and exploited. The Japanese have been good at this: seeing a niche, developing it, and building on it. For the middle, which is being rear-ranged, it's the only strategy we recommend. If you go out with a mass middle market strategy, appealing to everyone, you'll find that there are fewer people in this group than you imagined, and you'll end up appealing to no one.

A strategy that we don't recommend, except in special cases, is to expand your market by acquisition. I know that a lot of companies have been doing it, but that's one reason not to do it. By following the herd, you're likely to go over a cliff. If you have a choice, you're always better off developing a market than acquiring it. You have to be creative to develop a market, and if all you ever do is acquire the results of someone else's creativity, you won't be able to see new opportunities. You won't even be able to hold your market. That's why American companies have been losing ground in recent years—

they've been too busy shuffling around the pieces, instead of making them.

Some of our corporate leaders act as if they believe that bigger is better, and that merging two or more companies into one giant company will somehow improve their competitiveness. Well, this is an illusion. Bigger isn't better, and giant companies aren't noted for being agile, efficient, or innovative. Smarter is better, and the way to improve your competitiveness is to use more of your mental capacity.

The World

Most of our companies don't really see the global market until they face competition in the domestic market from foreign companies. In other words, they're on the defensive by the time they realize what has been happening in the world. Instead of proacting, they react. Instead of attacking foreign markets, they defend their positions in the domestic market. And they always end up losing ground.

If you want to prosper in the global market, you have to pursue an offensive strategy. You have to look beyond the borders of this country. You have to export to foreign markets or manufacture your product in those markets. You have to regard Germany as if it were as close to you and as much a part of your natural market as Illinois.

Just remember that Germany isn't Illinois, and if you want to sell there, you have to offer a product that meets the needs and tastes of that market. In this country, you have a large domestic market with few important regional differences. In most cases, you can sell the same product everywhere. You can't do that in the global market. You may have tried it, you may have failed, and you may have decided that it's not worth the effort to sell in those markets. But in the meantime foreign companies have decided that it *is* worth the effort to sell in your market. So unless you want to play the whole game in your territory, you should take another look at those markets and see what they want.

An important factor is design. In the first half of this century, we set trends in design. We created an American style. Now the trends are set by Europeans, who have created a Euro style. Now American suggests traditional and European is contemporary. You can see this, for example, in the kitchen cabinet market, where the traditional look is American and the contemporary is European. Here you can also see what I mean by defensive and offensive strategies. The Europeans came into our market with high-quality factory-made cabinets, the style of which was very contemporary. Americans eventually fought back with imitations of the Euro style. By then the Europeans had found that there was still a large market for the traditional style, especially with a country or antique look, and they had begun to make them. In other words, they designed products to meet the tastes of our market. Ironically, the wood they use is produced here, shipped to Europe, made into cabinets, and then shipped back. Like a Third World country, we provide the raw material and they add value to it. But we have a lot of companies that make cabinets as good as the ones from Europe, and they have certain advantages over the Europeans. So why aren't they selling in the European market? Because they're pursuing a defensive strategy.

An overrated factor is the cost of labor. As our companies have lost shares of the domestic market to foreign competitors, they have often attributed their losses to cheap foreign labor. Yes, in some cases it has been a factor. But four other factors are much more important: good management, efficient use of capital, new technology, and trained labor (as opposed to cheap labor). With advanced manufacturing processes, labor now accounts for only a small percentage of the cost of the product. Whatever advantage a foreign company may have with cheap labor, it may be no greater than the cost of shipping the product here. In the early 1980s I had an interesting conversation with a Japanese executive, who predicted that by the end of the decade the shipping cost would force them to make cars in the United States— that is, if they wanted to stay in our market. Though they make some cars here now, he was a bit ahead of time, having underestimated the ability of Japanese management to offset this and other disadvantages. The point is, they didn't do it with cheap labor.

A growing number of American companies export their products, having found that they can compete in terms of quality and value. This shouldn't come as a surprise, since historically our manufacturers have never had the advantage of cheap labor. In fact, it was our high cost of labor that stimulated Yankee ingenuity into creating what became known as the American system of manufactures—interchangeable parts, made by machines. We achieved our success with the most expensive labor in the world. So if you're setting up a plant in a foreign country just because of cheap labor, you're on the wrong track. If you have a market in that country, or if you can easily ship your product to countries where you do have markets, then it could make sense. But with few exceptions, you have more important factors than the cost of labor.

Of course, the most attractive foreign markets are Europe and the Pacific Rim. Whatever your business, you should look at them, study them, and redesign your products for them. You should set up plants in key countries, not to get cheap labor but to get better access to these markets. It will be a long time before the flow of trade between here and there is completely free. At the same time, you should be aware of opportunities in developing countries, despite their problems. After Southeast Asia, the region with the greatest potential is Latin America. The main problem there is politics. But with better government, debt reduction, and economic aid, the region could be turned around. So don't lose sight of it. Track trends there, and be ready to proact.

= 15 =

Personal Strategies

Finally, let's look at some personal strategies—strategies for finding a job, buying a house, starting a business, and investing. The objective is to profit, not only in a monetary sense but also in a broader sense. If you like your work, you're profiting. When I explain to people what I do, they always say it sounds exciting. And I agree with them. I love my work. But a lot of people hate their work, and no matter how much money they're earning, they're not profiting, not in the full sense of the word.

In surveys of college students 76 percent of the freshmen in 1988 identified financial success as their main objective, compared with only 39 percent in 1970. That's a trend, and it reveals a lot about the values of the 1980s. In contrast to the values of the 1960s, which were idealistic, the values of the 1980s were materialistic. The dominant passion of the 1980s was greed, which you could see being acted out from Wall Street to Hollywood. It reached the point where a lawyer representing a young man who had defrauded investors of almost $15 million could accurately describe him as a product of our times.

The values of the 1990s are going to be different. They're going to be like the values of the 1960s, only more pragmatic. People will have more realistic economic expectations. They'll still want money, but they'll expect less. And they'll want other things. They'll want rewarding work, free time, good health, and satisfying relationships. Above all, they'll want control over their lives.

The values adopted in the 1960s by the leading edge of the baby boomers haven't been lost, they've only been submerged. They'll rise again as these people, who are now in their early 40s, move into positions of leadership. The values of the 1990s will be defined by people with a Sixties mentality, just as the values of the 1980s were defined by people with a World War II mentality. So we're going to see an end to the "Me generation" and the beginning of the "We generation." We're going to see a greater sense of social responsibility and a broader consensus on vital issues, since people from all age brackets, all socioeconomic levels, and all ethnic groups share concern for the future.

Finding a Job

For people seeking jobs in the 1990s the good news is that there's going to be a labor shortage. The bad news is that at the same time there's going to be a relatively high rate of unemployment. This is because of the growing mismatch between the products of our educational system and the needs of our society. If you have an appropriate education, you'll have no trouble getting a job. If you don't have one, you'll risk being unemployed.

For those of you who are full-time students in your late teens or early 20s, this doesn't mean that you should get a narrow professional education. On the contrary, you should first study the liberal arts. And take courses outside of your major, as many as you can. If you're a science major, take courses in art, music, history, and philosophy. Be sure to learn a foreign language. Better yet, learn two foreign languages. Learn about foreign cultures, as much as you can. Whether you go into business, government, research, or the arts, your future will depend on your ability to function in the global market. So get a global education.

Despite the pressure you may be feeling from your parents, teachers, or peers, you don't yet have to decide what to do with your life. At this stage you probably don't know enough to make a good career decision. While you're in college, use the time to get to know yourself, discover your potential, develop your creative capacity, and learn to think for yourself. This is your chance to break away from the herd mentality and become your own person. Then, with a little experience, you can decide what you want to do.

One question I always get from students is whether you should be a generalist or a specialist. If you look at evolution, you see that at times of rapid change a generalist has a better chance of surviving. Our advantage as human beings is our big brain, which enables us to adapt to a wide variety of situations. So if you're a generalist, you have a better chance of adapting to changes. But you also have to learn how to do something in particular. Ideally, you should be a generalist who can move from one specialization to another, as the times require. For example, the smart people on Wall Street moved out of trading, where the big money was in the early 1980s, and into investment and corporate finance, where the big money is now. Proacting, they moved from one specialization to another.

Those of you who have jobs should continue your education. I don't mean going to an occasional seminar or workshop, I mean applying yourself to learn new things, as much as if you were getting an advanced degree. You may actually get an advanced degree, or do the equivalent by taking courses or studying on your own. Whatever you do, you should always be getting useful information, tracking trends, and anticipating changes. You should always be proacting to them.

One such change, which has already happened, is that you can no longer assume that if you work for a company and do well, you'll always have a job with them. Your father could assume this, but you can't. The bond of loyalty between employer and employee has been broken by the merger mania and the "lean and mean" response to global competition. If you work for a corporation, you can no longer sit back and enjoy the comfort of job security. If you're a top executive, you may have a golden parachute that will give you a nice soft landing. But if you're a senior executive, a middle manager, or just an employee, you have nothing to protect you other than your ability to get a job somewhere else. So you have to watch what's happening, and you have to anticipate the acquisition, the leveraged buyout, or the restructuring that could affect you.

As you track a social, economic, or political trend, you should ask yourself how it will affect your industry, how it will affect your company, and how it will affect your job. You should determine what, if anything, your top executives are doing about it. Are they proacting? Are they waiting until the trend overwhelms them? If they're doing nothing about it, and you're unable to change their policy, then you should start looking for another job, because you don't want to be there when the wave crashes down on them. You don't want be there when they react by cutting employees.

Where are the job opportunities now? They're everywhere, provided that you have the education, skills, and experience. But some areas offer special opportunities. In this respect, finding a job is like finding a market: there are niches just waiting to be filled. For example, if you look at the ads for teaching positions, you'll see a disproportionate number of ads for special education teachers and for counselors. If you've been following trends in the family and education, you won't be surprised. These job niches have opened up because of trends, and they're just waiting to be filled by those who proacted, who anticipated the need for such professionals.

In the 1970s and 1980s, the corporate jobs that led to the top were in marketing and finance, but this trend has matured. In the 1990s the glamour jobs will be in production, since the winners in the global market will be companies that can deliver quality and value. The global competition that we face will create a lot of opportunities for engineers, as the space race did 30 years ago. But unlike then, it won't be enough just to be an engineer, you should also have a broad liberal arts background, with a global perspective.

In all professions there will be niches that offer special opportunities. In law, there will be more demand for people with environmental knowledge, since this will be one of the biggest areas of legislation. In medicine, there will be more demand for people with alternative approaches, since these will be gaining acceptance. In computer science, there will be more demand for people with systems expertise, since this will be critical for successful linking and networking. Whatever the profession, if you look at the trends that will affect it, you can determine where the niche of special opportunity will open up.

In what are normally referred to as the trades, there will also be special opportunities. I'm talking about carpenters, masons, plumbers, and other people who work with their hands. I'm talking about people who make things and repair things. In fact, I don't make a distinction between a surgeon and a garage mechanic. They should both have the value system that goes with being a professional. For such professionals there will always be jobs, since there's a real shortage of them. If you've needed a plumber lately, you know this.

By tracking trends you can anticipate the job niches that will open up, and by continuing your education you can acquire the knowledge to fill them. As long as you keep learning, you can adapt to changes. And if you follow your interests, you can do something you like.

Buying a House

With the decline in average real income and the sharp rise in housing prices, the American dream of owning your own home has receded beyond the grasp of many people. Those who are able to buy a home pay a much greater percentage of their income for the mortgage and taxes than they would have 20 years ago. Still, the dream of home ownership hasn't died, and the motive hasn't changed: Americans want to be independent, just as they did at the beginning of our country. Home ownership is a way to gain some independence, even if it takes your whole life to pay off the mortgage. So people will stretch themselves to the limit, and beyond it, to buy a home.

Given this motivation and the problem of affordability, you can see why people are moving farther and farther away from the centers of large metropolitan areas. They can't afford to buy a home in the suburbs where they grew up, so they're fanning out in all directions, searching for affordable housing. In some cases, they're going into the cities and rehabilitating houses in blighted neighborhoods. But in most cases, they're going out to areas that were still country or to small towns that were still beyond commuting range less than ten years ago. And they're finding houses that they can afford.

This is lengthening their commuting time, just as moving from the cities to the suburbs lengthened the commuting time of their parents. A survey for Adia Services found that 40 percent of the people travel between one and two hours a day commuting to and from work, 15 percent travel between two and four hours, and 4 percent over four hours. Think about it. All those hours sitting in a car, or a bus, or a train. You have to wonder if there isn't a better way of living. I don't have an easy answer, I can only point out that finding a job and buying a house involve decisions that have some bearing on each other. That is, if you find a job in an area where there aren't any houses within a two-hour commute that you can afford, then maybe it's not the right job. From what I can see, more and more people are reaching such conclusions. If they're offered a job in an area where they can't afford to live, they're more likely to turn it down than they would have been a generation ago.

Companies are reacting to this trend. As they find it harder to fill positions in their urban or suburban offices, they're moving out farther from the cities, following their employees. This will eventually shorten commuting times. But instead of waiting for it to happen, you should proact. Unless you really enjoy commuting (or unless you believe the futurists who tell you that your car will become an extension of your home, complete with a microwave oven), you should take advantage of the opportunities to live within a short distance of your work. You might have to leave your present job or leave your present area, but if you look at the costs and benefits, you probably won't have much trouble making these decisions. Remember, there are a lot of jobs, and there are a lot of places to live. What stops most people from making a change is their inability to see beyond their present situation. I have a remedy for this: use your eyes and look around.

Working at home is another way to minimize commuting time. It also has other attractions. Most important, it gives parents more flexibility in caring for children. Of course, you can't perform a complex financial analysis while minding a toddler, but by working at home you can partition your hours in a way that will enable you to do both at different times. Instead of conforming to a rigid nine-to-five day, you can schedule your work to suit your particular needs.

With advances in office equipment, working at home is becoming more and more practical. It's also becoming more and more popular. According to the Bureau of Labor Statistics, 18 million people worked at home in 1988, an increase of about 40 percent since 1985. This figure includes employees who bring work home, employees who work primarily at home, and entrepreneurs who operate home-based businesses. Another survey, by Link Resources, put the number much higher. It found that every day about 25 million people get up and go to the office in their spare bedrooms, living rooms, and kitchens. This figure includes 15.5 million employees who supplemented their office work with work at home. The other 9.5 million were home-based, self-employed workers. Still another survey, by the American Home Business Association, found that in 1988 there were 13 million home-based businesses, one out of every seven businesses in the country.

This trend started at the top, with executives who bought personal computers, then modems, and then fax machines to use at home.

Professionals, especially lawyers, were also at the front of this trend, as were entrepreneurs who worked at home to save capital. But it has spread to employees now that the equipment has become more accessible. With further advances in technology, there will be a tremendous growth in the number of employees working at home. So it's something to consider when you buy or build a house.

Starting a Business

Our research indicates that the primary motive for starting your own business is to gain control over your life. And the more uncertain your future becomes with a corporate employer because of mergers and acquisitions, the more incentive there is to break away. Of course, if you do start your own business, you'll probably work longer hours than you ever have. But instead of working for absentee shareholders who are willing to sell out at any moment to the highest bidder, you'll be working for yourself, which at least will guarantee employer loyalty.

A lot of people are now starting their own businesses. It's a strong trend, and the number of entrepreneurs will grow as the baby boomers reach their 40s, the time at which people are most inclined to break away. As I said, they'll be driven primarily by the motive of gaining control over their lives, which is especially strong in the baby boom generation. And this, together with the demographic trend, will produce an entrepreneurial boom.

Many of the people who will start their own businesses in the 1990s will be women who have had enough of male-dominated corporations. You can see this happening already, and it hasn't been long since women in general began to acquire the necessary skills and experience for running a business. So the wave of women entrepreneurs is yet to come.

The basic strategies for starting a business are the same as those for finding a job: track trends to anticipate the niches that will open up and prepare yourself to take advantage of them. Usually, people do some kind of market study before starting a business. This may be helpful, but it's not enough, since it only focuses on the market, ignoring information from other fields. It may even be harmful, since it could mislead you into committing your limited resources to a market that will be adversely affected by a trend in another field. If you want to succeed, you have to think globally about the market for your product or service. You have to make connections. How will this market be affected by trends in the family? In education? In health? In the environment? In the economy? And how should you proact to these effects?

As you look at potential markets, remember that the merger and acquisition trend that destroys your job security at the same time creates your business opportunity. If you fill a hole with a lot of small grains of sand, there's hardly any space between them. But if you fill the same hole with a few boulders, there's all kinds of space between them. And this is what happens when large companies merge or acquire one another to fill a market: they leave all kinds of space between them, especially when they abandon segments of that market and concentrate on what they then define as their core business. They open up niches that you can move into.

Generally, you don't have to worry about competition from large corporations, as long as you don't fall into their habits. Most of them aren't looking ahead, aren't tracking trends, and aren't proacting. They're looking at monthly financial reports, they're focusing on their present markets, and they're reacting. If they enter into a market that you've created, they'll never understand it the way you do. And if you're still proacting, you'll be ahead of them. You'll be leading the moving target, while they'll be aiming at where it is, instead of at where it's going. So they won't hit it. Your big advantage as a small business is that you have a quicker response time. You're like a small boat that can adjust its course immediately to changes in the wind, while a large corporation is like a supertanker that needs a lot of time and space to make a turn.

Where are the opportunities? With all the talk about how we're becoming a service economy, entrepreneurs are likely to consider a service business. And without a doubt there are many opportunities in this sector. But don't ignore manufacturing, where there are special opportunities. In fact, we forecast a comeback in manufacturing, led by relatively small companies that find market niches, develop special products to fill them, and use the most efficient production techniques.

Whether you're in service or manufacturing, you have to find a market niche that you can fill. How do you find one? By tracking trends and seeing the needs that arise from them. For example, if you track trends in the family, you can see that working mothers need services that aren't being provided, and these may be niches that you can fill. What kind of services? Working mothers are trying to juggle a baby, a husband, and a job, with only so many hours in the day. They need services that save them time, that make their lives easier.

Instead of going through all the trends I identified and showing you how they lead to market niches, I've given you a directory of opportunities at the back of this book. For now what's important is that you know how to track trends and see the needs that arise from them. If you do, then you can find the niches yourself.

Investing

The primary motive for saving is concern about the future. Whether people save for contingencies, for college tuition, or for retirement, they're concerned about the future. Judging from our rate of saving in the 1980s, we haven't been showing very much concern. But this attitude is changing. As the baby boomers mature, they're going to be saving more of their income, not only because they'll be more concerned about the future but also because they'll be earning more.

Once you have savings, you can do two things with them: you can invest them, or you can speculate with them. By definition, people who invest take a long view, while people who speculate take a short one. You can make money both ways, but unless you're involved in a market on a daily basis, it's harder to make money speculating. So most people should invest their savings, rather than speculate with them.

I'm not going to give you stock tips. I'm going to give you investment strategies. If you pursue them, you can find your own stocks, and you'll be ahead of the people who later buy them on tips. But I don't want to imply that it's just a matter of buying stocks. In fact, stocks should only be part of your investment portfolio.

First, you should invest in things you can control. If you have your own business, or are planning to start one, this is probably your best investment. Then you should look at other businesses that you can get involved in. You should try to have some control over the way your money is used. If you want to invest in real estate, you shouldn't go into a limited partnership in which you have absolutely no control over what they do. Buy a piece of land yourself or with a partner. Retain some control.

Second, you should invest in things you understand. If you're an expert on computer systems, then maybe you can evaluate the products of the different companies in that industry. If not, then you have to rely on someone else's opinion or on blind luck. Since it's your money, you should know enough to make informed decisions on what you do with it.

Before you buy stocks, you should track trends and see how industries will be affected. For example, if you track trends in the environment, you can see how the chemical industry will be affected by public sentiment and eventually laws. You should see how the different companies are responding to these trends. Are they proacting? If so, then you might want to buy their stock. If not, then forget it.

Unless you limit your portfolio to Treasuries, you should take the same approach with bonds. You don't want to pay for an investment-grade bond that later turns into a junk bond because the management only reacted to changes. And with any corporate bond, you should have the right to put it back to the borrower if its rating is affected by a merger or acquisition. You don't want to end up with junk while the Wall Street deal makers walk off with millions of dollars in fees. Of course, with all bonds you have to be wary of inflation, which can destroy the value of your investment. Whatever the politicians say, with rising food and energy prices, inflation will be higher in the 1990s than it has been recently. So you should avoid buying bonds with maturities beyond five years.

With both stocks and bonds, you should look beyond the domestic market. You should take a global view. You should invest some of your money in Europe and some in the Pacific Rim. This strategy will protect you not only by diversifying your market risk but also by hedging your currency risk. If the dollar falls, your foreign investments will help to compensate your loss of purchasing power. Again, whatever the politicians say, as long as we continue to have such large trade deficits, the dollar will inevitably get weaker. So you should avoid having all your money in dollar securities.

As for real estate, you shouldn't expect it to be the winner that it was in the 1980s. The baby boomers, who created an unusually high level of demand for housing, have been absorbed by the market. And there isn't another wave of them coming along. In most areas the rate of appreciation in the value of single-family houses won't be much more than the rate of inflation. Of course, there will be special opportunities, with higher rates of appreciation. For example, if you invest in an exurban area that may become the next Princeton, you can make a lot of money. But you'll have to be selective. You'll have to consider how the area might be affected by present trends. This is critical if you're looking at land, a house, or a condo in an area where you might retire. Are they going to have a water shortage? Are they going to have fiscal problems?

The basic strategies, then, are to have control over your investment, to track trends before selecting stocks and bonds, to be wary of inflation, to diversify your security holdings with respect to markets and currencies, and to be selective with real estate. You should give the same consideration to investing your money as you would give to finding a job or starting a business. Your money represents time you've spent, time that you can never recover, so it should be invested with care.

Redefining Profits

In our society profits are usually defined in terms of money. This was especially true during the 1980s, which were characterized by materialistic values or, to put it more bluntly, by greed. For many people the business hero of the decade was Donald Trump, a deal maker, who seemed to turn everything he touched into gold, sometimes literally. What impressed people about Trump was not what he did but how much money he made. And they didn't care how he made it.

The media kept score on how much money people like Trump were making. They published lists of the wealthiest people. I remember talking to a man who hadn't made the cut for one of these lists. I think he was $10 or $20 million short of the minimum. It really bothered him, and he vowed that the next year he would make the list. He didn't make it. In fact, he lost money, and his net worth fell below $100 million. This devastated him because his only way of valuing himself was by his net worth. If he was worth less than $100 million, he wasn't anything.

We have in our file a newspaper article about a lawyer who used an expert witness in a trial to set a value on human life. The witness, an economist, said that compensation for lost income of an adult male should be in the range of $1 million dollars. To that he added $11 million for lost enjoyment. He put a dollar value on the joys of living. But we all know that this is ridiculous. The value of really important things can never be set in terms of money. Would you sell your health for money?

In defining profit, the dictionary doesn't mention money. It just says that profit is an advantage, gain, benefit, or return. It leaves open the choice of terms by which you should measure profits. In the future people will choose terms other than money. They'll redefine profits in terms of rewarding work, free time, good health, and satisfying relationships. Money will still be important, but it will no longer be the dominant measure. If anything, the dominant measure of profit will be having control over your life.

During the 1970s we saw the rise of the Me generation, the people who turned away from social responsibility and lived only for themselves. They were disillusioned by the 1960s or they were at the trailing edge of the baby boom. They became yuppies. They got a lot of media attention. But they were always a small minority. They represented at most about 5 percent of baby boomers, and they've already begun to recede into history. What's coming is the We generation, the leading edge of the baby boom who never turned away from social responsibility and felt powerless during the 1980s. They're going to have power in the 1990s, and they're going to be supported by people from other generations who share their values.

You Have the Power

As I said in discussing corporate strategies, you have two ways of proacting to changes: you can adapt to them, or you can try to reverse them. In some cases you should not only adapt to them, you should also try to reverse them. For example, if you adapt to the destruction of the ozone layer by using skin lotion and wearing sunglasses to reduce your risk of cancer and cataracts, it's not enough. If you value human life, you should also try to reverse the change by making government and industry attack the causes of the problem.

With information, you have the power to make them do it. Though they may take a while, they'll eventually respond to an aroused, informed public because politicians are afraid of losing elections, and business executives are afraid of losing markets. They need you more than you need them, and if you let them know that you won't vote for them or buy their product unless they do what you want them to, they'll respond.

Remember, in the Global Age information is knowledge, and knowing how to use information is power. So get information, track trends, anticipate changes, and proact to them. You can adapt to them, you can reverse them. You have the power.

DIRECTORIES

A Directory of
Profit Opportunities

Here's a directory of some profit opportunities. Instead of concentrating on a few areas, it covers a wide variety of possibilities. It gives you leads that you can pick up and follow, using our system.

If your particular interest doesn't appear in this directory, then review the major trends discussed in Part II—trends in the media, politics, the family, education, health, the environment, the military, the economy, and the world—and see how they might affect your interest.

Adult Care

As the population ages and the family continues to abandon its role of caring for the elderly, there will be a strong market for adult care services. Demand for workers in nursing homes and home care will grow, and salaries will rise, as we're now seeing in hospitals. There will also be a strong market for products like braces, walkers, and wheelchairs as well as special furniture and fixtures.

Air Conditioners

Demand for air conditioners will grow as the earth gets warmer. Because of the CFC problem, a substitute for freon will have to be found, but this is a good opportunity. Another good opportunity is the need for greater energy efficiency.

Air Travel

There will be more regulation of airlines in the early 1990s because of growing pressure from consumer groups to protect passengers. There will be a return to fresh air rather than the recirculation of cabin air, which poses health hazards.

In the 1980s air travel increased by 55 percent. In the 1990s we expect it to increase by an even greater rate as airports open up in exurban areas, making air travel like bus travel. To profit from this trend, identify large airports that are now being underutilized (such as Dulles in Virginia or Stewart in New York) as well as small airports with potential for expansion. Buy property near them. Airports that now seem out of the way will be future hubs.

Airports will become more like shopping centers, with more upscale products and more diversity. On each trip, passengers spend an average of 85 minutes at the airport. More and more, they'll kill time by shopping, and they'll be able to have their purchases sent home, as if they had ordered by catalog.

Airplanes

There will be more foreign competition in the manufacture of airplanes, especially from the Japanese and the European consortium. It will be like what happened in the auto industry, where three companies dominated the market and the Japanese slipped into the niches. Foreign competitors will probably gain entry with small aircraft and then move up. At the high end, the European consortium has already taken a position with its Airbus.

Alcohol

In the 1990s people will consume less alcohol. One reason is the health and fitness trend. Another is the aging of our population. Another is the safety trend, exemplified by Mothers Against Drunk Driving. So alcohol will generally not be a good business to get into. Within the market, the trend away from hard liquor will continue. Beer consumption will be flat, and wine consumption will grow moderately.

Allergies

As the air gets worse, allergies will increase, so there will be a growing market for protective devices and for treatments. This would be a good area of specialization for new doctors.

Apartments

There will be a strong market for apartments among middle and lower-middle single people, both young and elderly, who don't want the responsibility of owning a house or can't afford one.

Appliances

In the 1990s appliances will be computerized. They'll be designed to use less energy and less water, as both become scarcer and more expensive. The manufacturers that offer these features will capture a bigger share of the market.

Aquariums

With the growing demand for pets among elderly people, this will be a good business. For those who want a pet that requires a minimum amount of work, fish are ideal. You don't have to walk them or change their litter boxes. All you have to do is sprinkle food into the tank and make sure the filter is working.

Arcades

Though it's no longer growing, there will be a market for game arcades. To attract customers, you have to offer the latest products. This market is subject to fads, as makers of video games learned the hard way. But there's one product with staying power—the traditional pinball machine.

Architecture

In the 1990s there will be some changes in house and office building design. Because of the warming trend, houses will be designed to maintain comfortable temperatures, using styles and materials developed in the Mediterranean. They'll also be designed to use solar energy. Office buildings will be designed for greater energy efficiency.

Arts and Crafts

This market will continue to grow for several reasons. More people will be living alone, and they'll want to occupy their time. Also, people who are frustrated with their jobs will look toward arts and crafts as a means of fulfilling themselves. At one time people were artisans in their work, but now they're not, they only have jobs. Finally, people will use arts and crafts as a means of supplementing their incomes.

Astrology

In the 1980s interest in astrology was stimulated by the news that the Reagans used it. But other world leaders, such as Teddy Roosevelt and Winston Churchill, also used it. Astrology isn't just a passing fad. In fact, it's been around for thousands of years. In the 1990s interest in astrology will grow with the New Age movement.

Autos

The Japanese companies are pushing to gain a greater share of the midwestern market. They have as much as 50 percent in California, but only 15 percent in Michigan and 25 percent in Ohio. Now with Japanese factories opening in these areas, there will be a stronger push. Look for more Japanese cars in the Midwest and for further erosion of the American share of those markets.

There will be a strong market for a car that is inexpensive, well-built, trouble-free, and easy-to-fix, like the old Volkswagen Beetle. There hasn't been a replacement for that, and the market is crying for one. The growing number of people at the low end need a car that they can afford, a car that works, a car that has both form and function. The muscle cars now being promoted by Detroit are only fads.

We expect to see a global shakeout in the auto industry. There's excess capacity, and the growth of the 1980s won't be repeated in the 1990s. We don't recommend investing in auto companies.

Auto Insurance

Auto insurance will be a problem. Other states will follow California, which in the last election voted to roll back automobile insurance rates. It's just an extension of what has happened with liability insurance in general. And it's going to mean lower profits for insurance companies.

Baby Products

After the current baby blip the birth rate will decline, so the total market for baby products will be smaller. But with the concern for health, nutrition, and food safety, there will be a strong market for products that satisfy these needs, especially at the high end. There will still be a market for disposable diapers, but they'll have to be biodegradable.

Bakeries

With the health and nutrition trend, there will be a strong market for good wholesome breads. The local bakery will return, and it will be a good business. This will create a demand for bakers.

Banks

In the 1990s the banking system will have more problems, especially when the next recession hits, since many borrowers are overextended. If you want to invest in bank stocks, we recommend small banks in exurban areas that have growth potential. With good management, these banks will perform well, and they're likely to be acquired by large banks, which will pay a premium for them. Suburban banks may do all right, but the ones beyond the suburbs will do better.

The earnings of the larger banks will be affected by write-offs of loans to Third World countries as our government adopts a policy of debt reduction. If you want to invest in large banks, look for the ones with relatively low proportions of Third World loans. Some large banks will be so affected by these and other write-offs that they'll have to merge with healthier banks, under FDIC pressure.

Batteries

Demand for batteries will be strong as more tools and small appliances become portable. The growth in sales of portable computers will also be a factor. Battery disposal is becoming a problem, so they'll have to be recyclable or made with nontoxic compounds.

Beaches

Because of the pollution problem, the value of beach properties near densely populated areas will fall. As more and more people become aware of the problem, they'll head for the hills instead of the beaches. At the high end, people will go to beaches in remote areas, where property values will rise.

Beef

Beef consumption will continue to decline, both here and abroad. The main reason is the growing concern about cholesterol, but now people are also worrying about the hormones and other chemicals used in producing beef. We see the effect of this concern in the European refusal to import beef raised with the use of hormones.

Beer

Imports and domestic boutique beers will take the high end of the market. The losers will be the large breweries that dominate the shrinking middle, and the winners will be the small breweries that make premium beers for regional markets. The latter now have less than 1 percent of the market, but the consolidation phase is over, and the number of breweries is multiplying. By the mid-1990s there will be more than 200 of these small breweries. A recent development is the beer pub, where you can drink beer that was made in the next room. There are now at least 60 of these pub-breweries, mainly in the Great Lakes region and on the West Coast. Light beer has reached its peak and will start to decline, since it's neither a beer nor a health drink.

Bicycles

If the use of cars in urban areas is restricted because of air pollution, then bicycle transportation will become more popular. But the aging of our population will have a negative effect on the use of bicycles. On balance, these trends will probably offset each other.

Biotechnology

After years of waiting, investors in biotech companies are finally beginning to see results. Most of the research spending has gone to drugs and diagnostics, which take years to develop. But research is also being done on waste disposal and other environmental problems, which may have a quicker payoff. This industry is where the computer industry was 40 years ago, and it has a bright future.

Blinds

With the rising price of energy and the changing climate, window blinds will be used as heat collectors as well as reflectors. To conserve energy, people will collect heat in the winter and reflect it in the summer. This will be a good business.

Boarding Houses

As the population ages, housing for the elderly will be the fastest growing segment of the residential real estate market. There will be a rebirth of boarding houses for those who can't afford senior residences. Large old houses in urban and suburban areas, which can be converted for this use, will be profitable investments.

Books

The book market has been eroded by video, as it was by television. But it will be stable and even experience some growth, because as the baby boomers age they'll read more. This is the information age, and reading books is still the best way to get certain types of information.

Bowling

With the aging population and the changing climate, bowling will be a popular form of recreation. There will be a steady market for bowling alleys, apparel, and accessories.

Cable Television

The existing local monopolies of cable television will be broken up by the use of optical fiber telephone lines. This will hurt both the movie theaters and the video stores, since it will expand the market for pay-per-view video.

Cafés

In the 1990s there will be a strong market for cafés with live entertainment. With the changing family structure and the aging of our population, people will want to go to places where they can meet other people in a less harsh environment than they find in bars and discos.

Cameras

As the maturing baby boomers find more leisure time, there will be more demand for cameras. There will be continuing innovation in both still and video cameras. This will be a business with steady growth and little downside.

Camping

The market for camping will be very strong as people try to get back to nature. Makers and sellers of camping equipment, such as vehicles, stoves, and apparel, will benefit. Even in a recession camping will be popular, since it's less expensive than other ways of vacationing.

Car Washes

Because of the growing water shortage, more people will be restricted from washing their cars, as they already are in some areas, and more of them will have it done at car washes. This will be a good business, provided that you have the equipment to recycle water, which will be required.

Chemicals

The market for toxic chemicals and nonbiodegradable products will decline. Demand for chemical pesticides will fall as more people refuse to buy foods that have been exposed to them. Many of them will finally be banned. On the other hand, there will be a growing market for environmentally safe products, and this will be a good opportunity for chemists and entrepreneurs.

Childbirth

This area has changed a lot in the past 20 years, and it's still changing. There's a trend away from maternity wards and toward birthing centers. Fathers participate more in the process, babies are allowed to stay with their mothers. There will be less use of anesthesia, less use of cesarean sections, less use of forceps during delivery. There will be gentler and more humane ways of handling newborn infants.

Cigarettes

Despite lobbying efforts by the tobacco companies, cigarettes will be banned in more and more public places, as they have been in Canada. By the end of the 1990s we'll no longer see cigarette advertisements or smoking in public places. To offset their declining sales here, tobacco companies will push their products in developing countries and newly industrialized countries in the Pacific Rim.

Cleaning

This will be a very good business. Dry cleaning, office cleaning, home cleaning, rug cleaning, upholstery cleaning—all these businesses will flourish. The upper class won't want to do their own cleaning, and the elderly won't be able to. So this will be a good opportunity for entrepreneurs.

Clinics

Clinics will continue to grow at the expense of hospitals. For cost reasons, more and more people will have outpatient treatment rather than stay at hospitals.

Coffee

With the trend toward health foods, people will choose organic coffee over the coffee that is heavily sprayed. More people will drink decaffeinated coffee as its flavor is improved by technology. At the high end, there will be a strong market for boutique coffees. There will be a growth in coffee bars as places to meet and socialize.

Colleges

After the baby boomers passed through college, enrollment began to decline. It's still declining in the traditional age group (18–22), and marginal colleges are having problems. But as the needs of our society become more complex, enrollment in the nontraditional age groups will steadily grow. The older student will be the norm rather than the exception. At some colleges, the average age of students is now almost 30. For those who want to pursue a career in college teaching, the highest demand will be in the market of continuing education.

Commodities

In the 1990s the commodities market will be what the stock market was in the 1980s—an arena of wild speculation. Since the general trend of prices will be upward, there's an opportunity to make some profits. Track the trend, and then proact by taking a position in wheat, corn, or another commodity. There will be ups and downs, but the long-term trend in grain prices is going to be up.

Computers

The computer revolution has only just begun, and it will accelerate in the 1990s. As computers become more advanced, they'll be easier to use. At the same time, young people coming into the system will be accustomed to computers. With the World War II generation dying off, the new generation taking its place will be more willing to use computers in their everyday lives.

In offices the two big trends are networking (connecting computers to one another so that information can be passed around by a number of users) and interfacing (connecting computers to other devices so that information can be transmitted or accessed in various forms). These trends are changing the work place even more than mainframe computers did.

By the end of 1988 there were 23 million home computers. They were used for word processing, budgeting, money management, education, and entertainment. In the 1990s they'll be used for shopping as well as regulating temperature. Like automobiles, houses will become computerized.

The companies that think globally will be the big winners in this market. We believe that Nintendo has a winning strategy. They won the kids over with games, and now they're expanding into other services. By aligning with AT&T, they're positioned to profit from the merger of telephones and computers.

Consulting

As people seek control of their lives, they won't want to work for large corporations. At the same time, the large corporations are downsizing because of LBOs and mergers, relying more and more on outside services. So consulting work will continue to grow, and there will be more consulting franchises.

Cookies

We don't recommend investing in cookie franchises. They have their niche in malls and shopping centers. But that market is saturated. It doesn't need a new chocolate chip cookie.

Copying Centers

Demand for copying and duplicating services will continue to grow, but more slowly than it has in recent years, since more and more people will have copying machines in their homes.

Cosmetics

This will be a booming business in the 1990s. As the baby boomers age, they'll want to cover up the ravages of time, so there will be a strong market for any product that can make older people look younger. There will be an especially strong market for natural cosmetics, since people will be more careful about what they apply to their skin. By the end of the 1990s the government will regulate cosmetics to protect the consumer.

Cotton

With the trend toward natural fibers, there will be a great demand for cotton. At the same time, supply will be affected by the warming trend and the loss of farmland. So the price of cotton will go up.

Coupons

Coupon advertising will lose its appeal due to the number of coupons flooding the market. It started with only one or two supplements in the Sunday newspaper. Now there are more supplements than pages in the newspaper. Coupons will still appeal to the growing lower class and to the elderly, who are on fixed incomes. But the upper class won't use them much—they're just too busy.

Currencies

Until the twin deficits are eliminated, the dollar will continue to lose value over the long run. As a hedge, we recommend the Swiss franc and the German mark.

Day Care

As more women are driven into the work force by economic pressure, there will be more demand for day-care services. The supply of trained, reliable people will be limited, so the cost will go up. To keep good employees, corporations will have to offer day-care services or subsidies as part of their standard benefit plans.

Dental Care

There's an oversupply of dentists now, but in the 1990s their "busyness" problem will be solved by the aging of our population. There will be more demand for gum treatment, crowns, dentures, and other reconstruction procedures. Not only dentists but also makers of dental equipment and supplies will benefit from this trend.

Dieting

There will be a strong market for diet counseling and weight control programs. People with solid training in nutrition, as opposed to the pop diet hucksters, will be in demand.

Direct Mail

With rising costs and falling responses, the volume of direct mail will decline. Junk mail is like junk food. It has a market, but it's not hitting the high end because people just throw it out. Also, corporations have begun to throw out junk mail before distributing it. So this business will have to improve its techniques for directing mail toward real potential customers of a product or service.

Drugs

There are two kinds of drugs: the ones people take for escape, and the ones they take for health purposes. There will be a growing demand for the first kind, especially among the rapidly increasing underclass. There will also be a growing demand for the second kind, but at the high end people will seek alternative medicine, while at the low end they'll still accept the symptom relief medicine.

Education

Because of the declining public school system, there will be more demand for private educational services, which provide help in reading, math, languages, and other subjects. Concerned parents will expand the market for these services, and schools will find that in some areas it's more cost-effective to use private contractors.

Energy

With the rising cost of fossil fuels, there will be a strong market for energy systems, conservation, and management. There will be technological breakthroughs in areas such as superconductivity and solar energy. Even during the recent oil glut, there were advances in the efficiency of photovoltaic cells, and further advances in the 1990s will make them a competitive alternative.

Exercise

Though the market for public exercise facilities is saturated, the market for office facilities will grow. A lot of large offices already have them, and more will have them in the future. Medium and small offices will eventually have exercise rooms. So the demand for exercise equipment will come primarily from businesses, rather than from gyms and homes.

Export-Import

With world trade growing, we see a lot of opportunities for exporters and importers. Since most of our businesses haven't focused on exports, there's a lot of room for growth there. And you don't have to be big to export. More than 20 percent of our exports of manufactured goods are from businesses that employ fewer than 500 people.

Exterminators

As people become more concerned about the risks, there will be more restrictions on the use of pesticides in the home and office. Even without more regulations, people will be afraid to use them, so new nontoxic techniques will be needed.

Eye Care

This will be a very good business. As the baby boomers age, more of them will need glasses, and many of them will prefer to wear contact lenses. More of them will suffer from cataracts, not only because of age but also because of greater exposure to ultraviolet rays as a result of the destruction of the ozone layer. More people will suffer from eyestrain as a result of sitting at video display terminals. And more people will have other eye problems as a result of air pollution.

Face-lifts

Baby boomers, with their accent on youth, will be a very good market for face-lifts. At the high end, cosmetic surgery will become the norm. Facial treatments in beauty salons will also become more popular.

Farmland

Because of the warming trend, the price of farmland will fall in the Midwest, where there will be droughts, and in the West, where there will be chronic water shortages. The price of farmland will rise in the East and Northwest, where rainfall is more reliable. For the long-term investor, the East and Northwest will be the places to buy farmland.

Fax Machines

Fax machines will continue to proliferate, causing more stress in the work place. If you send a letter by overnight delivery, the other people have the ball for at least a day. But with the fax, they can throw it right back to you, so you're always under pressure.

Fertilizers

Because they damage the environment, chemical fertilizers will be used less and less in the future. There will be a trend toward organic fertilizers, which will open up the market to smaller companies, since they won't need billion-dollar chemical plants. Organic fertilizers will be a good business opportunity.

Filters

As air pollution gets worse, there will be more demand for systems in homes and offices that filter out material from emissions. There will even be portable systems for use in the cities. There will also be more demand for water filters.

Financial Planning

With the baby boomers reaching the age where they begin to think seriously about income after retirement, there will be a very strong market for financial planning consultants. Those who take a global view of investments will be the most successful and the most in demand.

Fish Farms

Because of the declining catch, more and more fish will be raised on farms. The highest prices will be paid for fish that are raised organically, so this will be a good business.

Fishing

Recreational fishing has grown in popularity. More than 30 million fishing licenses were issued in 1988, compared with 26 million in 1980. As maturing baby boomers turn to less strenuous activities and try to escape from urban congestion, fishing will become even more popular.

Food Products

With the health trend, food companies will want to claim that their products are nutritious. But they should be cautious. Remember what happened to McDonalds—they really got blasted for promoting their products as nutritious. We recommend that clients rethink their strategies, as Pepsi did. Rather than trying to sell a soft drink as a health product because it had a small amount of orange in it, they cut the percentage of orange and then marketed it as an orange-flavored soda.

Friends

A 20-year study at the University of Missouri, released in March 1989, found that investing time in friendships pays off in a life that's longer and happier than one spent chasing the material world. The study of 1,700 people found that the people who lived longest were those who said they found most happiness in social relationships. This is a profit opportunity for everyone.

Furs

Because of concern for endangered species and animals in general, demand for furs will drastically decline. It will start at the high end as furs lose status, and only people at the low end will want them, but they won't have the money to buy them. We don't recommend becoming a furrier.

Gasoline

By the end of the 1990s we'll be using less gasoline. It will be replaced by other fuels, like alcohol and hydrogen. By the turn of the century, we're going to see electric cars in urban centers that now have severe air pollution. Meanwhile, there will be new methods of filling gas tanks to protect customers from exposure to benzene.

Gold

As part of a diversified portfolio, we recommend that you buy some gold to protect the value of your savings. With inflation in the air, people around the world will retreat into gold, as they always have, and this will drive up its price. When it goes over $440 an ounce, we would start buying it.

Golf

Golf will be more and more popular as the baby boomers mature. It's not a strenuous form of exercise, and it's a good way to get outdoors. It's also a good way to do business.

Greenhouses

With advances in solar energy and glass insulation, greenhouse additions to houses will become more popular. In the hot summers of the 1990s people won't want to sit outside, but they'll want the feeling of being outdoors. A greenhouse cooled by solar power will meet that need. Of course, they'll also be pleasant places to sit in the winter.

Greeting Cards

The changes in this industry have mostly come from small businesses, which the major companies have copied. There will continue to be good opportunities for small, innovative businesses in this market.

Guns

As the crime rate soars, there will be more gun control legislation, despite the lobbying efforts of the National Rifle Association. So guns will not be a good business.

Hairdressers

This is a recession-proof business, and skilled hairdressers will always find work, since there's a shortage of them. After food, clothing, shelter, and health, getting your hair done is the next priority.

Hats

Remember how Kennedy started the trend of not wearing hats? Well, Gorbachev may start a trend of back to hats. In any case, as baby boomers lose their hair, they'll wear hats to keep their heads warm or hide their baldness. Hats will come back into style.

Herbs

With the trend toward alternative medicine, there will be a lot of books on the use of herbs for natural healing. This will create demand for herbs, including seeds and plants for home gardens and windowsills.

Health Insurance

The biggest growth area in health insurance will be for long-term-care policies. So far only about 600,000 have been issued nationwide, mostly to people over age 55. As they realize that neither the government nor their families will take care of them, younger people will buy these policies.

In general, health insurance will be a problem. Health costs will rise faster than the rate of inflation, and policies will be unaffordable for people who aren't covered by their employers. After requiring all employers to provide health coverage for their employees, the government will implement a national health plan for those who still don't have insurance. It will be another patch in the safety net.

Hispanics

This is the fastest growing ethnic market. About 20 percent of our population is now Hispanic, up 39 percent since 1980. With economic and political problems in Latin America, we're going to have more and more immigration from that region. But we're going to see a blending of culture, a hyphenation of the Spanish and American, like what happened in the 1950s with the Italians. Annette Funicello and Frankie Avalon weren't old-time Italians, they were modern, American Italians. And that's what will happen in the 1990s with the Hispanics.

Hobbies

For aging baby boomers hobbies like gardening, arts and crafts, and photography will replace more strenuous activities. Because of their health-motivated desire to grow their own food, they'll be especially attracted to gardening.

Hospitals

As more and more procedures are done in clinics, there will be less need for hospitals. Public hospitals will become places where old people go to die. They either don't have families, or their families don't know what else to do with them, so they're sent to the hospital. Private hospitals will become more specialized, but they'll still have trouble making money.

Home Improvements

As the baby boomers become less mobile, there will be less turnover of homes. More people will stay where they are and make improvements. This trend will be good for home centers and remodeling businesses.

Housing

The market for housing will be weaker, especially in the middle. Demand will be concentrated at the high end, as successful baby boomers trade up, and at the low end, as the lower classes grow and the pieces of broken families fall out of the middle class.

As our population ages, the fastest growing segment of the market will be housing for the elderly. There will be more senior residences, shared housing, and ECHO (Elderly Cottage Housing Opportunity) units. At the same time, housing will be designed and adapted for the needs of the elderly. There will be fewer stairs, and bathrooms will be easier for them to use.

In general, housing won't be as good an investment as it was in the early 1980s. In most areas prices of homes will barely keep up with the rate of inflation.

Incinerators

The market for incinerators will decline, since they pollute the air and leave residues of toxic ash. These burn plants don't solve the problem of garbage disposal, so we don't recommend investing in the companies that provide them. Other solutions, such as recycling, will prevail in the 1990s.

Interpreters

With the globalization trend, there will be a strong market for interpreters, especially those who know the languages of Eastern Europe and Asia.

Janitors

There will be a stable market for janitorial services. Labor will continue to be supplied by immigrants. Companies that provide the service as well as manufacturers or distributors of supplies and equipment will prosper in the 1990s.

Jewelry

As the baby boomers approach their years of peak income, there will be a growing market for jewelry. Many of them will prefer jewelry designed and made by independent craftsmen.

Junk Dealers

They won't be called junk dealers, they'll be called recycled materials dealers. Their business will grow as more and more local governments mandate recycling. As they invest in new processing technologies, the recycled materials will be very competitive. There is a very good profit opportunity.

Kitchens

Kitchens, where most of the household garbage is generated or collected, will be redesigned to facilitate recycling. New appliances will be required. Existing appliances will use less energy. Cooktops, grills, and free-standing ovens will replace stoves. Microwaves will be standard equipment. At the high end, the European style will dominate.

Labor Unions

In general, labor unions will continue to lose power in the 1990s. One reason is the trend away from manufacturing toward services. Another is the dispersion of people, which makes it harder for them to organize. Skilled workers in manufacturing will gain power, since there will be a relatively low supply of them. But unskilled laborers will have nothing to bargain with, and skilled workers in service jobs won't be a force.

Laundry Services

This will be a strong growth business, with more home delivery for the elderly and the growing upper class. Coin-operated laundries will become more inviting, like the laundry bars that offer drinks and snacks. Water-recycling systems for laundries will also be a profit opportunity, since they'll be required in many areas.

Landscaping

Environmental landscaping will be a growing field as people become more concerned about the effects of development. There will be more restrictions on land use, and these will challenge landscapers.

Law

The hot areas of law in the 1990s will be environmental law, antitrust law, and consumer law. The reason is that after a lapse in the 1980s, more regulations will be passed in these areas.

Lawns

With hotter, drier weather, lawns will be harder to maintain. There will be restrictions on watering lawns and on using chemical fertilizers. With less area devoted to grass, there will be less demand for lawn equipment, lawn care products, and lawn services. Because of concern about noise pollution, electric lawn mowers and weed cutters will increase their share of a shrinking market.

Lumber

With the loss of forests and more restrictions on cutting trees, the global supply of lumber will be lower, and with the growth in population, demand will be higher. So trees that can be harvested for lumber will be a good investment.

Magazines

The mass market magazines will decline in popularity, but there will be opportunities to find new niches. It will be like television, where the major networks have lost audience and cable channels have prospered.

Mail

Despite the boom in fax machines, we'll still depend heavily on mail, and as the postal service gets worse, there will still be opportunities for private services.

Maintenance

There will be a shortage of qualified people in this area, which requires some skills. At the same time, there will be a strong demand for maintenance services. If you can find and train employees, this will be a good business.

Marine Biologists

The growing demand for fish and seafood, along with the concern about polluting the oceans, will create jobs for marine biologists. Now that we've exploited the land to its limit, we'll have to turn more to the sea to feed the growing population of the world. In the future marine biologists will be like agronomists were in the 1950s and 1960s.

Marketing Services

Because of leveraged buyouts, downsizing, and the high cost of maintaining employees, large corporations will rely more on outside marketing services, including advertising, direct mail, market research, and sales promotion. This will be a very good business.

Martial Arts

The martial arts, including aikido, judo, jujitsu, kung fu, t'ai chi, and Okinawan te, will continue to expand in popularity as we become more attuned to Eastern cultures. They'll be practiced as forms of exercise, by young and old, as they are in China. They'll be among the programs offered by corporations to help employees cope with stress. For the less athletic and the elderly, t'ai chi will be popular.

Masons

At the high end of the housing market, there will be a strong demand for masons and a shortage of people who are highly skilled. Those who have the skills will earn very good incomes.

Mechanics

There will be a great demand for mechanics, not only for autos but for all kinds of machinery. There will also be a shortage of them, partly because of the trend away from working with your hands and partly because mechanics need a lot more education than they used to. We already have a shortage of them, and the situation will only get worse.

Medicine

Dissatisfied with our medical system, more and more people will seek alternatives. Practitioners who take a holistic approach will be in demand. Many of them will be trained in Eastern disciplines, including shiatsu and acupuncture. They'll use herbal remedies as well as drugs and surgery. They'll also know a lot more about nutrition.

Mental Health

Mental health will be a growing problem for various reasons: the breakdown of the family, economic hardship, and environmental stresses. For people who want to pursue careers in mental health, there will be a lot of opportunity.

Mergers

After rolling through Europe in the next few years, the merger wave will finally be over. There will still be mergers, but they'll be done for business reasons, instead of just for financial reasons. The loss of fees from this activity will hurt the earnings of Wall Street firms and some commerical banks.

Messenger Services

There will still be a need for people to carry items from one business to another, like long documents and sample products. Messenger services will still be a good business in the 1990s.

Metric

With the trend toward globalization, we'll have to go on the metric system. This will happen in the mid-1990s, and people will be needed to help with the conversion.

Microwave Ovens

Microwave ovens will become a standard kitchen appliance. Some people will never use them, but most people will. The market for microwavable meals will continue to expand.

Midwives

With the trend toward natural childbirth, there will be more demand for midwives. A lot of people will find that they get more attention from midwives than from doctors, and they'll prefer midwives. More and more people will want to have births in their homes.

Mobile Telephones

As prices fall and service improves, the market for mobile telephones will grow. One effect will be more traffic accidents, since people have a hard enough time looking at the road without fighting with their broker or sales manager. A mobile telephone, which you can use while commuting or driving somewhere, will increase your productivity. But it will also increase your stress.

Mobile Homes

This market will grow, since there will be more people at the lower income levels. Mobile homes will be the only housing they can afford. On the other hand, fewer communities will accept them, especially in the Northeast. So mobile home parks will tend to be located in marginal areas. But they'll proliferate, as young families and retirees at the low end turn to mobile homes.

Money Management

Because of the volatility in financial markets, there will be demand for professional money managers who have good track records. They'll have opportunities not only as managers of large funds but also as consultants and financial planners.

Movie Theaters

We don't recommend investing in movie theaters. Unless they find new ways to attract people, they're going to decline. People will prefer staying at home with their VCRs and high-definition TVs (HDTV) to sitting in a bleak oblong room with a flat screen in one of those six- or eight-theater complexes. There will still be movie theaters, since people will still want to go out. But with home delivery of movies through fiber-optic cables, they'll go out less frequently to see a movie.

Mufflers

The demand for muffler service will grow as people keep their cars longer and emission controls get tougher. There will be a trend toward multiservice businesses, which do more than just repair mufflers. Some will offer pickup and delivery services. But these businesses will have trouble finding people with the necessary skills.

Natural Foods

In a supermarket trade association poll, 76 percent of the people believed that chemical residues in food present a serious health hazard. So there will be a growing market for natural foods. The high-end supermarkets will offer natural foods as standard items. There will even be supermarkets that offer only natural foods. There will also be more natural foods in employee cafeterias as corporations try to reduce their health-care costs.

Neckties

As the climate gets warmer, neckties will become unpopular, as they are in most tropical countries. In hot weather, people don't want to button up their shirts and wear a tie around their necks. At some point we'll have a president who doesn't wear a tie, just as Kennedy didn't wear a hat, and that will kill the necktie business.

Needlework

This area will grow with legislation that allows women to do needlework for pay out of their homes. Also, as people turn more to arts and crafts, the market for needlework will grow.

Newspapers

At the low end, the market for newspapers is saturated, since most uneducated people get their news from TV. At the high end, there's potential for growth, especially for newspapers that take a global view. Educated people want information on current events in many fields around the world.

Nurses

The shortage of nurses for hospitals, nursing homes, and other health facilities will continue. Salaries will increase, but fewer people will want to do this kind of work. To meet the need, there will be more nurses from foreign countries. Eventually, our health care delivery system will be redesigned, with nurses having bigger roles.

Nursing Homes

With the aging population, the market for nursing homes will be very strong. The supply of facilities, managers, and workers will be less than the demand, so prices will go up. Those who are well-positioned in this market will profit.

Nutritionists

Demand for nutritionists will grow as more people make the connection between diet and health. The field of nutrition is still wide open, and those who can develop workable programs will flourish in the 1990s.

Office Buildings

There will be a glut of office buildings until the mid-1990s, especially in the cities and the near suburbs. The growth will be in exurban areas, with smaller buildings to meet the needs of downsized corporations and small businesses.

Office Equipment

There will a strong market for office equipment, especially for computers, copying machines, and fax machines. There will be more linking of office equipment. As more and more people work at home, there will be more demand for products that meet their particular needs. Competition and technological advances will keep prices down.

Office Furniture

The buzzword in office furniture will be ergonomics, the science of adapting working conditions to suit workers. We see a trend toward more comfortable and supportive seating for office workers, many of whom suffer from back and neck pains because of poorly designed chairs. The companies that make ergonomic chairs have a huge potential market, since more than 70 percent of workers now have sedentary jobs.

Oil

With less domestic oil production and more unity among the oil-exporting countries, the price of oil will be higher in the early 1990s. But as our environmental problems worsen, there will be more restrictions on the use of oil. By the end of the century, with breakthroughs in solar and hydrogen energy, we'll move away from fossil fuels as our primary source of energy.

Oriental

Our trade with China and the Pacific Rim will grow tremendously in the 1990s. Corporations and entrepreneurs who position themselves for this development will benefit greatly. Designs with elements of Oriental style will be popular, as they were during the era of the China trade.

Orthopedic

After years of jogging on hard pavements, the baby boomers will have problems with their legs and feet. If you plan to be a doctor, orthopedics would be a good speciality.

Packaging

Because of the garbage disposal problem, packaging will change drastically. There will be less bulk, less packaging for its own sake. There will be more paper bags and more reusable bags made of canvas and cotton, as you see in Europe, where people take their bags with them when they go shopping.

Paper

Paper bags will recover a lot of the market they lost to plastics. Even now at the checkout counters of supermarkets people are asking for paper bags. There will be more paper recycling, not only of newsprint but also of cardboard boxes and containers. Paper recycling will be a good business.

Paralegals

With the growth in litigation, this will be a very good profession to get into. Schools to train paralegals will also do well. In the 1990s there will be a shortage of people with the necessary skills for paralegal work.

Parcel Delivery

While mail delivery will lose some market share to fax machines, parcel delivery will continue to grow. It will be a long time before we can send parcels through the wires or air waves. So this will still be a good business, and it will be stimulated by catalog shopping and home shopping via computer or television.

Party Supplies

With the trend toward more home entertainment, there will be a strong market for party supplies, like cocktail napkins and paper plates. But plastic utensils, cups, and plates will be out of favor.

Patent Attorneys

As more research and development money is invested in consumer products and less in weapons, patent attorneys will be in greater demand.

Pawn Brokers

Pawn brokers are really just bankers who serve the low end of the market. With the growth of the lower classes, along with the declining standard of living, pawn brokers will flourish in the 1990s.

Personnel

With the shortages of qualified employees and the changes in benefits, there will be a growing demand for human resources professionals. Employment agencies, especially in the area of temporary work, will be good businesses.

Pesticides

The pesticides now used widely will be replaced by environmentally safe products. The latter are already being offered in catalogs for the home gardener, and before long they'll be used commercially on a large scale.

Pets

As more and more people live alone, there will be a strong market for pets. Dogs will be less popular, since they require a lot of attention. More people still buy dogs than cats, but cats are gaining. Birds and fish are also on the rise.

Physical Therapy

With the trend away from symptom relief medicine, more people will use physical therapy for aches and pains. For baby boomers, who have included exercise in their fitness programs, it will make sense to use physical therapy. Physical therapists, especially those who make house calls, will be in great demand.

Pizza

Pizza will continue to be popular. There will be a strong market for home delivery of a quality product, rather than just speed of delivery. Because pizza has such a high markup, this can be a profitable business.

Plastic

By the mid-1990s plastic bags and containers will be banned across the nation unless they're biodegradable. But they'll still be a problem, since even food waste isn't degrading in our tightly packed landfills. As anyone who makes compost can tell you, the process of biodegradation doesn't work without air. So we'll also have to change our landfills. Meanwhile, there will be less demand for plastics in packaging. But there will be more demand for structural plastics in machinery, equipment, vehicles, appliances, and other products.

Plumbers

Because of the trend away from working with your hands, there will be a shortage of qualified plumbers. This will be a good trade to get into.

Pools

As the climate gets warmer, demand for swimming pools will grow. Designers, contractors, and suppliers of equipment will profit from this trend. There will be a demand for new ways of purifying and recycling water.

Poultry

The consumption of poultry raised with hormones and other chemicals will decline. The fear of salmonella and other diseases from mass-produced chickens will also be a factor. At the high end, people will turn to free-range organic chicken, even though it costs more.

Printing

There will be a good market for specialty printing. Technological advances will require more highly trained workers. Among the larger printing companies, there will be a rapid globalization.

Property Management

This is a mature market that isn't going to change much. But there are a lot of buildings to manage, and people who can meet this need will make money.

Protection Services

With the growing number of uneducated, unemployed people, crime will increase, and so will the demand for protection services, not only in the cities but also in the suburbs. Companies that provide security guards, as well as companies that manufacture security equipment, will prosper in the 1990s. On the other hand, the need for these services will make our industry less productive and less competitive in the global market.

Publishing

For a while there will be more consolidation of publishing houses. The large media companies will absorb the remaining medium-sized independent houses. But there will still be small houses that focus on market niches. As the products of the giant companies become more homogenized, there will be more opportunities for the small houses. Like the major television networks, which catered to the common denominator of the mainstream, the giant publishers will lose some of the market to competitors that offer variety and quality.

Radio

Radio will be a good business, especially for those that deviate from traditional formats of news and music. For example, there's a strong demand for extensive business information, which none of the radio stations is providing. For many products, radio is the most cost-effective way of advertising.

Railroads

With the Euro tunnel and other steps to complete a network of fast, efficient rail transportation, the European Community will have a competitive advantage over us. So we have a strong incentive to upgrade our system.

Razors

There will be less demand for disposable razors. The industry will find better ways to sell blades, which are still what they make money on.

Real Estate

There will be a trend of people moving away from the city. With computers, modems, and fax machines, you don't have to be in the city. You don't even have to be in the suburbs. You can be anywhere. And people want to get away from the congestion of urban areas. Middle-class people left the city years ago, and now they're leaving the suburbs. They're moving to rural areas, they're settling in small towns. So this is where to invest in real estate—in outlying areas. The cities and the near suburbs will be inhabited mainly by the lower classes, along with those people who enjoy urban living and can afford a lot of protection as well as a second home in the country.

Recreation

Since the early 1970s, the time available for recreation has been declining. One important factor was the opening of retail stores on Sunday, which destroyed the tradition of family dinners and family outings. A lot of parents and teenage children now have to work on Sunday. Those who don't have to work often spend Sunday afternoon at the mall, which isn't exactly our idea of recreation. While we don't expect a return of the blue laws, which prohibited commercial activities on Sunday, we expect a decline in the popularity of malls—as the saying goes, if you've seen one, you've seen them all—and a return of other forms of recreation.

Resorts

There will be a growing demand for health spas and other resorts where people can take a "rest cure," as they used to call it. More and more people will take vacations just for rest and relaxation. This will be a good opportunity for the resort business.

Restaurants

With the globalization trend, there will be a strong market for restaurants with authentic cuisines of other countries. They'll follow the pattern of Italian restaurants, which have evolved from spaghetti and meatballs to linguine alla primavera. The same thing will happen with the cuisines of other countries. Like other markets, this one will polarize, with fine restaurants at the high end and fast-food joints at the low end. The middle will suffer.

Retirement

As our population ages, there will be a strong demand for retirement homes and communities. Many people will want the type of facility that combines independent living and health care. Some of the more affluent baby boomers will want to retire in other countries where the climate and other living conditions are more benign. There will also be a strong demand for financial planning services, since people can no longer expect their children or the government to take care of them in retirement. In our research we hear it all the time from single women who have good jobs or successful careers—they're afraid of ending up on the street.

Sales

There will always be a strong market for good salespeople, since sales are the lifeblood of a business. This won't change, no matter what happens.

Shipping

With the growth in world trade, there will be a strong market for shipping, especially ocean shipping. On land, railroads will capture more of the long- and medium-haul market as their service improves and trucking becomes more expensive due to fuel costs, emission controls, road congestion and labor shortages.

Shoes

The axiom in the shoe industry is that the shoe is the tail of the fashion dog, so whatever the dog does, the tail follows. This will change in the 1990s. There will be more emphasis on comfort, more concern about the health of feet. At the high end there will be more custom-made shoes and more use of natural materials.

Skiing

Aging baby boomers will do less downhill skiing and more cross-country skiing. They'll still be attracted to ski areas to get away from the city, but they won't be lining up at the lifts the way they used to.

Skin Care

With the aging of our population and the destruction of the ozone layer, there will be a very strong market for skin care products and services in the 1990s. These include skin treatments, skin protection, skin lotions, and other products.

Social Workers

As the family continues to break down and the underclass grows, there will be a great demand for social workers. People will have a higher social consciousness than they did in the 1980s, so more college graduates will want to go into this field. But there will still be a shortage here.

Soft Drinks

At the high end, people will consume fewer soft drinks. The market will grow only at the low end. The aging of our population will also have a negative effect on consumption of soft drinks. The opportunity for profit is in fruit drinks, especially if they are free of pesticides.

Solar Energy

This will be a hot area in the 1990s. People will make money on solar energy the way they did on oil, except they'll make it by inventing and commercializing new technologies, not by owning natural resources. The oil companies, which bought a lot of the solar companies during the 1970s, have mainly abandoned the field, leaving it open for entrepreneurs.

Sporting Goods

We don't recommend getting into this area. As the baby boomers age, the market for sporting goods will decline. With schools cutting their physical education programs, the next generation will be less interested in organized sports. But this trend could be reversed if the sporting goods industry gets involved in redesigning the school system.

Steel

Basic steel will be a Third World industry. Specialty steel will be our area, and American companies will be strong global competitors.

Stock Market

The stock market will languish in the 1990s, as it did in the 1970s. The bull won't return until we have bold leadership to steer the country in a new direction. Meanwhile, traders will make more money than investors.

Swimming

Swimming will be a popular sport, not only because of the warming trend but also because of the aging trend—it's a good, healthful activity for older people. Because of concern about pollution, people who can afford them will prefer to swim in their own pools.

Television

High-definition television (HDTV) will come in the 1990s. It will hurt movie theaters, but it won't fundamentally change the nature of home entertainment. It will just make the picture clearer.

Tailors

There will be a shortage of tailors in the 1990s. The market will be supplied by immigrants, mainly from China and Latin America. People with these skills will always have work. For the elderly it could be a good way of supplementing their retirement income.

Take-out Food

Take-out foods will be a good business. More and more, the service will include home delivery.

Teaching

With a higher priority on education, there will be opportunities for good teachers, especially in math, science, business, languages, and global studies. In most areas of the country teachers' salaries will improve.

Teenagers

More advertising will be aimed at teenagers. Even though they're losing in numbers, they're gaining in dollars. Remember, Mom and Dad both work, or single-parent Mom works. So the kids do a lot of the shopping, and they'll have the money to spend.

Telephones

In the 1990s telephones and telephone lines will be used for more and more purposes. Last year the telephone companies were permitted to offer households a variety of information services. They've been developing these services, and they've been laying fiber-optic cables that can handle greater volumes at faster speeds. These lines will deliver entertainment (pay-per-view cable TV), mail (fax, voice mail, and electronic mail), information (databases and libraries), and interactive services (shopping, banking, and ticket reservations). They'll also be used as an advertising medium to reach consumers, not in the present form of telemarketing but in a more advanced form of direct mail.

Toys

There will be fewer children, and this will hurt the toy market. Also, with declining real income, people will have less money to spend on toys. There will be a back-to-basics trend, continuing into the mid-1990s.

Travel Managers

Last year our corporations spent more than $100 billion on travel. After salaries and data processing, travel is the next most controllable expense. Yet less than a third of our large corporations have travel managers. This could be a good opportunity.

Trees

Planting trees will become an important activity as we try to reverse the greenhouse effect. It will be promoted by federal, state, and local governments, as well as by communities and corporations. Raising seedlings and planting them will be a good business.

Trucking

There will be reregulation of the industry, with stricter emission controls and higher safety standards. Shipping by truck will become more expensive, and business will be lost to the railroads.

Turkeys

Because of its low fat and low cholesterol, turkey is becoming more popular. It's no longer something you eat only on Thanksgiving. But the market for turkeys could be affected by concern over the use of hormones and other chemicals in raising them.

Vending Machines

Meeting the needs of our fast-paced society, vending machines are dispensing a variety of products from jeans to microwave meals to computer software. For those who can think of new uses for them, there's always an opportunity.

Ventilation

As people become more concerned over air quality, there will be more demand for ventilation systems. So makers of equipment, distributors, contractors, and servicers will do well in the 1990s.

Veterinarians

With the growing popularity of pets and the changes in the methods of raising animals for food, there will be a greater demand for veterinary services.

Videos

Until a new technology comes along, the market for home videos will continue to grow. The tapes will get smaller, as audio tapes did, and programming will get easier. VCRs will become more sophisticated. There will be good opportunities in video production, duplication, and distribution.

Vitamins

As more and more people make the connection between diet and health, there will be a strong market for vitamins and food supplements. Linus Pauling, who has made a case for greater supplements of vitamin C, will be vindicated.

Walking

According to a recent poll, every day 29 percent of Americans walk one mile or more. That's seven times the percentage of people who jog. So walking has become a popular form of exercise, and it will become even more popular in the 1990s.

Waste Disposal

There will be changes in this business: less hauling and less burning, with more recycling, more compacting, and more treatment. There will be good opportunities for people who can design and make the needed equipment, as well as for people who can manage the systems.

Water

With shortages and concern about safety, water will be a very good business in the 1990s. We recommend investing in water sources, distribution, purification—just about anything that has to do with water. Sales of bottled water and purification devices grew 68 percent over the past five years, and we expect them to continue growing at this rate over the next five years. Remember how in *The Graduate* the guy took Dustin Hoffman aside and told him what the big opportunity was? "Plastics," he said. Well, that was in the 1960s. Now it's water.

Wine

Domestic wines will capture more of the market as their quality becomes recognized and their prices become more competitive. A big factor is the weakening of the dollar, which will make imported wines more expensive. As wines from California, New York, and other states gain prestige, their price advantage will have some influence, even at the high end. Wine coolers have reached their peak.

Yogurt

Yogurt and yogurt products will continue to be popular in the 1990s as people become more health conscious, more weight conscious. Premium products will find niches in this market, as they did in the ice cream market.

Zoning

Zoning will be tougher, so real estate developers will have a harder time getting projects approved. The tougher laws will create more demand for zoning consultants.

A Directory of Information Sources

We're living in a world that depends on information. Whatever our field of interest, we have a growing need to obtain information from reliable sources. And the old storehouses of knowledge are being transformed into information markets.

Still, nothing in the foreseeable future will replace the newspaper as a daily source of information, so that should be your primary source for tracking trends. For more background and alternative views, you should use magazines. For additional information on specific subjects, you should consider using electronic sources.

We recommend that you change your sources of information from time to time, otherwise you risk getting into a reading rut. For this purpose, we deliberately rotate our primary sources, and we always try new alternative sources.

Also, we recommend that before you make an important decision, you review your files on the trends that could affect the matter at hand. And if you're looking for an opportunity, your files may suggest the answer. So be sure to use them. Unless you do, they're just a collection.

Newspapers

Asahi Shimbum (Tokyo), founded in 1879, has a careful layout and a broad perspective that make it the best choice in eastern Asia. The paper supports traditional values and serious views, with very few feature articles.

Berliner Zeitung (West Berlin) is one of five dailies owned by the Springer Group, the largest newspaper publishing group in continental Europe. *Berliner Zeitung* is politically independent, and Springer is a press giant, commanding almost 70 percent of Berlin's total circulation.

Corriere della Sera (Rome) was founded in 1876. Monetary demands by labor and for raw materials have brought hard times. *Corriere della Sera* now relies heavily on financial support from a financier/industrialist consortium. Solid writing, fine photos, and a focus on the regional and world news scenes make it the best of Italy's papers.

The International Herald-Tribune, published daily, is easy to get when you're traveling abroad. But when you're at home, there are more comprehensive papers to read.

Manchester Guardian Weekly (Manchester) excerpts special articles and reporting from the *Washington Post* and *Le Monde*. Some say it's the most literate and entertaining newspaper in the English language.

Le Monde (Paris), founded in 1944, was forced by sharp drops in ad revenues and rising operational costs to accept financial assistance from the government in 1983. Still, it's the leading Parisian source for local, national, and world news. It has a plain appearance and aims toward the educated reader. *Le Monde* remains one of the world's best dailies.

The New York Times (New York), founded in 1851, is respected as a powerful news source with large national acceptance. Printed in eight major American cities, it's noted for solid news reporting that is straightforward and well written. The New York edition provides in-depth local and regional coverage.

Pravda (Moscow), founded in 1912, has a circulation of 10.7 million. "Pravda" means truth and the paper operates as the organ for the Communist party. Editors are party members, which may explain why editorials are displayed like bulletins. The paper contains serious reporting on national and international affairs. With *glasnost*, it has become more interesting.

La Prensa (Mexico City), founded in 1928, is one of 20 dailies in the capital city. The paper contains general interest articles of regional as well as local focus. It's attuned to values of the established community. *La Prensa* concentrates coverage on Latin American affairs.

The Times (London) is an influential and highly regarded newspaper. Enlightened editorials and an excellent business section show that new ownership hasn't changed this informative and classic journal. Founded in 1785, *The Times* is a valuable research and index tool.

USA TODAY (Washington, D.C.), billed as the nation's newspaper, boasts that it is number one in the United States with 6.3 million readers every day. At the Institute, we say that "to learn about tomorrow, you need *TODAY*." The paper is filled with essential trend information covering a wide range of issues. We recommend that you supplement this paper with the *New York Times*, the *Washington Post*, the *Boston Globe*, the *Atlanta Constitution*, the *Chicago Tribune*, the *Los Angeles Times*, or another paper of comparable quality.

The Wall Street Journal (New York) is the American businessperson's talisman and is the premier financial daily information source in America. This paper's best-kept secret is its high-quality reporting on controversial issues, for which it devotes ample space to tell the whole story. Although perceived as a pro-business, "establishment" publication, the *Journal* pulls no punches when it comes to reporting controversial issues that may be detrimental to advertisers. Our guide to reading the *Journal* is to skip the "What's News" column and move on to the features.

Magazines and Weeklies

Today's world is a complex sphere drifting toward a changing tomorrow. Developing one perspective, or one level of understanding, isn't enough in the Global Age. Our lives are affected by events that require an in-depth knowledge based on information from different fields. Magazines explore a wide range of issues. Representing different views, this selection will help you to get the information you need.

Advertising Age and *Adweek* are published weekly. Over two-thirds of our gross national product is generated by consumer spending. If you're serious about selling products, whether wholesale, retail, or industrial, you should subscribe to either one of these magazines.

American Demographics is one of America's foremost publications on demography and marketing research. It contains interesting, informative articles on every aspect of American life and is a must for the serious trend tracker. It's not all numbers, it's a good read with a lot of analysis. Affiliated with Dow Jones & Co., Inc, this magazine is published monthly.

American Heritage is a magazine of history founded in 1954. Published bimonthly, it contains a variety of articles about history: a new look at the Emancipation Proclamation to reviews of historical restaurants. No subject is too trivial or too important to merit space within *American Heritage's* pages. Features vary in length and are illustrated with numerous photos. It's a popular magazine, with a clean layout, and is free of advertising.

American Opinion is a John Birch Society publication. Printed in full color, it frequently attacks the "liberal establishment." Articles range from casually factual and to sometimes scholarly views. The magazine is attractive and compact.

Asiaweek has a layout similar to a popular United States news magazine format, but the focus is from an Asian viewpoint. It's analytical and well written, with views on international affairs. Human interest stories and new book reviews round out this illustrated weekly.

Common Cause, a bimonthly published by the National Citizen's Lobbying Organization (NCLO), aims at more effective and responsive government. The magazine contains information on NCLO activities and feature articles on various issues. Political views are presented in an oppositional forum. News on featured citizen projects show how the system works effectively.

Counterspy reports on the snafus and wrongdoings of United States officials and agencies. The publication contains news on human rights violations and political science reports from around the world.

Current, an illustrated monthly founded in 1960, makes extensive use of reprints from all sources and contains relevant thought on today's problems, from space exploration to the automobile's impact on America. Half the articles are political in nature, but no single subject or ideology dominates.

Daedalus is a top American academic journal published by the American Academy of Arts & Sciences. Articles are devoted to contemporary society in the United States, scientific inquiry, and United States defense policies and leadership. Written by academicians, the scope is on society, politics, and intellectual thought.

The Economist, a complete, timely, and thorough magazine, goes beyond the borders of economics into global politics, finance, and science.

Encounter is concerned with domestic and foreign political affairs and social problems. Features include interviews with internationally known experts and politicians. The publication analyzes philosophy, literature, art, and contemporary life from an academic viewpoint.

Factsheet Five is a bizarre yet definitive directory of the alternative press. It contains anything and everything out of the ordinary. As such, it is published whenever Mr. Gunderloy feels like it (usually about five times a year).

Forbes is by far the most readable and the most interesting of the general business magazines. It's imbued with the spirit of Malcolm Forbes, who has an open mind and a way with words. While many of its articles are aimed at investors, it has penetrating features about major issues, some of which have been very accurate in forecasting the consequences of harmful government policies.

Harrowsmith is a how-to publication for the environmentally and socially conscious. Excellent investigative reports and feature stories include topics such as organic gardening, energy, and country life.

Human Events is required reading to learn about a particular slant on major foreign and domestic issues. We recommend this magazine to those who subscribe to the *Nation* to enable them to recognize the concerns of the other side.

In Context is the magazine of "humane sustainable culture." Environmental issues are the focus, with additional emphasis on related political issues. It's published quarterly as a cooperative project of the Context Institute.

In These Times is an attractive weekly on American life and foreign affairs. It also covers arts and entertainment. The writing and layout are top quality.

Multinational Monitor tells what the multinational corporations are doing throughout the world, focusing on their ethical behavior. Published monthly, it's a Ralph Nader "watchdog" publication geared towards anyone who follows the actions of large companies.

The Nation, founded in 1865, was voted best publication in the General Excellence category of the Alternative Press Awards. An excellent magazine, it focuses on politics.

National Journal is "what the leaders read" according to the masthead slogan of this magazine. The articles appeal to government officials, business administrators, labor unions, political think tanks, and research organizations.

National Review is a good source of information about international events and politics. Its viewpoints are consistent with the beliefs and policies of William F. Buckley, the publisher.

The New Republic reviews and comments on current events. Our analysis of this magazine differs from that of many people with strong ideological views. The magazine's editorial slant varies with the direction of the political wind.

Regardies is a well-written guide to rising and falling political stars. The "NewsReal" section focuses on the lighter side of reality. "Hotshots" features movers and shakers, while "City Slickers" zeroes in on Washington D.C.'s current newsmakers and political aspirants.

Rolling Stone, once the magazine for baby boomers, now appeals to a younger generation. It's the publication that tunes you in to the emotions, styles, and habits of young Americans. For advertisers who want to learn about this market sector and for organizations that rely on entertainment to drive their products, keep in touch with the *Rolling Stone* perspective.

Science News is the best weekly digest of news in science and technology. Very well written, it covers a range of fields from physics to behavior. It's an especially good source of information on the environment, providing research straight from the scientists, without any interpretation from politicians.

Utne Reader is the nation's fastest-growing general information magazine. A "Reader's Digest" of the alternative press, this publication deserves an A+. It appeals to people who like to think for themselves and want to broaden their views on major issues—and on life. It's published every other month.

Variety provides a good overview of what's going on in the entertainment area of the communications field. Movies, video, TV, radio, and music are covered. The biggest drawback is that the articles are written in entertainment jargon incomprehensible to the outsider—and possibly to the insider.

The Washington Monthly is an award-winning magazine focused on the political arena. It's an illustrated guide on presidential policies, federal agencies, congressional turmoil, and the courts. It contains a monthly "Who's Who in Washington." "Memo of the Month" provides insight and humor with bureaucratic interoffice memos. The magazine is popular and easy to read.

Washington Dossier is a tabloid layout covering the glamour, the intrigue, and the powerful personalities in our nation's capital. Top echelons are in the spotlight as the *Dossier* gives us the latest insider scoop from the halls of Washington.

Whole Earth Review has been a bible for over 20 years for those seeking social and spiritual information on a level different from that provided by the mainstream media. It includes reviews of books on living in balance with nature to reviews of computer magazines. It's published every other month.

World Press Review contains reprints and excerpts from major newspapers and magazines and serves as a digest on current world affairs. It gives a perspective of what the rest of the world thinks about major issues.

Newsletters

Rather than attempt to list all the newsletters available, we recommend that you use the *Newsletter on Newletters* to identify appropriate sources. Its address is 44 West Market Street, Rhinebeck, NY 12572.

Electronic Information

Gathering electronic information was once a luxury reserved for corporate executives, but an increasing number of smaller businesses are discovering that instant access is crucial to decision making at any level. With the latest technological advances, data retrieval methods are suitable for almost any business. Information bureaus use ever faster, more efficient methods of retrieval, so your immediate attention can be focused on the task of evaluation and decision making.

If there's a downside to this service, it's certainly the cost. Subscriber fees are relatively low, but user fees can make the service very expensive. User fees vary greatly, but you can expect to pay anywhere from $35 to over $100 per hour. With such a wide disparity in fees, it's important to shop around and ask questions. Time spent now selecting the best search service will later pay off on the bottom line. To see if an information service fits your specific needs, request a brochure explaining how the service works. In addition, two helpful references are found in most public libraries:

Directory of On-Line Data Bases, published by Cuadra Associates, Inc.

Encyclopedia of Information Systems and Services, published by Gale Research Co.

For companies that provide electronic informational services, check the yellow pages of your phone book.

Communications Networks

A number of data bases can be accessed using communications networks. You'll need a personal computer, modem, telephone, and communications software. Data retrieval is fast and simple using this computerized system. Two major networks are:

Telenet Communications Corp., 12490 Sunrise Valley Drive, Reston, VA 22096; 800/336-0437

Tymnet, McDonnell Douglas Network Systems, 2070 Chainbridge Road, Vienna, VA 22180; 703/356-6993; 800/336-0149

On-Line Services

Whatever information you're seeking—wire services, sports, weather, financial information, news, airline schedules, movie reviews, or computerized shopping—subscriber access is available to thousands of data bases worldwide. Many businesses offer free, "familiarization" time to learn the retrieval method. They also provide links to a variety of useful data base sources.

BRS Information Technologies, 1200 Route 7, Latham, NY 12110; 800/468-0908; 800/345-4277

CompuServe, 5000 Arlington Centre Boulevard, P.O. Box 20212, Columbus, OH 43220; 800/848-8199

Decisionline, USA TODAY Information Center, P.O. Box 450, Washington, D.C. 20044; 800/222-0990

Delphi, General Videotex Corp., 3 Blackstone Street, Cambridge, MA 02139; 800/544-4005

Dialog Information Services, Inc., 3460 Hillview Avenue, Palo Alto, CA 94304; 415/858-3810; 800/334-2564

Dow-Jones News/Retrieval Service, P.O. Box 300, Princeton, NJ 609/452-1511; 800/522-3567

Gannett/USA TODAY On-Line Library, Data Times, Parkway Plaza, Suite 450, 14000 Quail Springs Parkway, Oklahoma City, OK 73134; 800/642-2525

Newsnet, 945 Haverford Road, Bryn Mawr, PA 19010; 215/527-8030; 800/345-1301

Nexis, Mead Data Central, 9393 Springboro Pike, P.O. Box 933, Dayton, OH 45401; 513/859-5398; 800/543-6862

Orbit Search Service, 8000 Westpark Drive, Fourth Floor, McLean, VA 22102; 800/336-3313; 800/421-7229

The Source, 1616 Anderson Road, McLean, VA 22102; 703/734-7500; 800/336-3330

Vu/Text Information Services, Inc., 325 Chestnut Street, Suite 1300, Philadelphia, PA 19106; 215/574-4400; 800/258-8080

Electronic Mail Services

Electronic mail is a computerized delivery system for telegrams, mailgrams, cables, letters and overseas priority mail. It's very convenient and relatively inexpensive. Courier delivery is also available.

Dialcom E-Mail, Dialcom, Inc., 6120 Executive Boulevard, Suite 500, Rockville, MD 20852; 301/881-9020

EasyLink, Western Union, 1 Lake Street, Upper Saddle River, NJ 07458; 201/825-5000; 800/325-6000

Easyplex/Infoplex, CompuServe, Inc., 5000 Arlington Centre Boulevard, P.O. Box 20212, Columbus, OH 43220; 800/848-8199

MCI Mail, MCI Telecommunications Corp., Inc., 2000 M Street, NW, Suite 300, Washington, D.C. 20036; 202/833-8484

Quick-Comm, General Electric Information Services, Inc., 401 North Washington Street, Rockville, MD 20850; 301/340-4000

Telemail, Telenet Communications Corp., 12490 Sunrise Valley Drive, Reston, VA 22096; 800/336-0437

CD-ROM Data Bases

Compared with other forms of data transmission—telephone lines, satellite, and microwave—economic factors favor the use of CD-ROM, which means compact disk read-only memory. CD-ROM software applications are an economically viable retrieval method for home computer users and may be the choice for accessing large data bases and professional references. To replace microfiche and microfilm archives, many libraries are changing card catalog systems utilizing less expensive CD-ROM technology.

R.R. Bowker, 205 East 42nd Street, New York, NY 10017; 215/592-8601

Datext, Inc., 444 Washington Street, Woburn, MA 01801; 617/938-6667; 800/521-6667

Dialog Information Services, Inc., 3460 Hillview Avenue, Palo Alto, CA 94304; 415/858-3785; 800/334-2564

Grolier Electronic Publishing, Inc., 95 Madison Avenue, New York, NY 10016; 212/696-9750

Lotus Information Services, Lotus Development Corp., 55 Cambridge Parkway, Cambridge, MA 02142; 617/577-8500

Market Statistics, 633 Third Avenue, New York, NY 10017; 212/986-4800

OCLC, Inc., 6565 Frantz Road, Dublin, OH 43017; 614/764-6000

Psycinfo, American Psychological Association, 1400 North Uhle Street, Arlington, VA 22201; 703/247-7829; 800/336-4980

H.W. Wilson Co., 950 University Avenue, New York, NY 10452; 800/622-4002; in New York, 800/462-6060

Document Delivery Services

If you need the full text of an article or journal but lack the capacity to access the data base, you can now choose from the many suppliers operating as independent firms. These vendors offer copying, formatting, and delivery services.

Find/SVP, 625 Sixth Avenue, New York, NY 10011; 212/645-4500

Information on Demand, Inc., P.O. Box 1370, Berkeley, CA 94701; 415/644-4500

The Information Store, 140 Second Street, San Francisco, CA 94105; 415/543-4636

NASA Industrial Application Center (NIAC), University of Southern California, Research Annex, Second Floor, 3716 South Hope Street, Los Angeles, CA 90007; 213/743-6132

Electronic Bulletin Boards

As a means of exchanging information electronically, Bulletin Board Systems (BBS) are simply connection centers for members possessing a personal computer, phone, and modem. With BBS, individuals and groups in the United States can exchange ideas and information on over 1,000 systems.

Exporter's BBS, Export-Import Bank of the United States (300/1200/2400 baud); 202/566-2117

National Center for Health Statistics; 301/436-8500

Science Resources Studies, National Science Foundation; 202/357-9859

Notes

Preface

Page xiii—"We're now working . . . ." Harris Poll 1988.

Page xiii—"Recently, some other futurists . . ." *USA TODAY*, July 17, 1989.

Page xiii—Globalnomic®, a registered trademark of the Socio-Economic Research Institute of America, Inc.

Page xv—"That didn't happen . . ." *Poughkeepsie Journal*, March 12, 1989.

Chapter 1: Looking Ahead

Page 6—"On that occasion . . ." *The New York Times*, January 1, 1978.

Page 7—"In his autobiography . . ." Lee Iacocca, *Iacocca* (New York: Bantam Books, Inc., 1984).

Page 8—"At the end of 1986 . . ." *The Wall Street Journal*, October 24, 1986.

Chapter 2: Identifying Trends

Page 17—"Before his defeat . . ." *The New York Times*, September 11, 1983.

Chapter 3: Developing a System

Page 21—"At times headlines ..." *The Wall Street Journal*, June 22, 1989.

Page 21—"In the fall of 1987 ..." *The New York Times*, November 19, 1987.

Page 21—"In the summer of 1989 ..." *The Wall Street Journal*, July 26, 1989.

Page 25—"With the readership ..." Associated Press, January 3, 1988.

Page 27—"To show you how ..." *The New York Times*, September 6, 1988.

Page 30—"Remember, about 66 percent ..." *USA TODAY*, March 24, 1987.

Page 30—"Gene Mater ..." *Washington Post*, March 15, 1983.

Page 30—"In our files ..." *The New York Times*, November 13, 1985.

Chapter 4: Profiting

Page 33—"In fact, only 6 percent of the people ..." *USA TODAY*, January 6, 1987.

Page 34—"Between 1970 and 1985 ..." *The Wall Street Journal*, June 1, 1987.

Page 35—"For CBS, the story ends ..." *The New York Times*, October 21, 1987.

Page 36—"One-third of the 91 million ..." *The Wall Street Journal*, January 19, 1988.

Page 36—"A 1987 poll of adults ..." *USA TODAY*, February 20, 1987.

Page 36—"Sales of health publications ..." Socio-Economic Research Institute data.

Page 36—"In 1986 the border patrol ..." *USA TODAY*, August 19, 1986.

Page 37—"At the time of our study ..." *The New York Times*, April 20, 1988.

Page 37—"In 1989 they were given ..." *Poughkeepsie Journal*, June 24, 1990.

Chapter 5: The Media

Page 42—"NBC has started ..." *The New York Times*, June 18, 1989.

Page 42—"TeleCommunications ..." *The New York Times*, July 9, 1989.

Page 43—"This reduces public access ..." *The New York Times*, June 18, 1989.

Page 43—"We agree with Nicholas . . ." *The Nation*, March 27, 1989.

Page 43—"As Thomas Jefferson said . . ." *USA TODAY*, February 1, 1984.

Page 43—" 'A month ago today . . .' " *The New York Times*, September 25, 1983.

Page 43—"A few years later . . ." *The Nation*, May 23, 1987.

Page 44—"In 1987 the American . . ." *The Nation*, May 23, 1987.

Page 44—"That same year . . ." *The Nation*, May 23, 1987.

Page 44—"A report issued . . ." *Poughkeepsie Journal*, December 21, 1988.

Page 44—"For example . . ." *The New York Times*, May 8, 1989.

Page 44—"Dave Marsh . . ." *Poughkeepsie Journal*, October 28, 1983.

Page 44—" 'Most television executives . . .' " *USA TODAY*, December 19, 1983.

Page 45—" 'The reality is . . .' " *The New York Times*, July 2, 1989.

Page 45—"In an address at Middlebury . . ." *Poughkeepsie Journal*, May 27, 1985.

Page 45—"The trend toward news . . ." Joseph Persico, *An American Original* (New York: McGraw-Hill, 1985).

Page 45—"When TV critics . . ." *The New York Times*, June 10, 1985.

Page 46—"Network veterans . . ." *The New York Times*, December 4, 1984.

Page 46—"Commenting on . . ." *The New York Times*, April 15, 1984.

Page 46—" 'Since the mid-1970s . . .' " *The New York Times*, April 15, 1984.

Page 46—"Before he left CBS . . ." *Poughkeepsie Journal*, September 9, 1986.

Page 47—"For example . . ." *The New York Times*, July 28, 1989.

Page 47—"Extending the idea . . ." *Poughkeepsie Journal*, July 20, 1989.

Page 48—"Because they get news . . ." *Poughkeepsie Journal*, April 3, 1988.

Page 48—"In TV-land . . ." *USA TODAY*, December 6, 1983.

Page 49—" 'If anything . . .' " *Playboy*, January 1984.

Page 49—"In a recent poll 86 percent . . ." *The New York Times*, July 2, 1989.

Page 49—"For example, in our file on Japan . . ." *Poughkeepsie Journal*, October 21, 1985.

Page 49—"Ted Koppel . . ." *The New York Times*, January 9, 1985.

Page 50—"Another example . . ." Gannett News Service, April 24, 1988.

Page 51—"Ten years ago . . ." *Variety*, January 11, 1989.

Page 51—"Now that they're selling . . ." *Forbes*, December 12, 1988.

Page 51—"This is driving . . ." *The Wall Street Journal*, September 27, 1988.

Page 51—"Cable now reaches . . ." *The New York Times*, July 24, 1989.

Page 51—"VCRs are now found . . ." *The New York Times*, July 24, 1989.

Page 51—" 'Television has gone tabloid . . .' " *The Wall Street Journal*, May 18, 1988.

Page 52—"An estimated 2.2 million . . ." *Time*, August 17, 1988.

Chapter 6: Politics

Page 54—"I'm not talking . . ." Television Bureau of Advertising.

Page 55—"He cited the hundreds . . ." *The New York Times*, December 23, 1988.

Page 55—"It made headlines . . ." *USA TODAY*, March 18, 1985.

Page 58—"They were still debating . . ." *The New York Times*, February 5, 1989.

Page 58—"As the facts were revealed . . ." Scripps Howard News Service, February 22, 1989.

Page 58—" 'Members of Congress . . .' " *The Wall Street Journal*, February 7, 1989.

Page 59—" 'Old politicians . . .' " *The Wall Street Journal*, March 8, 1988.

Page 59—" 'I represent the mainstream . . .' " *Poughkeepsie Journal*, November 10, 1988.

Page 59—"As pollster Pat Caddell . . ." *The New York Times*, November 13, 1988.

Page 60—"The nonpartisan League . . ." *The New York Times*, October 4, 1988.

Page 60—"Eddie Mahe gives us . . ." *The New York Times*, November 4, 1988.

Page 60—" 'Polls have shown . . .' " *USA TODAY*, November 3, 1986.

Page 61—"In 1988 the presidential . . ." Federal Election Committee.

Page 61—"In 1988 they contributed . . ." *USA TODAY*, October 8, 1990.

Page 61—"For example, in the past three . . ." *The Wall Street Journal*, February 7, 1989.

Page 61—" 'The big story . . .' " *USA TODAY*, February 16, 1989.

Page 61—"In the 1990 elections . . ." *USA TODAY*, March 25, 1991.

Page 61—"A study by the Center . . ." *Poughkeepsie Journal*, June 23, 1989.

Page 62—"In the 1988 House . . ." *USA TODAY*, March 28, 1989.

Page 62—"Political action committees . . ." *The New York Times*, October 20, 1988.

Page 62—"Amitai Etzoni ..." *The New York Times*, June 19, 1988.

Page 62—" 'Here, sir ...' " *The New York Times*, September 25, 1988.

Page 62—"One of the many ..." *The New York Times*, December 17, 1983.

Page 63—"We saw an effect ..." *The New York Times*, June 4, 1989; June 12, 1989; June 21, 1989; June 30, 1989. *The Wall Street Journal*, June 2, 1989. *Poughkeepsie Journal*, June 21, 1989. *Newsweek*, August 7, 1989.

Page 63 —"After the 1988 election ..." *Los Angeles Times*, September 27, 1988.

Page 63—"For example, two former ..." *The Wall Street Journal*, March 7, 1989.

Page 64—" 'We are not attracting ...' " *The New York Times*, January 15, 1988.

Page 64—"Michael Deaver ..." *Poughkeepsie Journal*, February 2, 1988.

Page 64—"Edwin Meese ..." *The Washington Post*, January 17, 1989.

Page 64—"Jim Wright ..." *The Wall Street Journal*, October 26, 1989.

Page 64—"Mario Biaggi ..." *The New York Times*, December 19, 1988.

Page 64—"Harold E. Ford ..." *The New York Times*, December 19, 1988.

Page 64—"James Traficant ..." *The New York Times*, December 19, 1988.

Page 64—"Pat Swindall ..." *Poughkeepsie Journal*, June 21, 1989.

Page 64—"Dan Walker ..." *USA TODAY*, November 20, 1987; also, *New York Times*, January 10, 1988.

Page 65—"David Friedland ..." *USA TODAY*, December 28, 1987.

Page 65—"R. Budd Dwyer ..." *The New York Times*, August 27, 1987.

Page 65—"Robert Garcia ..." *The New York Times*, January 20, 1990.

Page 65—"Samuel Weinberg ..." *New York Post*, April 2, 1987.

Page 65—"In a 1989 poll ..." *USA TODAY*, June 2, 1989.

Page 65—"In the 1960 presidential ..." *The New York Times*, November 12, 1988.

Page 65—"In 1990 only ..." *The New York Times*, November 11, 1990.

Page 66—"Even blacks ..." *The New York Times*, October 27, 1988.

Page 67—" 'My greatest regret ...' " Associated Press, November 19, 1988.

Page 68—"In fiscal 1988 the total tax ..." *Forbes*, May 1, 1989.

Page 68—"Each year the Tax Foundation ..." The Tax Foundation, Washington, D.C.

Page 68—"Public reaction ..." *The New York Times*, June 17, 1988.

Page 69—"Responding to complaints ..." *The New York Times*, February 24, 1988.

Chapter 7: The Family

Page 70—"In the real world . . ." *Los Angeles Times*, July 21, 1988.

Page 71—"Single mothers . . ." *The Wall Street Journal*, June 28, 1988; also, *Poughkeepsie Journal*, July 3, 1988.

Page 72—"According to the Census . . ." *The New York Times*, March 20, 1988; June 16, 1988.

Page 72—"In 1960 one out of . . ." *USA TODAY*, February 16, 1989.

Page 73—"Almost 60 percent of all children . . ." *The New York Times*, June 2, 1989.

Page 73—"One out of two . . ." *The New York Times*, March 20, 1988; *Los Angeles Times*, July 21, 1988.

Page 73—"In fact, each year . . ." *The New York Times*, July 16, 1989.

Page 73—"For single mothers . . ." *Poughkeepsie Journal*, July 3, 1988.

Page 73—"A study by Sheila . . ." *The Wall Street Journal*, June 28, 1988.

Page 74—"It's estimated that the average family . . ." *American Demographics*, September 1989.

Page 74—"In April 1988 a task force . . ." *The New York Times*, April 18, 1988.

Page 74—"A 1985 survey in Los Angeles . . ." *The New York Times*, February 15, 1988.

Page 75—"Today about 3,300 companies . . ." *The New York Times*, February 26, 1989.

Page 75—"Large companies . . ." *The New York Times*, February 26, 1989.

Page 75—"But most women . . ." *Science News*, October 1, 1988.

Page 75—"The national Parent . . ." *The New York Times*, May 9, 1988.

Page 75—"In the years from kindergarten . . ." *USA TODAY*, March 20, 1991.

Page 75—"Both parents and teachers . . ." *USA TODAY*, September 3, 1987.

Page 76—"About 13 percent of children . . ." *The New York Times*, May 9, 1988.

Page 76—"Discretionary spending by teenagers . . ." *Poughkeepsie Journal*, June 24, 1990.

Page 76—"In a 1987 poll, 82 percent . . ." *USA TODAY*, May 27, 1987.

Page 76—"A survey conducted . . ." *USA TODAY*, September 14, 1988.

Page 76—"A study released in 1987 . . ." Associated Press, June 4, 1987.

Page 77—"The number of children . . ." *The Wall Street Journal*, February 3, 1989.

Page 77—"A 1987 government study . . ." *Poughkeepsie Journal*, July 15, 1987.

Page 77—"A survey conducted . . ." *The New York Times*, August 10, 1988.

Page 77—"Another survey of 11,000 . . ." *USA TODAY*, August 10, 1988.

Page 77—"Still another survey . . ." *USA TODAY*, September 14, 1988.

Page 77—"In a 1988 survey . . ." *USA TODAY*, November 28, 1988.

Page 81—"By the end of the 1990s . . ." *American Demographics*, September 1989.

Page 81—"Somehow they do . . ." *The New York Times*, May 14, 1989.

Page 81—"About 1.5 million . . ." *The Wall Street Journal*, January 29, 1988.

Page 81—"Data show that 70 percent . . ." *The Wall Street Journal*, June 30, 1988.

Page 82—"Most of the elderly . . ." *Poughkeepsie Journal*, May 11, 1988.

Page 82—"When a 70-year-old . . ." *USA TODAY*, December 23, 1988.

Page 82—"At present there are only about 500,000 . . ." *The Wall Street Journal*, December 15, 1987.

Page 83—"A large number . . ." *The New York Times*, September 20, 1988.

Page 83—"The estimates are now . . ." *USA TODAY*, August 16, 1989.

Page 83—"From 1981 to 1986 HUD funding . . ." *The New York Times*, March 25, 1989.

Chapter 8: Education

Page 87—"In a survey by the Carnegie . . ." *The New York Times*, December 12, 1988.

Page 87—"At entry level . . ." *The New York Times*, July 22, 1989.

Page 87—" 'The severe crisis . . .' " *Poughkeepsie Journal*, August 24, 1983.

Page 87—" 'For the most part . . .' " *The New York Times*, August 13, 1983.

Page 87—"The quantity of people . . ." *Poughkeepsie Journal*, July 2, 1987.

Page 88—"The training of teachers . . ." *The New York Times*, March 24, 1988.

Page 88—" 'The crisis has to do with . . .' " *Los Angeles Times*, May 22, 1988.

Page 88—"Among the causes of the problem . . ." *Los Angeles Times*, May 22, 1988.

Page 88—"So while spending on education . . ." *The New York Times*, March 3, 1991.

Page 88—"Terrell Bell, secretary of education . . ." *Poughkeepsie Journal*, April 24, 1988.

Page 89—"In 1988 we spent . . ." *Forbes*, June 26, 1989.

Page 89—"About 30 percent of our children . . ." *The New York Times*, February 16, 1988.

Page 89—"A report by the Department of Labor . . ." *Washington Post*, July 31, 1988.

Page 89—"A study of dropouts . . ." *The New York Times*, February 16, 1988.

Page 90—"With 50 percent to 60 percent . . ." *Poughkeepsie Journal*, October 27, 1988.

Page 90—"According to the Department of Education . . ." *The New York Times*, February 20, 1988.

Page 90—"Estimates of the cost of illiteracy . . ." *The New York Times*, February 20, 1988.

Page 90—"The Business Council for Effective . . ." *Poughkeepsie Journal*, February 28, 1988.

Page 90—"Illiteracy in the work force . . ." *Poughkeepsie Journal*, October 9, 1990.

Page 91—"Assessing his effort . . ." *Poughkeepsie Journal*, April 24, 1988.

Page 91—"A report from the Carnegie . . ." *The New York Times*, March 16, 1988.

Page 91—"Its 1987 report, entitled . . ." *The New York Times*, September 6, 1987.

Page 91—"But now the children . . ." *The New York Times*, April 20, 1988.

Page 92—"A report from the National . . ." Associated Press, August 24, 1988.

Page 92—"The Department of Education found . . ." *USA TODAY*, October 29, 1987.

Page 92—"You've heard of the lost . . ." Gilbert M. Grosvenor, Speech at National Press Club, July 27, 1988.

Page 92—"The Committee for Economic Development . . ." *USA TODAY*, October 27, 1987.

Page 92—"A study conducted by the Center . . ." *The New York Times*, October 25, 1983.

Page 92—"Some companies, recognizing . . ." *Poughkeepsie Journal*, February 28, 1988.

Page 93—"The National Alliance of Businesses . . ." *Forbes*, November 28, 1988.

Page 93—"For example, the Motor Vehicle ..." *The New York Times*, July 26, 1988.

Page 93—" 'The educational foundations ...' " *A Nation at Risk*, National Committee on Excellence in Education, April 26, 1983.

Page 94—"A study released by the National Science ..." *The New York Times*, February 16, 1988.

Page 94—"Another study ..." *The New York Times*, September 23, 1988.

Page 94—"Still another study ..." *USA TODAY*, February 1, 1989.

Page 94—" 'Public education has put this country ...' " *New York Times*, October 27, 1987.

Page 95—"Addressing teachers ..." *Poughkeepsie Journal*, July 3, 1988.

Page 95—" 'The 1983 reforms do not change ...' " *USA TODAY*, October 29, 1987.

Page 95—" 'There's a wonderful trend ...' " *The New York Times*, May 2, 1988.

Page 95—" 'I think ...' " *Advertising Age*, January 16, 1989.

Page 96—"In several states ..." *The New York Times*, August 20, 1989.

Page 96—"South Carolina ..." *The New York Times*, August 20, 1989.

Page 96—"Many corporations have formed ..." *The New York Times*, August 20, 1989.

Page 96—"In 1989 about 20 CEOs ..." *USA TODAY*, February 3, 1989.

Page 97—"They're spending $25 billion ..." *USA TODAY*, February 3, 1989.

Page 97—"Businesses don't want that ..." *The New York Times*, January 11, 1989.

Page 97—"To meet the needs of our society ..." *The New York Times*, March 1, 1989.

Page 97—"In its April 1989 supplement ..." *The New York Times*, April 9, 1989.

Page 98—"Another trend we see ..." *The New York Times*, August 14, 1989.

Chapter 9: Health

Page 100—"Last year we spent ..." *The New York Times*, July 13, 1989.

Page 101—"Two-third of all visits ..." *The New York Times*, November 5, 1989.

Page 102—"Many of the unknown victims ..." *The New York Times*, February 15, 1989.

Page 102—" 'Most older people ...' " *Poughkeepsie Journal*, February 16, 1989.

Page 102—"Recent studies have found ..." *The New York Times*, February 13, 1989.

Page 103—"Then in 1988 it issued ..." *The New York Times*, July 26, 1988.

Page 103—" 'We really need to change ...' " *Poughkeepsie Journal*, March 13, 1988.

Page 103—"Another study found that about 25 percent ..." *Poughkeepsie Journal*, November 29, 1986.

Page 104—" 'Medical schools tended ...' " *The New York Times*, June 15, 1983.

Page 104—"Studies have found that 40 percent ..." *The New York Times*, June 15, 1983.

Page 104—"At one point, they tried ..." *USA TODAY*, April 5, 1989.

Page 105—"Commenting on the report ..." *USA TODAY*, July 20, 1988.

Page 105—"For example, the Public Voice ..." Associated Press, August 28, 1988.

Page 105—"In response to this criticism ..." Associated Press, August 28, 1988.

Page 106—"A study by *Consumer Reports* ..." *Consumer Reports*, October 1986.

Page 106—"It's the fastest growing breakfast food ..." *New York Times*, May 13, 1987.

Page 106—"George A. Hormel has a line ..." *Advertising Age*, November 7, 1988.

Page 107—"A 1987 report from the National ..." *The Wall Street Journal*, June 23, 1988.

Page 107—"According to a 1988 study ..." *Poughkeepsie Journal*, October 4, 1988.

Page 107—"In defense of its policies ..." *The Wall Street Journal*, June 23, 1988.

Page 107—"Those shiny apples ..." *The New York Times*, June 29, 1988.

Page 107—"In processing, about 3,000 ..." *The New York Times*, March 28, 1989.

Page 108—"Our meat is produced ..." *Poughkeepsie Journal*, July 25, 1985.

Page 108—"In early 1988 we picked up ...." *The Wall Street Journal*, January 29, 1988.

Page 108—"A month later the *Journal* reported ..." *The Wall Street Journal*, February 5, 1988.

Page 108—"A few months later the Reuters ..." Reuters News Service, April 13, 1988.

Page 109—"For example, 30 years ago ..." *The New York Times*, July 30, 1989.

Page 109—"This isn't just hypothetical ..." *The New York Times*, July 30, 1989.

Page 109—"In a 1981 report the General ..." *The New York Times*, January 31, 1983.

Page 109—"Two years later the Associated Press ..." Associated Press, February 1, 1983.

Page 110—"In the same year a report by Ralph Nader ..." *The New York Times*, January 31, 1983.

Page 110—"In 1988 the Gannett News Service ..." Gannett News Service, November 4, 1988.

Page 110—"If you do, you'll be a victim ..." *The New York Times*, December 7, 1988.

Page 111—"In the northeastern United States the maple trees ..." *The New York Times*, October 3, 1988.

Page 111—"In the St. Lawrence River ..." *The New York Times*, January 12, 1988.

Page 111—"We were tracking this trend ..." *The Wall Street Journal*, October 25, 1988.

Page 111—"Also, children who are ..." *USA TODAY*, July 26, 1989.

Page 112—"Americans spent $4.2 billion ..." *The New York Times*, April 1, 1991.

Page 112—" 'Clearly it's a boom industry ...' " *The New York Times*, July 16, 1989.

Page 113—"If you read the lists ..." *The Utne Reader*, January/February 1988.

Page 114—"In a 1989 poll conducted ..." *In These Times*, December 6–16, 1989.

Page 114—"In the late 1970s ..." *The New York Times*, December 7, 1989.

Chapter 10: The Environment

Page 116—"In this country we generate . . ." *USA TODAY*, November 27, 1990.

Page 117—"The EPA estimates that by 1995 . . ." *Forbes*, November 28, 1988.

Page 117—"In New Jersey shopkeepers . . ." *The New York Times*, March 18, 1988.

Page 117—"One response to this problem . . ." *The Wall Street Journal*, September 1, 1987.

Page 117—"Remember the barge from Philadelphia . . ." *USA TODAY*, November 29, 1988.

Page 117—"At the beginning of 1991 . . ." *Forbes*, March 18, 1991.

Page 118—"In addition to garbage . . ." *The New York Times*, October 23, 1988.

Page 118—"The General Accounting Office . . ." *The New York Times*, July 30, 1989.

Page 118—"A 1989 study by the Department of Health . . ." *The New York Times*, February 5, 1989.

Page 119—"Our use of fossil fuels . . ." *Science News*, May 7, 1988.

Page 119—"We now spend about 11 percent . . ." *Science News*, May 7, 1988.

Page 119—"Nor are they encouraging . . ." *The New York Times*, September 13, 1988.

Page 119—"A 1988 survey found that 22.5 billion . . ." *The New York Times*, April 13, 1989.

Page 119—"What's startling is that this . . ." *USA TODAY*, June 9, 1985.

Page 120—"It's estimated that 75 percent . . ." *The Wall Street Journal*, January 24, 1985.

Page 120—"Here's a story from our files . . ." *USA TODAY*, May 26, 1988.

Page 120—"Here's another . . ." *The New York Times*, June 20, 1988.

Page 120—"An enormous volume of toxic chemicals . . ." *The New York Times*, August 2, 1989.

Page 120—"According to an Illinois . . ." *The New York Times*, August 2, 1989.

Page 120—"From our file on the subject . . ." *The New York Times*, October 4, 1985.

Page 121—"In January 1988 there was a major . . ." *The New York Times*, January 2, 1988.

Page 121—"Of the 1.4 million underground ..." *The New York Times,* April 3, 1988.

Page 121—"In October 1988 the leaks..." "ABC News," October 17, 1988.

Page 122—"In the early 1980s researchers ..." *USA TODAY,* March 1, 1989.

Page 122—"Every year about 2.6 billion ..." *USA TODAY,* January 27, 1988.

Page 122—"In 1972 Congress passed a law ..." *The New York Times,* October 17, 1987.

Page 122—"They still haven't all been tested ..." *USA TODAY,* July 26, 1985.

Page 122—"A study by the National Resources ..." *Science News,* March 4, 1989.

Page 122—"Then there's the story ..." *The New York Times,* July 6, 1983.

Page 123—"It's also formed in the process ..." *Science News,* February 18, 1989.

Page 123—"In September 1987 AP reported ..." Associated Press, September 30, 1987.

Page 123—"For example, EDB was used ..." *The New York Times,* March 6, 1986.

Page 123—"In recent tests of farmland ..." *The New York Times,* March 6, 1986.

Page 123—"A 1987 study by the Consumers' ..." *The New York Times,* October 17, 1987.

Page 123—"One reason why the EPA ..." *USA TODAY,* January 27, 1988.

Page 124—"In 1983, when the astronauts ..." Associated Press, April 23, 1983.

Page 124—"According to the EPA, 110 million ..." *USA TODAY,* July 28, 1989.

Page 124—"More than one-third of Americans ..." *Science News,* April 1, 1989.

Page 124—"In a 1989 hearing ..." *The New York Times,* March 1, 1989.

Page 124—"But there's mounting evidence..." *The New York Times,* March 1, 1989.

Page 125—"In 1989 a Senate subcommittee ..." *The New York Times,* April 22, 1989.

Page 125—"The American Lung Association ..." *The New York Times,* April 22, 1989.

Page 125—"Half of the drinking water..." *The New York Times,* December 14, 1988.

Page 125—"A study by the EPA found . . ." *The New York Times*, December 14, 1988.

Page 125—"Another study, by the National Wildlife . . ." *The New York Times*, December 13, 1988.

Page 125—"Here's one from our files . . ." *USA TODAY*, November 17, 1983.

Page 126—"Here's another . . ." *The New York Times*, August 8, 1984.

Page 126—"In the summer of 1988 the New Jersey . . ." *The New York Times*, July 3, 1988.

Page 126—"According to . . ." *USA TODAY*, August 10, 1989.

Page 127—"In July 1988 the New York State . . ." *The New York Times*, July 7, 1988.

Page 128—"The commissioner of the state's . . ." *The New York Times*, July 7, 1988.

Page 128—"Christian Rice, a spokesperson . . ." *The New York Times*, July 7, 1988.

Page 128—"Here, and in Canada . . ." *The New York Times*, May 22, 1988.

Page 128—" 'I think we need to do more . . .' " *The New York Times*, May 13, 1982.

Page 128—"In 1986 the Brookhaven National Laboratory . . ." *The Utne Reader*, September/October 1989.

Page 128—"Canada's environment minister . . ." *The New York Times*, September 18, 1987.

Page 129—"As recently as October 1983 . . ." *The New York Times*, October 21, 1983.

Page 129—"In fact, the 1980s accounted for . . ." Scripps Howard News Service, February 4, 1989.

Page 129—"In June 1988 James E. Hansen . . ." *Science News*, July 2, 1988.

Page 130—"Other climatologists agree . . ." *Science News*, April 30, 1988; June 10, 1989.

Page 130—"In August 1988 W. Moulton Avery . . ." *USA TODAY*, August 18, 1988.

Page 130—"The farm belt will become . . ." *The New York Times*, June 26, 1988.

Page 130—"In October 1988 the EPA released . . ." ABC, CBS, and NBC News, October 20, 1988.

Page 130—" 'Major changes will be here . . .' " *The New York Times*, October 18, 1983.

Page 130—"More recently, they recommended ..." *Science News*, March 25, 1989.

Page 131—"In March 1988 the *New York Times* wrote ..." *The New York Times*, March 28, 1988.

Page 131—"A treaty signed by 47 countries ..." *Science News*, September 26, 1987; *The New York Times*, March 3, 1989.

Page 131—"Data collected by NASA ..." *U.S. News & World Report*, October 31, 1988; *Science News*, December 17, 1988.

Page 132—"The number of cases of melanoma ..." *USA TODAY*, May 20, 1988.

Page 132—"Further, some scientists ..." *USA TODAY*, December 5, 1989.

Page 132—"Instead, they considered ..." *The New York Times*, May 28, 1987.

Page 133—"In Florida ..." *The Wall Street Journal*, July 20, 1988.

Page 133—"Such laws have been passed ..." *The New York Times*, July 26, 1989.

Page 133—"We're seeing a wave ..." *USA TODAY*, August 23, 1989.

Page 133—"In a 1989 poll 77 percent ..." *USA TODAY*, August 23, 1989.

Page 133—"In California ..." *The New York Times*, February 22, 1988.

Page 133—"In the summer of 1988 ..." *The New York Times*, August 25, 1988.

Page 133—"In his first budget message ..." *The New York Times*, February 10, 1989.

Chapter 11: The Military

Page 135—"When that war ..." *Forbes*, October 31, 1988.

Page 137—"In 1988 I noticed ..." *USA TODAY*, October 26, 1988; "NBC News," November 14, 1988.

Page 138—"When later asked ..." *The New York Times*, February 16, 1984.

Page 138—"Studies have found ..." *USA TODAY*, June 14, 1983; *The Wall Street Journal*, April 24, 1984.

Page 138—"Defense spending ..." *Forbes*, February 20, 1989.

Page 138—"A 1983 study ..." *USA TODAY*, June 14, 1983.

Page 138—"A 1988 report ..." *The New York Times*, December 10, 1988.

Page 139—" 'What the economy gets ...' " *Forbes*, March 20, 1989.

Page 139—"The Department of Defense ..." *The New York Times*, November 28, 1988.

Page 139—"Most of the defense contracts . . ." *The New York Times*, April 14, 1985.

Page 139—"We spend more than . . ." *The New York Times*, March 6, 1988; July 3, 1989.

Page 139—"When a commission . . ." *The New York Times*, October 5, 1983.

Page 140—"The government had paid . . ." *The New York Times*, June 13, 1984.

Page 140—"In February 1984 . . ." *The New York Times*, February 23, 1984.

Page 140—"Trying to head off . . ." *USA TODAY*, June 26, 1984.

Page 140—"Now and then . . ." Associated Press, April 5, 1985.

Page 141—"The commission . . ." *The New York Times*, July 28, 1988.

Page 141—"In July they threw . . ." *The Wall Street Journal*, July 16, 1986.

Page 141—"Later that year . . ." *The New York Times*, September 21, 1986.

Page 141—"In February 1987 . . ." Associated Press, February 13, 1987.

Page 141—"In June they threw . . ." *The Wall Street Journal*, June 24, 1987.

Page 141—"In August . . ." Associated Press, August 6, 1987.

Page 142—"At the same time . . ." *The New York Times*, August 24, 1987.

Page 142—"Toward the end . . ." *Poughkeepsie Journal*, October 24, 1987.

Page 142—"Meanwhile, the Air Force . . ." *Poughkeepsie Journal*, August 5, 1987.

Page 142—"In March 1988 . . ." *The New York Times*, March 25, 1988.

Page 142—"A few months later . . ." *The New York Times*, June 7, 1988; June 17, 1988; June 20, 1988; July 1, 1988; July 10, 1988; August 3, 1988; August 9, 1988. *The Wall Street Journal*, June 23, 1988. *USA TODAY*, June 20, 1988.

Page 142—"In October Sunstrand . . ." *The New York Times*, October 13, 1988.

Page 142—"In fact, according to . . ." *Washington Post*, January 17, 1988.

Page 142—"In late 1988 . . ." *The New York Times*, December 20, 1988.

Page 143—"But meanwhile . . ." Associated Press, April 1, 1985; *The New York Times*, July 30, 1986.

Page 143—"Senior military officers . . ." *The New York Times*, March 24, 1987.

Page 143—"When Eisenhower . . ." Farewell Address, January 29, 1961.

Page 143—"About 40 percent . . ." *In Context*, Winter 1989.

Page 143—"About two thirds . . ." *In Context*, Winter 1989.

Page 143—"A little-known arm . . ." *The New York Times*, March 5, 1989.

Page 143—"In the fall of 1988 . . ." *The New York Times*, October 19, 1988; June 23, 1988.

Page 144—"In late August 1989 . . ." *The New York Times*, August 23, 1989.

Page 144—"Now, bear in mind . . ." *The New York Times*, November 18, 1989.

Page 145—"On November 17 he proposed . . ." *The New York Times*, November 18, 1989.

Page 145—" 'For all its risks . . .' " *The Nation*, October 9, 1989.

Chapter 12: The Economy

Page 152—"From early 1985 . . ." *USA TODAY*, January 15, 1987.

Page 152—"Paul Volcker . . ." *The New York Times*, February 3, 1987.

Page 152—"In a poll conducted . . ." *The Wall Street Journal*/"NBC News," April 1987.

Page 153—"Commenting on . . ." *The New York Times*, August 7, 1987.

Page 153—"The July deficit . . ." *The New York Times*, September 12, 1987.

Page 153—"In fact, it shrunk . . ." *USA TODAY*, January 15, 1987.

Page 154—"In June 1987 . . ." *The New York Times*, June 23, 1987.

Page 155—"It has been estimated . . ." *The Wall Street Journal*, December 5, 1988.

Page 156—"In June 1985 . . ." *The Wall Street Journal*, June 3, 1985.

Page 156—"By the end of the year . . ." *The Wall Street Journal*, December 27, 1985.

Page 157—"According to . . ." Associated Press, January 2, 1986.

Page 157—"Instead of growing . . ." *The New York Times*, January 26, 1986.

Page 157—"In February 1986 . . ." *The Wall Street Journal*, February 10, 1986.

Page 157—"The good times . . ." *The New York Times*, March 16, 1986.

Page 157—"Lines formed . . ." *The New York Times*, March 23, 1986.

Page 157—"In April a new Gallup . . ." *The New York Times*, April 11, 1986.

Page 158—" 'No one expected this . . .' " *The Wall Street Journal*, September 12, 1986.

Page 158—" 'White House Unruffled . . .' " *The Wall Street Journal*, September 15, 1986.

Page 158—"On the same day . . ." Associated Press, September 15, 1986.

Page 158—"In the real world . . ." *The Wall Street Journal*, September 2, 1986.

Page 159—"Factory orders . . ." *The New York Times*, December 5, 1986.

Page 159—"But Reagan maintained . . ." *The New York Times*, October 26, 1986.

Page 159—"The next day . . ." *The New York Times*, January 9, 1987.

Page 159—" 'With the stock market . . .' " *The Wall Street Journal*, January 9, 1987.

Page 159—"John Mendelson . . ." *The Wall Street Journal*, January 19, 1987.

Page 159—"With the Dow . . ." USA TODAY, January 8, 1987.

Page 160—"On January 22 . . ." *The New York Times*, January 22, 1987.

Page 160—" 'Raging Bull . . .' " USA TODAY, March 25, 1987.

Page 160—"Showing concern . . ." Associated Press, October 15, 1987.

Page 161—"On October 18 . . ." NBC News, "Meet the Press," October 18, 1987.

Page 161—"On October 19 . . ." *The Wall Street Journal*, October 19, 1987.

Page 161—"That morning . . ." USA TODAY, October 19, 1987.

Page 161—"Before getting into . . ." "ABC News," October 19, 1988.

Page 162—"Walter B. Wriston . . ." *The New York Times*, October 22, 1987.

Page 162—"We found an equally . . ." *Poughkeepsie Journal*, October 21, 1987.

Page 162—"Their action . . ." *The Wall Street Journal*, October 26, 1987.

Page 163—"When asked . . ." *The New York Times*, November 11, 1988.

Page 163—"To placate . . ." *The New York Times*, October 22, 1987.

Page 163—"By then the crash . . ." Associated Press, April 25, 1988.

Page 163—"Of course, people . . ." *The Wall Street Journal*, May 1, 1989.

Page 164—"In reality . . ." *The New York Times*, October 31, 1987; January 30, 1988; July 30, 1989. *The Wall Street Journal*, March 7, 1988.

Page 164—"That sounded like . . ." *The Wall Street Journal*, October 16, 1989.

Page 164—"Encouraged by . . ." *Forbes*, October 31, 1988.

Page 164—"On top of that . . ." *The New York Times*, October 15, 1988.

Page 164—"At the same time . . ." *The New York Times*, October 19, 1989.

Page 165—"While more and more . . ." *The New York Times*, March 21, 1988; July 16, 1989.

Page 165—"This trend ..." *The New York Times,* July 16, 1989.

Page 165—"Between 1973 and ..." *The Utne Reader,* September/October 1989.

Page 165—"Another measure ..." *USA TODAY,* June 23, 1989.

Chapter 13: The World

Page 169—" 'President-elect ...' " *The Wall Street Journal,* November 16, 1988.

Page 170—"In September 1987 he said ..." *The New York Times,* September 25, 1987.

Page 170—"Gorbachev also suggested ..." *Poughkeepsie Journal,* November 25, 1988.

Page 171—" 'There are certain periods ...' " *The New York Times,* October 28, 1988.

Page 172—"In his first meeting ..." *The New York Times,* October 25, 1986.

Page 172—" 'None of this would have ...' " *The Wall Street Journal,* November 11, 1989.

Page 173—"According to ..." *Newsweek,* November 7, 1988.

Page 174—"As of June 1989 ..." *The New York Times,* June 9, 1989.

Page 174—"In early 1988 ..." *The New York Times,* July 28, 1988.

Page 174—"By the end of 1992 ..." *The Wall Street Journal,* December 29, 1988.

Page 174—"Combined, the 12 ..." *The Wall Street Journal,* July 7, 1988; December 29, 1988. *The New York Times,* October 9, 1988.

Page 175—"But Willy Declerq ..." *The Wall Street Journal,* August 1, 1988.

Page 175—"Nestlé has acquired ..." *USA TODAY,* August 5, 1988. *The Wall Street Journal,* December 29, 1988.

Page 176—" 'It will enormously ...' " *Newsweek,* November 7, 1988.

Page 176—"General Electric has committed ..." *Newsweek,* November 7, 1988. *USA TODAY,* September 9, 1988. *The New York Times,* October 9, 1988.

Page 177—"As recently as ..." *The New York Times,* May 9, 1989.

Page 177—"Of the world's ..." *USA TODAY,* July 26, 1989.

Page 177—" 'We are now talking ...' " *The Wall Street Journal,* December 5, 1986.

Page 177—"At the leading edge ..." *The New York Times*, February 2, 1989.

Page 177—"When Hamish Maxwell ..." *The New York Times*, November 18, 1988.

Page 177—"J. Richard Munro ..." *Poughkeepsie Journal*, March 7, 1989.

Page 178—"Other potential ..." *Advertising Age*, March 17, 1989. *The New York Times*, March 19, 1989. *USA TODAY*, April 13, 1989.

Page 178—"New York Life ..." *The New York Times*, October 18, 1988.

Page 179—"In 1988 they burned ..." ABC News, October 19, 1988.

Page 179—"We'll not only lose ..." *Los Angeles Times*, July 26, 1989.

Page 179—"Brazil has been ..." *The New York Times*, March 23, 1989; June 29, 1989.

Page 179—"As one of its presidential ..." *The New York Times*, March 23, 1989.

Page 180—"We saw evidence ..." *The New York Times*, July 30, 1989.

Chapter 15: Personal Strategies

Page 205—"In surveys of college ..." *The New York Times*, January 14, 1988.

Page 209—"A survey for Adia ..." *USA TODAY*, May 20, 1988.

Page 210—"According to the Bureau ..." *American Demographics*, December 1988.

Page 210—"Another survey ..." *The New York Times*, October 16, 1988.

Page 210—"Still another survey ..." *American Demographics*, December 1988.

Index

Single-parent family. *See also* Working
    mothers
    economic status of, 71, 72, 73
    need for child care in, 73–74
    school dropout rate and, 89–90
    as social trend, 72–73
Sloane, James D., 65
Snack food industry, 35
Soft drinks, 106
South Carolina, 96
Southwest, water shortage in, 127
Soviet Union
    changes in system in, 29, 67, 170,
        171–172
    demilitarization and, 144, 167, 170,
        198
    U.S. defense spending and, 135, 137
Special interest groups
    corporate strategies and, 187
    environmental issues and, 115, 128
    political spending and, 54
    political trends and, 61–62
    waste in Pentagon and, 143
Specialization
    employment flexibility and, 207
    parental involvement in schools and,
        86–87
Spin-offs, from defense spending, 138–
    139
Standard of living, 164–166
Star Wars, 138
States, and educational reform, 96, 98
Stock market
    as indicator of public opinion, 155–
        161
    strategies for investment in, 213–215
Strategies. *See* Adaptive strategies; Corpo-
    rate strategies; Corrective strategies;
    Personal strategies; Strategy imple-
    mentation
Strategy implementation, 35
    in advertising, 34
    in domestic politics, 33
    in Globalnomic system, 31
    Iran crisis and, 32
    news broadcasting and, 35
    in snack food industry, 38

Stress reduction, in workplace, 193
Sugar, 103
Suicide, among teenagers, 77
Sundstrand, 142
Swindall, Pat, 64
Symptom relief
    as approach to health, 101–102
    as government response, 5, 56, 58, 84,
        132, 147, 151
Symptoms, versus cause, 7

Tandy Corporation, 95
Tax Reform Act of 1986, 68
Tax system
    injustices in, 68–69
    reform movements and, 68–69
Teaching, 86–88
Technology
    educational needs of society and, 92–
        93
    network television and, 52
Technology transfer, 178
Teenagers
    food shopping by, 106
    household responsibilities of, 76
    as market, 190
    mental health problems and, 77
    problems of, 76–77
    spending by, 76
    steroids and, 137
Television. *See also* Cable TV
    attitude toward public in, 44–45
    future of, 51–52
    intellectual skills and, 94
    junk food commercials on, 106
    latchkey children and, 75
    marketing and, 185
    network audience share in, 51
    politics and, 53–54
    as source of information, 30, 184
Textron, 141
Third World. *See* Developing countries
Thrift industry
    bailout of, 27–28
    government influence and, 187
    politics and, 55–58
Time, 26

FOR YOU TO TREND TRACK THE 1990'S

you need to know what's going to happen and how to plan for it. We at The Socio-Economic Research Institute have designed a unique newsletter that will help you profit from tomorrow's trends TODAY.

THE TRENDS JOURNAL is the world's only newsletter that:

- Keeps you in touch with the real trends shaping your future
- Shows you how to profit from trends
- Updates trend identification procedures

In this world of rapid change, *THE TRENDS JOURNAL will* help you plan for change and position yourself to profit from change.

OTHER INSTITUTE SERVICES:

The Institute applies Globalnomic® Forecasting and trends analysis to business marketing, product and concept development and organizational trend training services. Our work takes the forms of commissioned research and analysis studies, custom-tailored conference presentations and seminars.

For more Information on how you can receive *THE TRENDS JOURNAL* and other Institute services, call 914-876-6700 or write The Socio-Economic Research Institute, Salisbury Turnpike, Rhinebeck, NY 12572.

WARNER BOOKS INC. IS NOT AFFILIATED WITH THE SOCIO-ECONOMIC RESEARCH INSTITUTE OR *THE TRENDS JOURNAL.*